FIFTY

C000096303

About

For five years Tim Bullamore was the music critic of
The Bath Chronicle. His time at the newspaper coincided
with the first five years of the Bath Festivals Trust, the
organisation established to rescue the ailing Bath International
Music Festival in 1993.

Tim first visited Bath while working at Ibbs and Tillett Ltd as
a manager of classical musicians. He accompanied artists such
as the Takács Quartet, the Franz Liszt Chamber Orchestra, and
the pianist Mikhail Pletnev to the city, and settled there
himself in 1993.

In the musical world he is best known for bringing the Russian
pianist and Shostakovich interpreter Tatiana Nikolayeva from
the obscurity of Moscow to her acclaimed series of Wigmore
Hall concerts in 1991, and her remarkable concerto début at
the BBC's *Last Night of the Proms* the following year.

Born in 1966 and brought up in Leeds, Tim's colourful career
has included spells working for Barclays Bank,
the Youth Hostels Association and the Really Useful Group.
He is now a freelance writer. Publications he has written for
include *The Times*, *The Sunday Times*, *The Daily Telegraph*,
The Independent, *The Guardian*, *Classic CD*
and *BBC Music Magazine*.

FIFTY FESTIVALS

The History of the Bath Festival

by

Tim Bullamore

Mushroom Publishing

First published by
Mushroom Publishing in 1999

156 Southlands
Bath
BA1 4EB, UK

mail@mushroompublishing.com
http://www.mushroompublishing.com

ISBN 1-899142-29-0

British Library Cataloguing in Publication Data
A catalogue record for this book is available from the
British Library

Printed and bound in Finland by WSOY.

CONTENTS

ACKNOWLEDGEMENTS

Without the help, support and encouragement of a great many individuals this book would never have come into being.

In particular I would like to thank the staff – both past and present – of Bath Central Library and the Bath & North East Somerset Record Office, whose meticulous record keeping has proven invaluable to my labours.

Others to whom I am indebted include Bath Festivals Trust and *The Bath Chronicle* who have both allowed me access to their files, archives and pictures.

Individuals to whom I am grateful for sparing time to be interviewed, to proofread, or to generally offer words of encouragement include – in no particular order – Tim Joss, Tim Hobbs, Jonathan Dimbleby, David Gledhill, Bel Mooney, Julie Peacock, David Pratley, Mark Sparrow, Amelia Freedman, Ken Broadhead, Paul Perry, Barbara Robertson, Sir Ian Hunter, Sir William Glock, Ruth Hayden, Mary King, Jack Phipps, Sir Robin Buchanan, Naomi Buchanan, Chris Head, Luke Rittner, Harriet Arkell, Christine Allanson-Bailey, Martyn Folkes, Helen Folkes, Nod Knowles and the late Lord Menuhin, who sadly died as this book was going to print. If I have omitted anyone, it is entirely unintentional.

To my predecessors at *The Bath Chronicle* – particularly Morley Pooley, who passed away in 1994 – and correspondents from other newspapers, journals and magazines, who for half a century have recorded the day-to-day ups and downs, arguments and disputes, successes and spectaculars of the festival, I remain indebted. Contemporary archive and personal recollections have been fused with festival promotion material collected over the years to produce this history. To all those who have contributed, knowingly or otherwise, a big thank you.

Every effort has been made to contact copyright holders and authors of letters or other correspondence to seek their permission for reproduction. Unknown or untraced copyright holders are requested to contact the publisher so that they might be credited in any future edition.

Except where otherwise stated, credit for all the pictures featured is *The Bath Chronicle* who have generously permitted their reproduction in this book.

The appraisal of the Bath Assembly on page 24 from *The Times Educational Supplement* of May 16, 1948, is used with permission and copyright © Times Supplements Limited.

Dame Ruth Railton's recollection of the National Youth Orchestra's concert in Bath on page 21 is copyright © Random House Publishing.

Henry Raynor's description of Yehudi Menuhin's relationship with Pierre Boulez on page 81 is copyright © Robert Hale & Co.

During the writing of this book, accuracy has been my primary objective and I hold myself solely responsible for any errors or misunderstandings that may have arisen.

Tim Bullamore

FOREWORD by Jonathan Dimbleby

It is terrific to be able to celebrate the fact that, after 50 years, the Bath International Music Festival is going from strength to strength.

As residents of Bath, my wife Bel Mooney and I have long been "festival groupies". For 20 years we have seen the festival grow, evolve and adapt into one of Europe's finest displays of the arts.

What particularly delights us is the enormous breadth of disciplines represented in today's festivals: flamenco, jazz, and Indian music stand side-by-side with opera, classical and contemporary music.

While the festival continues this diversification – and long may it do so – Tim Bullamore's book is a welcome opportunity to remind ourselves of how the festival has reached this point. Personally, I was astonished to discover that the festival's first concert of Indian music took place some forty years ago in June 1959, and I did not know that jazz was first heard in the festival the year before that. What a marvellous heritage we are building upon.

Like many music lovers, I am an amateur listener; I hear with my emotions more than my intellect. I allow music to waft across my day, quite often as background to routine activities – for example when I am driving or dealing with correspondence. The joy of live music in general, and the Bath International Music Festival in particular, is that it requires me to park the car or put down my pen, and absorb myself thoroughly in the music. Spared the intrusion of the telephone, the fax or the doorbell, I can truly immerse myself in the vitality of live performance.

And can you imagine a more glorious setting than Bath in which to indulge in such pleasures? Even in the rain, the city is a jewel in this lovely country. It is an immense privilege to sit beneath the chandeliers in the Assembly Rooms or the portraits in the Guildhall, listening to some of the world's greatest musicians, and one of which I never tire.

But an increasingly important feature of the Bath International Music Festival is that it also stretches much further than these elegant surroundings. Concerts in community centres, workshops in classrooms and, of course, the free opening night celebrations in front of the Royal Crescent, are as much a part of the present festival programme as the events in the grand Georgian rooms I have described.

No organisation achieves this much without facing difficulties along the way. In the course of fifty festivals, the Bath International Music Festival has been through struggles and turbulent times. There were even a pair of festivals in the mid-1950s that didn't happen. It would be easy to produce a list of artistic triumphs and ignore the reality of funding crises, political obstacles and public opinion. Thank goodness this book does not gloss over the hard times; the author examines them in detail and shows how on so many occasions the festival has managed to defeat its problems and to move forward.

8

After fifty festivals, it is our intention not only to keep the flame alight, but to ensure that it burns more brightly than ever. The festival offers a spectacular and imaginative choice of events – at the last count there were some 165 scheduled over 17 days in 1999 – and truly is open to all. It is frustrating, therefore, that there are many potential enthusiasts in and around Bath who have yet to discover this gold-mine of artistic activity that comes round year after year. I do hope that when you have read this book you will tell them what they have missed in the past: Sir Thomas Beecham, Jacqueline du Pré, Elisabeth Schwarzkopf, Margot Fonteyn, Rudolf Nureyev, Yehudi Menuhin, Jessye Norman, James Galway, Evelyn Glennie: the names read like a roll-call of the musical world. There are similar delights this year, as there will be long into the new millennium.

With jazz, world music, contemporary music and opera now essential parts of this wonderfully diverse festival, I sincerely hope that more and more people will cherish an event that in truth belongs to the entire community.

Chalking up fifty festivals is a remarkable achievement and the result of great determination, sometimes in the face of apathy and even hostility. I would like to pay tribute to all those who have persevered over the past half century. In particular, I am grateful to Tim Bullamore – who has spent some 13 months researching, interviewing and writing this book – for his effort, and to applaud his determination. He has explained clearly and succinctly how the Bath International Music Festival came to be the world-renowned institution it is today.

Work is already well underway on the first of the next 50 festivals and – like you, I hope – Bel and I look forward to spending many more happy days and evenings listening to world-class music played by the world-class musicians who are visiting the world-class Bath International Music Festival.

Jonathan Dimbleby
Chairman, Bath Festivals Trust
April 1999.

INTRODUCTION

What would Bath be without its festival? The two words – Bath and festival – are almost synonymous.

Sir Thomas Beecham conducting opera, Yehudi Menuhin playing solo Bach in the Abbey, Dame Margot Fonteyn and Rudolf Nureyev on the stage of the Theatre Royal, Sir Michael Tippett's Blues Festival, recitals by Jessye Norman and Elisabeth Schwarzkopf – the catalogue of great performances by world-class artists seems endless. And still the show rolls on, bringing new talent and famous names to the city each year.

Across the world there are people who know of Bath primarily from reading about, or hearing recordings and broadcasts from, what is truly one of the most important of international festivals. Musicians and artists lobby to be given the opportunity to appear in the Bath International Music Festival, while visitors and tourists make a beeline to the city to enjoy the atmosphere of a city *en fête*.

But the festival's path has rarely been a smooth one. Finance, artistic direction, and public perception have often proved to be major stumbling blocks. That the festival has reached its marvellous golden jubilee is little short of a miracle and a tribute to the hard work and tenacity of a great many people.

* * *

What started out as a straightforward project to sum up fifty years of festival history through newspaper cuttings, archives and interviews, has turned into a far more complex and demanding exercise.

The discovery that music festivals were held in Bath intermittently throughout the nineteenth century and in the 1930s throws into turmoil the notion that 1998 marked the fiftieth anniversary of the first festival and 1999 the fiftieth festival. But, not wishing to spoil the party, we can perhaps dub these the fiftieth anniversary and fiftieth festival 'of the modern era'.

For those puzzling over why the fiftieth festival comes after the fiftieth anniversary, my mathematics has not gone awry. During the 1950s two consecutive festivals fell by the wayside, as the would-be annual extravaganza of music suffered its worst crises.

While attempting to examine the cause of such difficulties and subsequent uncertainties, I have also tried to capture some of the spirit of the Bath Festival. For those expecting or hoping for a comprehensive list of who appeared where and in what year, I am sorry but you will be disappointed. This is an anecdotal book rather than an academic tome, although it has been my aim to ensure that accuracy has prevailed.

Many of the great milestones in artistic development and the famous names who have visited the city are recorded on the pages that follow – how I wish I had seen and heard them. Maybe you did, and this book will bring back fond memories. Or perhaps you participated in the 'Roman Orgy', 'La Serenissima' or 'La Ronde', some of the festival's great social events. More recently, the evolution of the opening night celebrations into the city's biggest annual party, the visit by the Val Reef Choristers from South Africa, and a standing ovation for the famous Borodin String Quartet from Russia, are all memories I personally treasure.

Too often the importance of the Bath International Music Festival to the economy, to education and to tourism is not adequately recognised by those who live here. Politicians have complained at the cost, detractors have chided the perceived elitism of great art, and residents have been apathetic to its ideals. Yet both in this country and beyond its shores, there are many who envy the rich cultural jewel we have inherited here in Bath.

'What good does the festival do the city?' cry its critics. One economic survey after another has silenced the doubters, but how can you measure the goodwill and publicity that the festival brings to Bath? How can you quantify the lifelong love of colour, spectacle and sound which is instilled in young people who spend a day working with an artist? As long ago as the 1960s, Yehudi Menuhin was working with school children in and around Bath, as well as finding time for his intense schedule of evening concerts. Many people I have talked to for this book cherish such memories, and speak warmly of their appreciation for music born of those days. We must continue to find the means to allow the current festival team to carry on taking great art, literature and music into the community and into our schools.

The story of the Bath International Music Festival's continual development may not be a blueprint for how to run a successful festival, but it does provide an insight into the workings of one of the nation's greatest cultural gems.

I trust you will enjoy reading *Fifty Festivals* as much as I have enjoyed writing it.

CHAPTER ONE

For centuries people have considered Bath to be the ideal setting for a festival of one sort or another. The reasons can clearly be attributed to the city's architectural charm: Georgian crescents sweep effortlessly across the visitor's gaze; the local stone oozes a sense of warmth and tranquillity; and the city nestles comfortably in the surrounding seven hills.

With its famous spas and royal connections, Bath draws many visitors: the rich and the famous, the royal and the aristocratic, the humble and the curious. The city has long sought ways to persuade them to linger longer and to open their purses and wallets further. One way of keeping the tourists – and their cash – is to lay on a programme of entertainment. Music, in all its forms, has often fitted the bill.

The history of music in Bath is documented in many diverse sources, and a survey of it will provide a useful background to understanding how the Bath International Music Festival that we see today came into being.

Even before the city became a fashionable resort, Queen Elizabeth I visited the then roofless Bath Abbey, where choristers from Wells sang for her. Not long afterwards the diarist Samuel Pepys made his way to Bath. Arriving on June 12, 1668, he noted that: '...by and by comes musick to play to me, extraordinarily good as ever I heard at London almost anywhere.'

However the first musical events of any note took place when in 1704 Richard 'Beau' Nash, a well-documented impresario and the city's Master of Ceremonies, arranged for a group of five or six musicians to perform under large trees in 'The Grove' (Orange Grove). They were each paid a guinea a week. In due course physicians treating patients at the Pump Room persuaded Nash to move his ensemble there, and before long the band was performing for the infirm in the morning and at the Assembly Room balls in the evening – very often the same clientele.

Nash recognised the importance of music as one of the means of making Bath attractive and ensured a constant round of entertainment during the season. In later years he enlarged and maintained his orchestra by means of a 'voluntary' subscription, which no man of class in the city would dare refuse to pay.

The earliest musician of note working in the city was Thomas Chilcot, composer and organist of Bath Abbey from 1728 until his death in 1766. He ran a thriving business as a composer, instrument dealer and teacher. One of Chilcot's most important pupils was Thomas Linley – composer, harpsichordist, music director and teacher. Together with Henry Harington, Richard Sheridan and the organist of the Octagon Chapel, William Herschel (who in due course forsook composition to pursue his calling as an astronomer and discover the planet Uranus), Linley entertained fashionable society in the grand drawing-rooms of the city.

The ageing George Frideric Handel had been due to leave London for Bath on April 7, 1759 in order to take the waters. Unfortunately he was confined to his bed and died a week later without having made the journey. News of Handel's work had nevertheless reached Bath. *The Bath Advertiser* of November 13, 1756 contained an advertisement for performances of both *The Messiah* and *Judas Maccabeus* to be given eleven days later by the husband and wife duo of Giuseppe and Christina Passerini.

The famous Italian male soprano Venanzio Rauzzini settled in Bath in 1777 and, together with the violinist Franz Lamotte, managed the subscription concerts at the New Assembly Rooms in succession to Thomas Linley. Rauzzini exerted a strong influence on the music of the city and was particularly active at St James's Church, then an important musical centre in the city.

Although a summer season of music had been established for more than a century, Rauzzini directed the first musical gathering to be called a 'festival' in the area. 'The Bath and Somersetshire Grand Musical Festival' of 1809 included performances of the *Dettingen Te Deum* by Handel, and selections from *The Creation*, *Judas Maccabeus* and *The Messiah*. However, it came at a time when the city's fortunes were gradually waning. Nevertheless, the years 1820 to 1830 saw a good deal of musical activity, and the renowned conductor Sir Charles Smart was a regular visitor. He is known to have conducted a musical festival in the city in 1824.

Subsequent years saw a procession of grand names through Bath: Johann Strauss the Elder turned up with his orchestra in both June and August 1838, while the brilliant pianist Sigismond Thalberg visited in 1839. Thalberg's great rival for the title of pre-eminent pianist of the nineteenth century, Franz Liszt, came to Bath in September 1840 with a programme that included the *Grande Marche Hungroise* and the *Morceuax Choisis*. Although Bath had lost some ground as a major destination for royalty and the aristocracy, musical life continued. The Pump Room Orchestra gave daily performances, and concerts were regularly held in the various halls around the city.

* * *

In terms of major innovation we must skip almost a century until the first Festival of Contemporary Arts, which was held largely in the Pump Room between March 20 and April 5, 1930. It covered a wide spectrum of the arts including concerts, theatre, paintings, drawings, literature and photography. The opening event brought the violinist Albert Sammons to the city. Considered by many to be the finest English virtuoso of his generation, Sammons performed Delius's *Violin Concerto*, of which he was the dedicatee. *The Daily Telegraph's* review of his performance was glowing:

> *... Albert Sammons played with his usual beautiful accuracy of pitch –*
> *he has never been off the middle of the note in his life and his bow was*
> *born without original sin, so innocent is it of the slightest scratching –*
> *and the tone glows like the varnish on an old violin.*

But this was to be a festival of some artistic scandal. William Walton's new work for chanteuse and orchestra, *Façade*, received its first provincial performance, with the poems of Edith Sitwell recited through a megaphone by the well-known English composer Constant Lambert. *The Daily Telegraph* reported: '*Façade* has been performed twice – once this afternoon and again this evening – and there have, I think, been a good many casualties.' According to the local newspaper, *The Bath Chronicle,** the audience merely laughed.

But the *Western Daily Press* grew hot under the collar about those members of the public who became restless with the modernity of the festival:

> *At the afternoon concert several elderly people who did not understand and would not try to understand the very modernistic world of Gavin Gordon, talked continuously while the guest conductor was leading his own* Divertimento. *Those who wanted to hear the interesting composition had their attention distracted. It was a work with distinctiveness that embraced a new idiom.*

That the festival, the first of its kind in the city, attracted so much press coverage was remarkable. If both *The Daily Telegraph* from London and the regional newspapers were prepared to give it so much attention, then clearly it had something to say. This then was no quaint, provincial rendition or exhibition of popular classics. It was, for its time, cutting-edge contemporary British art. As the syllabus said: 'it will please some, and probably infuriate others – but no one will find it dull.'

So successful had the exercise been that five years later the city mounted the second Festival of Contemporary Arts between April 24 and May 8, 1935. Distinctly more international in scope, it was opened by the Belgian poet Professor Emile Cammaerts. He contended that it was not enough to preserve the glories of the past; it was also necessary to watch for what life can bring today. Arguing that 'unpleasant originality' was always better than 'pleasant conventionality', he told his audience that a nation gets the art, music and literature it deserves. He went on to congratulate Bath on the bold step of 'opening a window on the present and the future,' and, after an allusion to the 'ghosts' of the great figures associated with Bath's past, declared: 'It is probably a good thing that this fine city should be shaken from her graceful complacency by the strident voice of modernity. The stream of life brings, I know, a great deal of wreckage, but from time to time among the wreckage floats a treasure which we have no right to ignore because it doesn't answer to our expectations.'

Strong words; but these inter-war years were a time of adventure, experimentation and breaking new ground, particularly in the world of the arts.

---

* The local daily newspaper in Bath, today called *The Bath Chronicle*, has had several titles during the history of the festival including *The Bath and Wilts Chronicle and Herald*, *The Bath and Wilts Evening Chronicle*, and the *Evening Chronicle*. For ease of reading I have referred to it throughout as *The Bath Chronicle*.

Among the contributions to the 1935 festival, there was a concert by the famous violinist sisters Miss Jelly d'Arányi and Madame Adila Fachiri, both great-nieces of the legendary nineteenth century violinist Joseph Joachim. They gave the first performance of a new concerto for two violins by Alexander Brent-Smith. There was also the first performance of the *Symphony No.1 in E minor* by a 22-year-old Derbyshire composer named Roger Sachervell Coke, and a children's day with the pianist Eileen Joyce. A 23-year-old Australian, Joyce had been found playing barefoot in the Australian outback by a priest who felt sure the girl must be talented, and sent her to England to be educated. She went on to become one of the great keyboard names of the century.

The now defunct *Evening World* newspaper summed up the second Bath Festival of Contemporary Arts beneath the triple headline 'Reputation Of Bath Greatly Enhanced – Spectacular Finale To Season – Attractions For The Summer':

> *Today was the last day of the Festival of Contemporary Arts in Bath. At present it is impossible to give a financial result of the festival, but from the cultural point of view it can be said that the event has been a great success and has enhanced largely the reputation of Bath in the world of music and the arts. Famous artists have appeared at the concerts, famous writers have been represented in the manuscripts displayed, and outstanding paintings have been represented in the varied exhibitions of paintings and etchings that has enlivened the corridors of the Pump Room and the walls of the concert hall.*

The 1935 festival ended with a moment of high drama when a daring raid on the festival's art treasures was foiled by an attentive security guard. Attracted by a noise on the terrace above the Roman Baths, just at the entrance to the exhibition, a man on night duty flashed his torch through the glass door and saw two men crouched in the shadows. He raised the alarm and tried to capture them, but in the darkness they escaped. The police were on the scene in a couple of minutes, but there was no sign of the two men.

Even outside festival time, Bath in 1935 was becoming something of a hotbed of culture. The list of famous artists who appeared in the city at other times of the year included the pianists Alfred Cortot, Solomon (then still known as Solomon Cutner) and Cyril Smith; the Portuguese cellist Guilhermina Suggia; the violinists Daniel Melsa, Jan Kubelík, Joseph Szigeti and Jascha Heifetz; and the Rothschild and Lener Quartets.

Enthused by their artistic successes, the city's Spas Office decided to make the festival an annual affair. The Bath Spring Festival of 1936 took 'The Art of Three Centuries' as its theme, and included symphony concerts, an organ recital, chamber music, drama (*A Man's House* by John Drinkworth, performed by the Bath Festival Players) and a substantial exhibition of paintings. Among the musicians appearing were the well-known pianist Harriet Cohen and the viola player Lionel Tertis.

So it continued in similar vein and, on the eve of the Second World War, the Bath Spring Music Festival was held from March 18 to 25, 1939. The Pump Room Orchestra was enlarged to become the Pump Room Festival Orchestra, and among the visitors were the conductors Sir Adrian Boult and Sir Henry Wood as well as, once again, the violinist Albert Sammons. The soloists in the opening performance of *The Messiah* included Isobel Baillie (later Dame Isobel Baillie) and Astra Desmond (later awarded the CBE). Writing in the introduction to the programme book, a copy of which sits in Bath Central Library, Sir Henry Wood refers to the success of the previous year's spring music festival. The BBC broadcast many concerts, or parts of concerts, and such was the demand among the ticket-buying public in Bath that some of the performances were given at 3pm and repeated at 8pm.

But even the festivals of pre-war years were not without financial headaches. The *Evening World* of March 26, 1936, related the story of a patron of the arts who lived in the West Country and who was among the audience at the opening concert of the festival at the Pump Room. He was warm in his praise for the festival in a conversation with Mr John Hatton (spas director) after the concert. He was horrified to discover, however, that running a music festival did not make any financial sense, and subsequently sent a donation to the city. In an accompanying letter he said: 'I think these festivals are not only very enjoyable, but have real educational value. If I lived a little nearer to Bath I should be in and out of the Pump Room every day.'

* * *

It was against this background (and before the 1939 festival even took place) that, on October 14, 1938, a meeting was called in London to consider a proposal to establish 'an international festival of music, drama and the allied arts in the city of Bath.' But why? Was it that, despite some impressive names, the existing festival was not international enough, and failed to bring in overseas artists? Was there a general disdain for anything organised by the corporation, such as the Spring Festival? Or was it simply a matter of one faction of musical opinion within the city trying to outsmart another faction?

Given that the Mayor of Bath was associated with both the existing festival and the new proposal, the latter two answers would seem unlikely. It seems there was a desire for something on a far larger scale and with a much greater international flavour. Writing in *The Bath Chronicle* in April 1966, journalist Dick Ledbury recalled being assigned as a cub reporter to cover the meeting, which took place at the Royal Opera House, Covent Garden:

A genteel and impressive gathering made this decision. It included Sidney Bernstein, Lady Diana Cooper, John Gielgud, Owen Mase, Capt. Bruce Otley and the Hon. James Smith. The whole thing was rather overpowering to a poor scribe... I came away feeling that Salzburg would have to look to its laurels, but a certain Austrian had different ideas. So this festival, with its glittering promise, was killed by the imminence of war.

While the Covent Garden meeting certainly attracted the great and the good from (and associated with) Bath, it was clearly not a discussion to which the ordinary man or woman of the city was invited, nor were their views even considered. Behind the bid was Charles B Cochran, the well-known theatrical producer. Part of his motivation had been the re-opening of the Assembly Rooms by the Duchess of Kent in October 1937. His idea, not least the need to raise a guarantee fund of £50,000 of which £10,000 was to come from the city, was aired in *The Bath Chronicle*, and in December 1938 Cochran briefed the city's Chamber of Commerce on his plans. At a subsequent reception the Mayor of Bath, Captain Adrian Hopkins MC, spoke of the proposal as the beginning of a 'brighter Bath'. Certainly, Cochran had it in mind that Bath should rival Salzburg, and quickly overtake it, as the major festival city of Europe. At this time there were just a handful of other festivals in Britain.

Indeed there were then, and still are now, good comparisons to be drawn between Salzburg and Bath. Both are cities of exceptional beauty and steeped in history; they are of similar size; and, then at least, they had similar facilities for visitors. The difference was that in 1938 Salzburg had a hugely successful festival, which attracted strong local and civic support and a great many visitors.

The Mayor of Bath's appeal did well. By writing personally to his many contacts, Alderman Hopkins raised £4000. Meanwhile names being bandied about for the Bath Festival of 1939 included the conductors Bruno Walter and Leopold Stokowski. There were, however, complaints in the press that the proposed dates clashed with the drama festival at Malvern and the recorder festival at Haslemere.

On January 4, 1939, Cochran announced his plans to the country at large through a letter in *The Times*, emphasising the eighteenth century wonders of the city. Two days later a response in the same newspaper from eleven signatories including Stephen Spender, Graham Greene and Rebecca West, criticised Cochran for the 'one or two archaeological signs which suggest that the works of art in the Bath Festival will be mainly those made safe by time.' They continued:

> ...it is twice the duty of the promoters of an international festival to see that the genuine art of the present stands by the genuine art of the past. The Bath Festival is a big opportunity in the Europe of 1939, but it ought to be really international and really vital, and really concerned with the arts.

However, in a letter to *The Times* of January 14, 1939, a Major Benton Fletcher, disagreed:

> The plea to make this festival an international and up-to-date affair is to defeat the object of its promoters. Truly British, insular, and self-contained, the city of Bath should not stoop to compete with her academic or commercial sisters, nor be exploited in rivalry with Continental festivals.

But Miss Bateman of the Royal Crescent, Bath, corrected the Major:

The suggestion that the Festival of Arts, under the aegis of Mr Cochran, should be 'international and up to date' is not an innovation but definitely a return to the conditions that obtained in the period whence Bath now reaps her glory. Insularity, a quality ascribed to Bath by Major Fletcher, although formerly of considerable value geographically, has never been anything but catastrophic when applied to matters artistic.

Signing himself 'Your Music Critic', a further letter writer to *The Times* on January 18 concluded that although Cochran could undoubtedly provide conductors of international repute, 'he could promise nothing else, not even an orchestra of national repute for them to conduct.' He continued: 'This is not the first time that the municipality of Bath has sponsored a musical festival. Once bitten twice shy!'

But before the festival plans were aborted, an advance brochure – complete with colour picture on the cover – was printed, advertising that a 1939 international festival of the arts would run from July 17 to August 12. A company of French players were to attend, and a morality play was to be produced outside the Abbey; Sir Thomas Beecham had examined the Pavilion and was quite content with the acoustics of the hall; there was to be an evening of Mozart by candlelight in the Assembly Rooms and a Handel concert on an illuminated barge. Ledbury recalled that many years later the Handel concert did take place 'played on a barge which was pulled along the Avon banks in a downpour of rain, scowled at by J B Priestley, who with myself had come to behold'.

However, with the arguments about the style a festival should take already rumbling in the press, and the proposals being considered in far-away London, was the seed already sown for the charge that has continually haunted the Bath Festival: namely that it is – or has been – elitist, snobbish and inaccessible and contains very little for the ordinary citizen of the city? In the context of the aborted 1939 festival, that question becomes all the more pertinent when looking at the mayor's own remarks in a Chamber of Commerce speech a month after the Covent Garden meeting. He justified the timing of the festival by saying 'the people whom one wanted to attract – the people of fashion – had finished the London season and were free to go their own way.'

Adolf Hitler ensured that the 1939 Festival was never to be – and more's the pity given the line-up of interested artists, which included Cecil Beaton, Rudolf Bing, Constant Lambert and Edith, Osbert and Sacheverell Sitwell.

First, there was a war to be fought. The money that had been raised for the 1939 festival was returned to its donors, and all hopes of an international arts festival were laid aside for many years.

CHAPTER TWO

Across the post-war arts world, the name Ian Hunter appears time and again. Edinburgh Festival, Glyndebourne Festival Opera, Hong Kong Festival – not to mention the musicians' management agency Harold Holt Ltd – Ian Hunter has run with them all.

He was awarded the MBE for his wartime services, and knighted for his services to music in 1983. Moreover, half a century after the festivals in Edinburgh and Bath began, he is still an active mover and shaker in the musical world.

In March 1947, Ian Hunter had been staying at his brother's home near Reading and, by his own account, spent one wet Sunday afternoon browsing through a book describing the Georgian architecture of Bath. He immediately saw the city's potential as a backdrop for a major new arts festival. Hunter was already heavily involved in the Edinburgh Festival, of which that year's was to be the first, but Edinburgh was principally to be a Scottish outlet for Glyndebourne Opera. Hunter had a wider vision for Bath. Although at that stage he had never visited Bath, he believed that the city's historical buildings could be brought to life with a children's festival – a series of artistic events geared towards young people.

Financially unable to work alone on the project, Ian Hunter thrashed out his ideas with John and Audrey Christie, the owners of Glyndebourne, and Rudolf Bing, general manager of Glyndebourne and the first artistic director of the Edinburgh Festival. Using a family connection, Hunter wrote to the then Member of Parliament for Bath, Sir James Pitman, outlining his ideas. A positive response was received, and on May 17, 1947, Hunter was invited to Bath to meet with the city's spas director, John Boddington, to explain his ideas more fully. On his way to the meeting, Hunter stopped at Corsham Court to lunch with Lord Methuen, a keen supporter of the arts, whose enthusiasm encouraged Hunter in his quest for civic backing.

Sitting in Boddington's office beneath a portrait of Beau Nash and over-looking the King's Bath, Hunter was brimming with the idealism and energy of youth. He later described what happened:

> *Boddington told me that something similar had been proposed before the war, but it had come to nothing. I assured him that if he could get support from the city, I could produce the goods.*

A week later, Hunter was back in Bath with his proposal for 'The Bath Assembly', a festival of the arts for young people, and within a couple of months a public meeting was convened in the Guildhall to raise interest and enthusiasm. At that meeting Alderman William Huntley, chairman of the Spa Committee, explained Ian Hunter's proposals in detail. He also went on to discuss the wider hopes for the festival and to examine the difficulties it might face. He told the city's business community that drama, concerts and entertainment alone do not necessarily constitute a festival – it also needs atmosphere. He added: 'I believe you can help us very materially.'

During his speech, Huntley also conceived the need for what would later be termed 'the fringe', to complement the main focus of the festival. He said: 'numerous other attractions could be and should be arranged during the same period.'

By Christmas 1947, a formal structure was taking shape. A company limited by guarantee was to be established, and the liability of the city council limited to £3000 (subsequently reduced by the council to £2000). The country's newly formed Arts Council would be approached to offer a similar guarantee. They came up with £750 which, if necessary, would be available before the city's funds were drawn upon. But the difficulties were potentially great. Two years after war had ended many of the hotels in Bath were still being used as government offices. Consequently there were precious few beds to accommodate the hoped-for visitors at festival time. Rationing of many essential goods and services was also still in place.

A trophy was offered to the organisers of the festival to be awarded to the artist securing the greatest number of votes from the public in respect of his or her performances. Mercifully, a director's meeting on February 25, 1948 turned down that well-intentioned but inappropriate offer.

At about the same time Ruth Railton (now Dame Ruth Railton), who was in the process of founding the National Youth Orchestra, was in contact with Ian Hunter. With the Bath Assembly's emphasis on youth, where better than for this orchestra – which over the subsequent half century was to gain such a prestigious reputation – to make its début?

However, her involvement with Hunter's enterprise nearly backfired as he explained:

> Ruth strongly objected to the idea of a press conference to boost the small number of tickets we had sold in advance. However, the press were called to a rehearsal and a large number turned up. The following day the Daily Mirror had a large picture and a good story: they blew up the hand of one of the young violinists who had only three fingers and captioned the story 'Johnny plays with three fingers.'
>
> It was in poor taste and Ruth justified her stance, but the concert sold out.

Ironically, not long after this incident Railton married Cecil King, the proprietor of *The Daily Mirror*.

For Ruth Railton, the National Youth Orchestra's début concert in Bath was the culmination of many months hard work. Railton had spent the first three months of the year trawling the country for youngsters who demonstrated potential as much as talent. On April 13, 1948, 110 of them – many of whom had never before left their home cities or even travelled by train – descended on Bath. Waiting to coach them were musicians of the calibre of Henry Holst,

Douglas Cameron, Lionel Tertis and Frank Probyn. Tertis was astonished: 'All this young talent on the viola!' he exclaimed.

But the week's preparations were not without problems: Tertis walked out feeling ignored (he later returned apologetically with a bunch of flowers for Railton), the oboists and clarinettists were barely up to the job, and the youngsters' instruments were totally unprepared for six hours of rehearsal a day. In her book *Daring to Excel*, Ruth Railton tells of the end result:

> *The culmination of two years' thought, planning and hard work arrived on 21 April 1948, bringing the first public concert of the National Youth Orchestra of Great Britain, which was also the opening concert of the Bath Assembly. The Lord Mayor, many local dignitaries and the London press were going to be present for this exciting occasion.*[1]

The concert took place in the Pavilion. The programme was Weber's *Oberon Overture*, Mozart's *Piano Concerto K488*, Malcolm Arnold's *Suite for Youth*, Beethoven's *Symphony No.2 in D major*, and Elgar's *Pomp and Circumstance March No. 4*.

Railton later recalled the evening: 'The concert made a great impression. This was due to the atmosphere the orchestra created rather than the actual standard achieved by such young players in one week.'[2] *The Times* was cautiously welcoming: 'The orchestra as a whole was able to do considerable justice to a typical symphony orchestra programme with Malcolm Arnold's first work cleverly scored.'

And so the first Bath Assembly, with its offices at 8 Abbey Church Yard, was launched. The attractive two-colour brochure designed by Edward Ardizzone, of which 33,000 were distributed overseas and 67,000 in this country, included photographs of many of the artists taking part, as well as an introduction by the author Horace Annesley Vachell who lived at Widcombe:

> *Why has Bath quintessential claims to hold a Festival of All the Arts?*
> *1. The Queen city is incontestably an international heirloom.*
> *2. The gracious curves of its architecture are a joy for ever.*
> *3. Eloquent of care-free yesterdays, it whispers confidentially of merrier tomorrows.*
> *4. It has been a sanctuary to the giants of old.*
> *5. It was – and will be again – an enchanting Garden City.*
> *Edinburgh rose and gripped a great opportunity. We must do the same. Pilgrims of yore were admonished to see Naples and die. Let us say to all the world: 'Come to see Bath and live'.*

In addition to the National Youth Orchestra, the BBC Symphony Orchestra conducted by Sir Adrian Boult performed Prokofiev's *Peter and the Wolf*, Stravinsky's *Firebird Suite* and Strauss's tone poem *Till Eulenspiegel*. The London

---

[1] From *Daring to Excel* by Ruth Railton, published by Secker & Warburg, 1992, p.58.
[2] *ibid.* p.59.

Philharmonic Orchestra conducted by Karl Rankl appeared with a veteran visitor to Bath, the viola player Lionel Tertis, performing the soloist's own arrangement of Mozart's *Clarinet Concerto*. The London Philharmonic Orchestra returned for a second concert. This time they were conducted by Victor de Sabata making his first visit to England, with the great Italian violinist Gioconda de Vita, also making her British début, playing the Brahms *Violin Concerto*.

The City of Bath Bach Choir, recently formed by Cuthbert Bates to mark the forthcoming bicentenary of the death of Johann Sebastian Bach in 1950, performed their calling card, *The Matthew Passion*, in the Abbey in two parts. The first began at 2.30pm, the second at 5pm. The choir, conducted by Bates, was accompanied by the Boyd Neel Orchestra, with Bath's long-serving organist Ernest Maynard at the console of the Abbey's organ. The Boyd Neel Orchestra also gave their own concert, with the famous oboist Leon Goosens.

Many of the concerts took place in the Pavilion, a dank, hangar-like building, which has not changed much in the past half century. But there was more to the Assembly than music. The station was bedecked with flowers and banners welcoming visitors to the city; the Abbey, the Empire Hotel and Pulteney Bridge were illuminated (a rare feat in those years of energy rationing, requiring special dispensation from the Government); the Skupa Puppet Theatre from Prague was in town; Sheridan's *The School for Scandal* was presented at the Theatre Royal; the Children's Theatre presented *The Immortal Lady* by Clifford Bax; Bath Choral and Orchestral Society presented *Hiawatha*; and Glyndebourne Opera gave six performances of *Die Entführung aus dem Serail* by Mozart conducted by one of the great musicians of the century, Berthold Goldschmidt.

Away from the serious business of the music was the Costume Ball on April 23, which had a waiting list for places of 700 – almost as many as there were tickets sold (800). The ball was a nostalgic look at Bath in its eighteenth century heyday. Among those 'appearing' were Beau Nash, Sarah Siddons and Elizabeth Linley.

A Festival Club was organised at the Pump Rooms. According to the brochure it was to '...provide a rendezvous for patrons of the Assembly where they may meet their friends at all times and enjoy relaxation and refreshments in congenial surroundings.'

The Bath Chronicle was full of advertisements placed by local traders wishing the Assembly well. Indeed *The Bath Chronicle* was supportive in its own right. At the top of the front page there was a bright red message each day wishing the Assembly success.

The Assembly received the royal seal of approval with a visit by its first patron, Princess Margaret. The 17-year-old princess was on one of her first unaccompanied public engagements, and visited Bath for most of the festival's final day. *The Bath Chronicle* described her appearance and renamed the day 'M-Day' – *M* for Margaret Day and *M* for May Day:

> *Over a pale pink dress, Princess Margaret wore a fitting Spring coat in off-white. The slightly old-fashioned look of the new hat styles was charmingly achieved by her pastel-pink hat, fitting at the back like a*

jockey cap over her brown curls and having large roses on the off-the-face peak. There was no crown to the hat. Matching spot veiling was tied under her chin – the New Look indeed! Her skin shoes had plat-form soles and were toeless.

In the evening Princess Margaret visited the London Philharmonic Orchestra's concert in the Pavilion, where Gioconda de Vita's performance of Brahms's *Violin Concerto* conducted by Victor de Sabata almost had to be abandoned in mid-flow because of hailstones on the roof. The day – and the festival – ended with a fireworks display over the Recreation Ground at 10pm: a spectacular send-off to a successful first festival. In an end of festival interview with *The Bath Chronicle*, Moran Caplat, manager of Glyndebourne Opera, said: 'There is no reason why the Bath Festival should not rapidly achieve the magnitude and importance of the famous international festivals – after all Salzburg is no bigger than Bath.'

Although it may seem that Hunter's initial aim for the festival as a children's event had been sidelined, more than 10,000 young people were bussed in to experience concerts and rehearsals. At the Odeon Cinema (where the Southgate Shopping Centre now stands) there was an International Festival of Children's Entertainment Films which, as the title suggests, included offerings from far and wide. Among the 16 films shown in groups of four were *Bush Christmas* from Australia, *Magic Globe* (Czechoslovakia) and *The Boy who Stopped Niagara* (Canada).

Also for young people was a little reported or publicised 'live' trans-Atlantic radio discussion organised and broadcast by the BBC – an advanced feat of engineering for its time – involving teenagers at the Pump Room in Bath and at the WHEC studio in Rochester, upstate New York.

But what had happened to the Assembly's overall appeal to youth? For those from a cultured background or with a particular interest to pursue, it was fine. However, some of Ian Hunter's popular idealism had evidently disappeared. And, true to subsequent form, the 1947 Assembly was not without a row. As the Assembly began, it transpired that a circus had been given permission to set up camp in a field opposite the Pavilion. In those days performing animals were the norm. Hasty efforts were made to relocate the tents and livestock elsewhere, but the circus was certainly present during the BBC Symphony Orchestra's concert with Sir Adrian Boult. After his performance Sir Adrian denied any disturbance, but the *Daily Express* breathlessly reported that:

...the 100-strong symphony orchestra paused for three beats. Conductor Sir Adrian Boult stood, baton raised. The strings held their bows. The winds held their breath. The audience sat silent. Then came a strident trumpet call – but not from the orchestra. It was ten-ton Dinah, star elephant of a circus moving into a field opposite Bath's Music Pavilion. At the top of Dinah's call, Sir Adrian brought down his baton. And the BBC Symphony Orchestra crashed out all the proper notes to end Prokofiev's whimsical Peter and the Wolf.

Although this first Bath Assembly had limited overseas marketing, the city welcomed visitors from America, Portugal, Finland, Holland and the countries of the Empire. *The Times Educational Supplement* offered a positive and constructive review of the Assembly, but one which hinted that feuding about what the festival was meant to be about, and who it was for, was already apparent:

> *No finer setting for a festival of the arts could be found. Its one danger was that it raised hopes extravagantly high. The Bath Assembly, a first venture, prepared only over nine months, limited financially, was approached by some critics as though it ought to have equalled and outstripped the most famous festivals of pre-war Europe.*

The article went on to point out that it was in fact a small festival for beginners. Bath itself was a beginner; it had never held a festival of this sort before. Many of the audiences were beginners. Not only were a large number of children at all performances, but the region around Bath had not enjoyed the facilities for an active cultivation of the arts. The organisers themselves were also beginners, in the sense that they had no access to the finances open to those who run established European festivals. The *TES* continued:

> *Taken as a regional festival it was a first-class success. In Bath and the country around, the rougher London critics are judged to be unaccountably wolfish men. Although the Assembly shed in the course of preparation something of its originally intended direct appeal to youth, what remained of it was exactly to the surrounding taste. Clearly the development of the festival on international lines is beyond Bath's own resources. It is work for the State or some private Croesus, if any is left. But if annual festivals are being planned it would be a fiddling piece of egalitarianism to allow Bath to rise no higher than the other regional centres. Inherited wealth may be under a cloud, but inherited beauty ought still to have its claims respected.*

Writing in the magazine *Time and Tide*, Philip Hope-Wallace was not so kind:

> *Bath, nestling in the verdant hills, is a festival in itself. The stone stares back sleepily in the spring sunshine, dazzling like a Sickert picture; there is a powdering of blossom; window boxes, pennants and an occasional pink geranium. No Assembly Rooms, alas, but the exquisite Pump Room in spite of decorous boogie-woogie and too much in the dainty-tea line, makes a fine if ill-attended festival club. Festivalisons!(sic) but, let us also be practical: the three best hotels are still in Government hands; there is no really good concert hall (the Pavilion is little more than a glorified drill-hall) and the theatre though genuinely en style is not specially well-suited.*
> *Is it, after all, such a good place for a festival – even a festival for*

young people, which surely cannot be held to imply that lowered or puerile standards are to prevail? What a rumpus there would be if watered milk were sold as suitable for young people; frankly if I were a young person and had come from, say, Italy (where the thing is advertised) I think I should have been rather disappointed. The concerts were quite good though ordinary, but the Mozart and the Sheridan were unworthy, much nearer to the kind of shows put on by undergraduates in the summer term.

Financially the final results showed there was little to complain about. The council's guarantee of £2000 was not going to be exceeded, and only the opera turned in a loss. Nevertheless, the moans and groans soon followed. Cllr Charles Shadwell pointed out at a subsequent council meeting that the ordinary person had no opportunity of attending some of the shows without losing time from work, to which Cllr Alleyne Berry replied that in the case of orchestras, they had to return to London after their performance, which rather determined the starting time of concerts.

Just three years after Europe had come to the end of six years of devastation, Bath had its own festival subsidised by the municipality but controlled by men of high artistic ideals. The city was only a year behind Edinburgh in getting off the mark. Surely it could only go from strength to strength?

CHAPTER THREE

Ian Hunter had every reason to be pleased with himself after the 1948 Bath Assembly. A firm foundation had been laid; audiences had responded enthusiastically, and even if the press hadn't always been encouraging, financially he had kept within his remit. He therefore felt he had every reason to expect to be asked back to repeat the exercise in 1949. He wasn't. And to this day he doesn't know the true reasons why.

The minutes of the board of directors dated June 21, 1948, report simply this:

> *1949 Festival: The board further considered the question of the organisation of this festival, and decided that the spa director and his staff should undertake it, and that the offer of the Arts Council of Great Britain to co-operate in matters concerning the programme be accepted.*

Ian Hunter said:

> *The first festival was certainly a success and I had every reason to expect that it would be the first of many that I would direct. Accompanied by Rudi Bing, we went down to Bath on June 9 (1948) to meet the Spa Committee and to discuss a festival in 1949. There would indeed be a festival and they were delighted with the success of the first festival. On the other hand, Bath had its Spas Director and an Entertainments Officer and the Spa Committee felt that they had sufficient expertise to run a festival themselves, but they would like to engage me and Glyndebourne as 'artistic advisors'. Rudi and I quickly concluded that this would not work. For me it was a sad blow to see what we at Glyndebourne had created passing into the wrong hands.*

Hunter's was not the first scalp to be claimed by the Bath Festival, nor would it be the last. And it would not be the only time Hunter would leave the festival in high dudgeon. Clearly the city felt embarrassed that it had been unable to muster such an event itself. Locally there were bruised prides and damaged egos to be repaired. But it takes more than excellent administrative skills and a collection of addresses to make a festival work; it needs a profile and a presence in the artistic world to bring it all together. Sadly, no one either elected to or working for the council had that ability – although for the next few years they tried. The results were not always dismal, and the city attracted some top name musicians – but festivals they were not.

The spas manager, John Boddington, to whom responsibility for organising the subsequent Assemblies fell, arrived in Bath for his final appointment before retirement after a spell managing the spas at Buxton. He had been a pupil-teacher at the age of 12, and subsequently studied at Manchester University. Following a spell as a classics master in Northern Ireland he enlisted in the army during the First World War. As a lance-corporal in charge of the battalion snipers, he was granted the rare honour of a commission in the field with the Manchester Regiment and was soon promoted to captain. Wounded, he returned to England as brigade education officer, establishing the first technical classes to equip returning troops for civilian life. During the Second World War he was in charge of a Derbyshire Home Guard numbering 800 men, finally retiring with the rank of major.

None of this had prepared Boddington for the role of running the Bath Assembly, which was foisted upon him by his political masters. In an interview for this book in 1998, Ian Hunter said: 'He felt that if the festival was going to go on, he ought to be running it. He really knew very little about the thing, as the following year showed.'

An editorial in *The Bath Chronicle* of April 23, 1949, was supportive of the local authority's efforts to continue with the Bath Assembly:

> *Economic theorists may deplore the expenditure of money on enter-tainment when so much stringency and austerity still exist, but if the city spent not a penny on a Bath Assembly no more bricks would be laid, nor would a single family be rehoused any the more quickly. While many Bathonians will be unable to attend any of the Assembly events, the Festival is worthy of the active support of all, and it is encourag-ing to the promoters to receive such ready co-operation from local theatre managements and the businessmen of the city.*

An extended programme for 1949 was presented to the world in January of that year. Sensing murmurings of criticism about how the previous Assembly had been perceived by some, Cllr Alleyne Berry, chairman of the Spa Committee, fired a pre-emptive shot: 'Let us enjoy it and not make it merely a snobbish exhibition,' he said. The second Bath Assembly, he insisted, would build upon the success of the first.

One of the most important innovations was the inclusion of the Forum cinema as a venue for orchestral concerts. It had first been used for that purpose in 1935, when the Pump Room Orchestra conducted by Edward Dunn performed a midnight matinée in aid of the Royal United Hospital. On that pre-war occasion, the programme had included Gershwin's *Rhapsody in Blue*, and the same work came around again in the second Assembly. On this occasion it was performed by Geraldo and his Concert Orchestra before an audience estimated at 2000 people.

Opera, always an expensive medium to promote, was out. But there was the Ballet Rambert for one week at the Theatre Royal and many other events including the Busch String Quartet, the London Symphony Orchestra performing Lennox Berkeley's *Piano Concerto* with soloist Colin Horsley, and the Hallé Orchestra with John Barbirolli offering Brahms's *Symphony No.1*. The Hallé included two works by the composer John Ireland (*Prelude: The*

Forgotten Rite; and *Symphonic Rhapsody: Mai-Dun*) who was present to hear them performed. For the first time a foreign orchestra, the Amsterdam Concertgebouw, with their conductor Eduard van Beinum, visited the Bath Assembly. They gave two concerts, and included in their programmes were Bartók's *Concerto for Orchestra*, and the 'Four Sea Interludes' from *Peter Grimes* by the promising young composer Benjamin Britten.

It is fascinating to note how much contemporary music of the day appeared in the mainstream programming of these early festivals, and it undoubtedly attracted good audiences. One work in the 1949 Assembly, which has slipped from the repertoire, was the *Concerto for oboe and strings* by the Somerset-based composer Rutland Boughton, performed by Leon Goosens and the Boyd Neel Orchestra.

The City of Bath Bach Choir's offering in 1949 was Bach's *B minor Mass*, while at the Theatre Royal the young Peter Ustinov appeared with Brenda Bruce in a new play called *Love in Albania* by Eric Linklater. Fifty years later the Ustinov Studio behind the Theatre Royal is named after Sir Peter.

The children's film festival ran as before, while at the Victoria Art Gallery there was a major exhibition of works by Thomas Gainsborough, a one-time resident of Bath, and a Linley-Sheridan exhibition was held at the Old Sessions Court in the Guildhall. The BBC broadcast an edition of the radio programme *The Brains Trust* from the Pump Room, with a panel that included the young poet and Bath enthusiast John Betjeman.

Although sponsorship as we understand it today was non-existent, the need for patronage over and above ticket sales was acknowledged. A Festival Luncheon was organised, and members of the Festival Club – resident at the Pump Room once again – were invited to purchase tickets.

The social highlight of the festival was the Assembly Ball, held at the Pump Room but with a totaliser hut (as used at point-to-point meetings) erected in Abbey Church Yard for the buffet. The Film Ball, a similar occasion, but clearly aimed at a different sector of society, brought 1200 people to the Pavilion, where among the guests were Lana Morris (star of *Spring in Park Lane*) and Paul Dupuis (*Johnny Frenchman*).

The city responded to the 1949 Assembly with gusto. Large areas were dressed in flowers, including a magnificent harp-shaped display at Colmers on Union Street. Shop windows were packed with photographs of visiting musicians, and the station was once again adorned with welcoming banners. Fireworks at the Recreation Ground rounded off the celebrations and were described by *The Bath Chronicle* of May 30, 1949: 'On Saturday night as the brilliant colours of the fireworks drifted gently down over the centre of the city, already glowing with the floodlighting of the Abbey and the weirs, Bathonians witnessed the close of the Bath Assembly.'

The 1949 Assembly emulated its predecessor and tied up a few loose ends, but did it move the festival on any further? In the post-war climate, could Ian Hunter have fared much better? He would almost certainly have secured Glyndebourne's services for opera, but probably not a lot more besides.

Even before the 1949 Assembly got underway, shots were being fired: was it for highbrows, lowbrows or middlebrows? This question has continually haunted the festival. In catering for the so-called highbrows, they stand accused of elitism. Pursuing a programme for the so-called lowbrows does nothing for the advancement of either the arts or the city as a cultural destination of international repute. And when trying to please everyone, the result is invariably failure.

In *The Bath Chronicle* the debate raged. On April 28, 1949, Bruce Johnson of Monkton Combe advocated what he called a 'poor-man's Assembly' instead of the proposed programme:

> *Without question, the working class, much as they would like, cannot afford to patronise more than, say, one of the magnificent performances which are being presented. To them the Assembly means very little. Enchantment is obtained from the floral displays, the floodlighting is admired, and the milling crowds, outside the ballroom in order to catch a glimpse, are endured. Here they stay, on the fringe, but beyond all this they felt that they would like to be in it somewhere. Is this thought to be possible?*

A letter-writer signing himself merely HNP concurred (May 5):

> *So many of the local people look upon the Assembly as something that is just not for them, but rather for the highbrows only. Mr Johnson seems to have the knack of being able to appeal to all. I hope that the powers-that-be will see their way clear to adapt at least some of his suggestions.*

John Boddington tried to appease the critics but in so doing shot himself in the foot:

> *All arts festivals, in whatever part of the world they have been organised, are specifically for the highbrows, or shall I say those interested in the arts. There is always at least one exception to every golden rule, and among festivals there is a glorious exception and I am pleased to say that the exception is the Bath Assembly. Surely this is obvious to anyone examining the programme. There is something for all in the Bath Assembly. Now I am afraid – or am I – that someone will accuse us of catering for the lowbrows.*

Writing from Oxford University, Kenneth Gregory retorted:

> *What a situation when the Spa Director of a city which prides itself on its cultured heritage is more or less obliged to apologise for organising an arts festival.*

Another correspondent, F B Donovan, expanded that view in the paper:

> *Why should Bath be ashamed to be known as a centre for highbrow entertainment if, as I assume, by highbrow is meant the highest and the*

best of its kind? Salzburg and Bayreuth or even Glyndebourne in this country did not gain their great international reputation by pleading that the entertainment they offered was not so very highbrow after all. There is always, and not only at the time of festivals, abundant entertainment available for lowbrows, and there seems no need for organised effort to cater for them. I speak as one who is broad-browed enough to enjoy some forms of so-called lowbrow entertainment on occasion. Let Bath set out frankly to raise the taste, and to provide opportunity for the many (not of one class only, as some of your correspondents appear to imply) who want to hear the best music and drama by the best performers. It will thus best serve its citizens, even though some of them may not recognise it and, at the same time, increase its fame in the world at large.

Even the Church of England attempted to wade into the debate. At the festival service in Bath Abbey, the Venerable Edwin Cook, archdeacon of Bath, said from the pulpit:

It ought not to be an insoluble problem to ensure that those with small incomes should be able to benefit to the full from a festival such as this. Good music and good drama are often so very expensive. I have no solution to offer but I do suggest that this is a problem which ought to be faced by all who are concerned, for quite clearly the will of God concerns every man.

The Bath Chronicle, supportive as always, wrote of the festival as a business in its leader on June 1, 1949:

There are many criticisms which can and ought to be made, but there is also a lot of ill-informed talk as to the 'unnecessary luxury' of a festival of the arts at this juncture in the city life – or, indeed, at all according to some. So let us be clear about one thing – the Assembly is very much part of the city's 'business' as the premier spa in Britain. Naturally it needs the patronage of Bath citizens, and it is there for their own enjoyment; but its main purpose is to keep the city on the map of outside interest and to attract visitors to the city, not only for the Assembly but thereafter. It is unlikely that such festivals can be run on a completely self-paying basis, but this cost has to be weighed against the returns received in the shape of publicity and influx of those who want, at one time or another, to come to our city. One thing is certain – the Assembly must go on.

The debate over who the festival does and should cater for is perhaps the one constant in its chequered history. At times it would swing incredibly highbrow and in so doing put both the festival and the city firmly on the international map. At other times the festival might attract less attention from beyond the city walls, but be felt by local people to be more inclusive. A happy medium – should one actually exist – has rarely been found.

* * *

Over the coming years, as the memory of wartime austerity began to fade, the Assembly did not progress significantly in any direction. The same tried and tested formula was used, and the same orchestras and their conductors turned up. Soon it all wore rather thin – although that is not to belittle the quality of the artists who did appear.

The 1950 festival brochure gave a poor impression. It was little more than a list of dates and programmes. Even in 1948, descriptions of performances, a strong element of design, and black and white photographs, had been incorporated into the Assembly's publicity.

Opera returned in the form of *The Secret Marriage* by Cimarosa, performed by the London Opera Society at the Theatre Royal. There were also performances of *Prima Donna* by Arthur Benjamin and *Susana's Secret* by Wolf Ferrari. The Assembly Ball had a Georgian theme and guests were invited to attend appropriately dressed. Fears of gatecrashers led to several members of the local police force attending in evening dress.

The Birmingham Symphony Orchestra with George Weldon performed Grieg's *Piano Concerto* (soloist Kendall Taylor); Malcolm Arnold's *Concerto for Clarinet and Strings* was played by Frederick Thurston with the Jacques String Orchestra under Dr Reginald Jacques; Sir Thomas Beecham brought the Royal Philharmonic Orchestra with the pianist Betty Humby-Beecham; the Hallé and Sir John Barbirolli came with Sir John's wife, Evelyn Rothwell, performing Mozart's *Oboe Concerto*; and the Bournemouth Municipal Orchestra were in town conducted by Rudolf Schwarz playing Beethoven's *Piano Concerto No.1* with soloist Franz Osborn.

Barbirolli received five recalls to the platform after his performance of Beethoven's *Second Symphony* in front of a packed audience at the Forum, while a special plea was put out before Beecham's concert urging members of the audience to arrive early, as seating 1800 people in just ten minutes would be impossible.

In 1950 there was a major boost from Queen Mary. As a mark of gratitude for the kindness and hospitality received in Bath by Her Majesty during the war when she lived at Badminton, the home of the Duke and Duchess of Beaufort, the Queen lent a panel of her own needlework for an exhibition during the Assembly. It was the only time outside of London that the tapestry had been seen, and more than 1000 people came to view it each day. The panel measured 2½ft by 2ft, and depicted a crane-bird fishing with a frog caught in its beak.

Alderman Alleyne Berry, chairman of the Assembly, told a press conference (held in London) that the Assembly was to be a curtain-raiser for the 1951 Festival of Britain celebrations. He went on to allude to the highbrow/lowbrow problem once again:

> *The object of the Bath Assembly is to enable people – all the people –*
> *to enjoy themselves. If they do not care for symphony concerts they can*
> *ignore Sir Thomas Beecham and Sir John Barbirolli and go and hear*

Geraldo's concert orchestra. If opera bores them they can enjoy the marionettes. If they think a Molière play is too highbrow they can see instead a new film or a display of athletics or eighteenth century dancing. Not everyone will want to afford a 30-shilling ticket for the Assembly Ball at the Pump Room – so they can go to the special dance at the Pavilion for a modest 3s 6d, and enjoy an equally excellent band. Bath has endeavoured to retain and develop all the pleasant characteristics of her eighteenth century glory. The only difference is that the entertainment and happiness she now offers are no longer privileges confined to the exclusive few.

But the national press were beginning to show signs of losing interest. According to *The Sunday Times* of May 14, 1950, Bath, while a beautiful place, had very little to offer in artistic terms that was unique. Describing the outstanding setting, the writer continued: 'The festival that can live up to these surroundings needs to be very special indeed; and, to speak the truth, the present Assembly is not, or not yet, quite that. Beau Nash, I fear, must be longing to come back and take charge.'

Morley Pooley, *The Bath Chronicle's* long-serving music critic and news editor, whose career with the paper spanned five decades, decided to undertake a round table interview which appeared on May 23, 1950:

To hear what ordinary people are saying of the Assembly let us eavesdrop for a while at a little round table which I shared recently with an overseas visitor, a resident of Bath of long-standing, and another who was brought here fairly recently by the Admiralty.

A young attractive raven-haired student from overseas is speaking: 'Even if this Assembly cost £2000, what of it?' she asks aggressively. 'It has afforded people like myself from the Colonies an opportunity of seeing the loveliest bit of England, and at the same time thrilled my very soul with operatic performances, the like of which I am never likely to see or hear again. I shall return to my people to preach the gospel of the mother country.'

The elderly Bathonian is not amused: 'I know only too well what we have given you,' he counters pointedly, 'but what contribution have you made to Bath? What have you spent in our shops? Not a thing... For the most part, traders have done less business than in any other fortnight of the year.'

'You're taking far too parochial a view,' chimes in the Admiralty man. 'You are thinking solely of immediate results rather than taking the long-term view. That's the trouble with the people of Bath, they cannot see further than their own noses.'

'The Assembly ignores the man in the street and caters solely for the very few highbrows,' declares the old Bathonian. 'Until it takes note of the ordinary people it will always be a drain on the rates and a white elephant to the people of Bath generally'.

Some traders were also having their doubts, but their gripes were of a different sort. An anonymous letter writer to *The Bath Chronicle* (March 20, 1950) wrote that: '...far from attracting customers, the Assembly empties my shop.' The paper rebuffed him by carrying out a survey that showed the opposite. The president of the Chamber of Commerce, Mr J E McKeon, said: 'I think that as the Assembly becomes better known and we attract more visitors, it will be of growing importance to the business community of the city.' A former Chamber president, Mr Albert Manns, managing director of the music shop Duck, Son and Pinker, conceded that he didn't actually do any extra business as a result of the festival, but said, 'such events must do the city and the business community a lot of good.'

He continued:

> *People cannot come into a place like Bath without spending money in some way or other. I have heard it said by a lot of business people that the Assembly does not do the city any good. I don't know how they can say this.*

John Boddington recognised the good that just one event in the festival – the Assembly Ball – did for the city. He said:

> *Just think how much money is spent by the 400 women who attend the Ball, in the week preceding it. Nearly all of them will visit the hairdresser for a perm, or at least a wave and set. Many of them will buy powder paint and perfume and have their nails manicured. There are many who will buy a new dress for the occasion – and possibly a lot of other items of clothing as well. For the men there will be haircuts and dress shirts, collars, ties and shoes to see to.*

The Church had its own axe to grind, voiced at the end of the festival from the pulpit by the archdeacon, the Venerable Edwin Cook. He complained that during the festival there had been a play which portrayed the vice of the seventeenth century: 'The fact that this play has aroused no comment is indicative of the ease with which we accepted a standard which was not of the highest order.'

There were problems too with the children's film festival. A pair of Czech films which were due to be shown were suddenly withdrawn by the government in Prague. A spokesman for the J Arthur Rank Organisation, which was arranging the festival, described the move as 'purely political'.

But the Assembly ended happily enough with a May Fayre finale at the Recreation Ground lasting from 3.30pm to 10.30pm. It featured folk-dancing, the Dagenham Girl Pipers, Speedway, fencing, bridge building by local scouts, country dancing, Scottish dancing, and finished with a spectacular firework display.

In summing up the 1950 Assembly, *The Bath Chronicle* called for greater visibility:

Could it not begin with a carnival that would bring in the whole city right at the start and make all citizens fully festival-minded? Could not triumphal arches grace the way into the city as well as flags and flowers decorating the street? Would not the revival of a Master of Ceremonies add a touch of colour in keeping with the eighteenth century traditions? Such an office might obviate some of the awkwardnesses on the social side which have occasionally made themselves apparent.

Within weeks of the end of the 1950 festival there was clearly much feuding going on. A motion was debated by the city council which, if passed, would have barred the chairman of the council's Spa Committee from being chairman of Bath Assembly Ltd, the company which, with certain financial guarantees from the local authority, ran the Assembly. It was tantamount to a vote of confidence in Alderman Alleyne Berry who occupied both posts. After a heated debate, much of it in private session, he survived. Nevertheless he conceded that the council of management should be renamed The General Council of the Bath Assembly and placed on a broader basis by including people representing different organisations and varying walks of life. That move, at least, would appear to have come as a result of pressure from the Arts Council who, in reality, were selecting and paying for many of the artists appearing at the Assembly.

Writing in *The Critic*, a short-lived local arts and gossip magazine, the journalist Dick Ledbury said:

It is not enough, in my judgement, that for one fortnight in the year Bath should preen herself with a festival, which is at the highest the playground for those fortunate enough to possess something of a musical or highbrow inclination. Of course the 'art' people would hold up their hands in horror were I to timidly suggest that in these days when people have little to go with their bread, circuses and variety provide quite a welcome 'sauce'. One applauds the engagement of famous orchestras and the like, but, even with the reconstituted committees – and have they been reconstituted enough? – one fails to find a broadening of public interests which should make a profit and not a loss to the ratepayers of Bath. Bath should be the Salzburg of this country, for it has all the advantages of a lovely situation, and it should be en fête for the visitor, not for a fortnight only, but for the whole year.

A fraught discussion by the board of directors on February 28, 1951, concluded that Assemblies should continue to be held annually, but they should be shorter except in every third year. Alderman Alleyne Berry made a spirited defence of the annual festival in a lengthy speech to the Chamber of Commerce. However, he admitted that it was impossible to quantify the good it did the city: 'But we have reasonable proof that over one third of the seats were taken by people outside Bath. Only eight counties in the whole country did not have bookings. Applications for seats also came from Australia, the United States, New Zealand and South Africa.' He also reported that in 1950 the publicity value of the Assembly had been such that, worldwide, 327 newspapers and periodicals had carried reports.

The Festival of Britain, marking the centenary of the Great Exhibition, fell in 1951, and Bath was selected to be a regional centre, but a certain malaise had set in at the Assembly. It was reflected in a series of mishaps. Both Ralph Vaughan Williams and Josef Krips pulled out of a concert by the London Symphony Orchestra, and the actor Hedley Goodall withdrew from Shakespeare's *A Midsummer Night's Dream*. The numbers attending the opening day of the Children's Film Festival – again barely unchanged in concept since 1948 – were tiny. It subsequently transpired that the event was taking place on a school day.

On the first day of the 1951 Assembly, crowds gathered for the opening of the Octagon on Milsom Street as a cultural centre (now part of the Royal Photographic Society). As part of the city's role in the Festival of Britain, a choir of 340 voices from all over the West Country sang a festival service in Bath Abbey. The city was once again floodlit at night during festival time. Bath's first woman mayor, Cllr Miss Kathleen Harper, led a procession along an underground passage leading through the east gate of the city into Parade Gardens, to undertake the ceremonial switch-on.

An emphasis on West Country music pervaded the orchestral programmes. The Hallé Orchestra under Sir John Barbirolli performed a Rhapsody written by Frank Tapp, composer and pre-war director of the Pump Room Orchestra, for two pianos and double string orchestra. Meanwhile, the Bournemouth Municipal Orchestra under Rudolf Schwarz played Reginald Redman's *West Country Suite* with the BBC West of England Singers.

The one truly international name was Alfredo Campoli, the outstanding Italian violinist who, with the Bournemouth Municipal Orchestra, offered his calling-card, a spellbinding account of Mendelssohn's *Violin Concerto*. Dame Myra Hess's all-Beethoven piano recital at the Forum, in front of an audience said to number 2700, was a special occasion requiring three encores. Morley Pooley summed it up in *The Bath Chronicle*: 'It was more than a great evening of music: it was a musical occasion.'

Sir Thomas Beecham was in a bit of a grump after his concert in the Forum, refusing any encores: 'If you are expecting us to play something else, that is entirely out of the question,' he said on being recalled to the stage for the fourth time. 'The temperature of this hall is at least 200 degrees. I am not going to say anything about the architecture of this building, but it is not a concert hall, and I want to know why you presume to have a festival without having a concert hall. I am here under false pretences.'

Over the years, many have clamoured for a concert hall in Bath. While in the current era of lottery largesse the capital funding would most probably be available, few have addressed the financial aspects of running such a venue and keeping it busy year round. Nor have they considered the moral obligation that would then be on promoters to use a modern concert hall in preference to the city's Georgian rooms·which, for all their limitations as concert venues, exude an irreplaceable and exquisite charm and atmosphere.

On the River Avon a barge carrying the Boyd Neel Orchestra performed Handel's *Water Music*, while at the Theatre Royal, the Ballet Rambert included in their programme the world première of *Fate's Revenge*, a ballet especially designed for the Assembly by David Paltenghi, the company's ballet master and premier danseur. It was based on a satirical poem by a Mr Goosequill about social life in Bath during the middle of the eighteenth century. Among the distinguished visitors to this fourth Bath Assembly were the former government minister and founder of the National Health Service, Aneurin Bevan, and his wife Jennie Lee MP, later to be arts minister in the Labour Government of the 1960s.

An innovative event came in the form of a 'serenade concert' given by the City of Bath Bach Choir to an audience of 500 across the water of the Roman baths. *The Tatler* was there to snap the great and the good, so too was *The Times* which approved:

> *Although it lost its Assembly Rooms in the air-raid, Bath is still rich in rooms of beauty and distinction suitable for music. The Romans who built the baths, however, could hardly have had such a purpose in mind among the civilised amenities they projected for their building. It was left for Mr Cuthbert Bates and his Bath Bach Choir to discover that the colonnades round the main pool of the Roman baths form an excellent auditorium. To hear* Palestrina *sung in a Roman bath by an English choir of today is to realise how constant is the spirit of man in its search for beauty – and how successful.*

Away from the music, a spectacular exhibition of more than forty Gainsboroughs – including two lent by King George VI from Buckingham Palace – graced the Victoria Art Gallery. The show ran for an extra week to cope with demand. Sir Alfred Munnings, the celebrated painter, orator and former president of the Royal Academy, opened the exhibition. He criticised the Royal Academy for failing to loan the painter's self-portrait, saying that if the Earl of Sefton could lend a picture to Bath, then others could: 'I hope you will all see, and may it shame the Academy, the picture which has been lent by Earl Sefton. If he can lend that picture of Bath, then many others can and the Academy should have lent the picture of Thomas Gainsborough.'

Long before Tony Blair had captured the prefix 'a people's...' for his Government of the late 1990s, Morley Pooley had lined up the accolade for the 1951 festival: 'Far more than any of its forerunners this was a people's Assembly. Far more was offered to the ordinary man-in-the-street.'

He also hit the nail on the head with his question about whom the festival was for: 'Would it not also be fair to say, however, that its national appeal was correspondingly less than at any previous Assembly?' Already, Bath was struggling to work out who its festival should be aimed at. Should it be to provide a spa city – fighting intense competition for popularity with other British spas – with the type of publicity which will arouse the interest of potential visitors and residents? Or is it to provide a fortnight's festival for people living in the immediate vicinity? The latter might well be people who could pay a flying visit to Bath and hear a particular programme and dash back home afterwards – in other words, people who would not stay and spend their money within the city. But should this type of visitor be discouraged? Pooley concluded: 'The Assembly must go on, aiming ever higher, combining the two ideals of international publicity for Bath with a festival in which the citizens themselves can play an ever-increasing part. Bath, a city of priceless jewels, must tell the world of them or run the risk of being passed by.'

Summing up the 1951 festival, *The Bath Chronicle* highlighted the 'blitzed corners of Bath which were made to bloom' and expressed delight that the city was intending to remain in this state of floral decor. The paper's leader pointed out that 7000 people saw the Gainsborough exhibition, 5000 went to the architectural exhibition, and nearly 3000 heard Dame Myra Hess play Beethoven. It continued:

> *There are those – they are to be found in Edinburgh also – who condemn outright such festivals as the Assembly and affect to believe that they are for the 'snobbish few', that they have nothing to offer the 'man in the street'.*
>
> *These figures speak for themselves. They represent not 'the few' but 'everyman'. To say that there should not be opportunities such as the Assembly, to hear some of the best that the arts of civilisation can offer because they are not generally wanted, is to condemn everyone down to the cultural level of filling in pools coupons. The argument is as absurd as it is untrue.*

Despite all the encouragement, by 1952 the Assembly was down to just one orchestra, the Royal Philharmonic conducted by Sir Thomas Beecham, giving two concerts. And, said the Assembly directors, all the orchestral and choral programmes had to be based on the music of Haydn and Mozart. Stagnation was clearly setting in. The Arts Council's response was to reduce its support to £500. (It had previously been £750 except in 1951 when £2500 had been given, because Bath was considered part of the Festival of Britain.)

Bath Choral Society with their conductor William Jackman offered Haydn's *Creation* in the Abbey, while the City of Bath Bach Choir with Cuthbert Bates sang at the same venue a programme of Vaughan Williams's *Benedicite* and, as a tribute to the late King, Brahms's *Requiem*. There was just one token chamber music concert, given by the Griller Quartet with the pianist Colin Horsley. The Grillers had been regular wartime visitors to Bath when Lady Noble had organised a series of concerts in the city, while Horsley had premièred Lennox Berkeley's *Piano Concerto* in the city in 1949.

In a preview in May 1952, *The Bath Critic* noted this tokenism in a somewhat disdainful fashion:

> *This is a concert not to be missed. With the music in the hands of the Griller Quartet and Colin Horsley we may look forward to a memorable afternoon. But the failure to provide more than one concert of this kind can only be described as an artistic blunder of the first magnitude. Why must the intelligence and taste of the listening public be underrated in this fashion? A city like Bath should know better.*

The 1952 Assembly Ball, a distinct money-spinner which again took place at the Pump Room and around the baths, had a Roman theme and included a production of Shakespeare's *Coriolanus*, which had been running there all week on a specially erected stage over the waters. It was a *bal masque* and the guests, who had each paid 30 shillings to be there, were not allowed to unmask until after the judging at 11pm. The dancing, to Geraldo and his Orchestra, went on until 2.30am. Down at the Forum a popular young singer had been engaged to take part in a concert of light music. Julie Andrews, then 16, sang a range of songs with the Melachrino Orchestra.

The fame of Bath as the cradle of the modern postal service was explored in a postal history and postage stamp exhibition mounted at the Octagon. A special postmark was employed for letters mailed at the venue. The exhibition celebrated the work of Ralph Allen (1693-1764) who organised the bye and cross posts, the mail coach pioneer John Palmer (1742-1818), and Thomas Musgrave, who as postmaster of Bath from 1833-54 probably licked the very first adhesive postage stamp.

Although, as mentioned, the musical programme was curtailed in 1952, it included a violin and piano recital at the Forum on May 28 by a 36-year-old violinist and his brother-in-law. *The Bath Critic* reviewed it thus: 'If this concert had consisted simply of the movement from the *'Kreutzer' Sonata* which was given as a third encore, the audience would have had their money's worth.' The pianist was Louis Kentner and the violinist Yehudi Menuhin. It was Menuhin's first involvement with the Bath Festival, and an association which, while cursory at this stage, would continue until 1968 and put Bath firmly on the international map as one of the world's leading festivals.

Despite the Assembly's limited programme, organisers exceeded their £1000 guarantee from the city by almost £300, largely due to the reduction in the grant from the Arts Council, which was notified after the programme had been publicised. A heated council meeting on July 29, 1952 brought much argument as councillors struggled to set a figure for 1953.

Cllr George Stevenson felt there were too many other demands on ratepayers, and the Assembly attracted the wrong type of people anyway: 'I believe that restaurants which kept open to provide meals after the events had to close for lack of customers. The people we attract are not the type who spend money in Bath; and I don't think it can be said that the increase in the numbers at the Roman Baths is due to publicity from the Assembly.'

Cllr Albert Whitcher felt that the Assembly had been given enough time to become self-financing: 'It is no use saying that they must get a bit more from the ratepayers; the people who run the Assembly must get down to facts and run it on a self-supporting basis and not keep coming for these continual rises.'

Others mounted a spirited defence. Alderman Adrian Hopkins said that the press coverage of the Assembly more than justified the cost: 'Once you stop advertising, I am absolutely convinced that you may as well pack up. There would be no need for the city council to meet, for there would be no city to administer. The Assembly is the finest advertising medium this city has ever had.' By 24 votes to 18 the Assembly survived and received a grant for 1953, but the walls were closing in.

* * *

Coronation year, 1953, brought the first theme or motif to the festival. Perhaps unsurprisingly it was 'Royal Occasions', and much of the music had been written for regal events. The highlight, in social terms, was the now traditional Assembly Ball where guests dressed as past monarchs, including Helen of Troy, Queen Victoria, and even Oberon and Titania. The Hallé Orchestra conducted by Sir John Barbirolli gave three concerts, including one at the conductor's request with only the orchestra's string section in the Banqueting Room of the Guildhall. Cellist André Navarra performed the Elgar *Concerto* at one of their Forum concerts, while Clifford Curzon played Brahms's *Piano Concerto No.2* at the other.

Kathleen Ferrier was booked to sing in Bach's *B minor Mass* with the Bath Bach Choir conducted by Cuthbert Bates. Alas illness overtook the great contralto and she cancelled. In October of that year she died, and was soon immortalised as one of the greatest singers of the century, cruelly stolen from her adoring fans. Her place was taken by Kathleen Joyce.

A rare concert of fifteenth, sixteenth and seventeenth century music was given at the Guildhall by the London Consort of Viols and The Tudor Singers. The Tudor Singers had been founded by Cuthbert Bates in 1923, and he had directed them until they became a wartime casualty in 1942. He also led them for two years after the war until he came to the West Country as an inspector of music in schools. In this concert they were directed by Harry Stubbs, although Bates was an appreciative member of the audience.

The first ever television broadcast from the Assembly was not of a musical event, but of a fashion show at the Octagon in Milsom Street, arranged by the Everyman Club of Bath, a group that raised money for charity through social events. There was only room inside the building for an audience of 270 among all the broadcasting equipment, and large crowds gathered on the road outside to witness the models arrive in a convoy of vintage cars. Still at the Octagon, Mary Lee Epling, wife of Hollywood actor Douglas Fairbanks Jr, opened the 'Splendid Occasions' exhibition, and Dame Sybil Thorndike gave a poetry recital with her husband Sir Lewis Casson.

The bicentenary of the death of John Wood the Elder was marked in the 1954 Assembly. Representatives of ten countries, including three ambassadors, gathered to pay tribute to the architect's genius at a special festival lunch. Coinciding with the opening of the festival came news of the discovery of 41 original letters written by John Wood, found at a house in Tibberton, Hereford, which Wood had built for a cousin of the Duke of Chandos. They were considered a major find, shedding considerable light on the thoughts of the man who set the architectural tone for much of Bath.

At the Theatre Royal, 'Joyce Grenfell requests the pleasure' was a popular event. The Assembly's music policy had been quietly relaxed, allowing a greater range of orchestral music. It included, for the first time, the Liverpool Philharmonic Orchestra with Sir Adrian Boult. In *The Bath Chronicle*, critic Morley Pooley enjoyed contrasting the difference in conducting styles between Sir Thomas Beecham and Sir Adrian Boult:

Sir Thomas, given the usual ovation from a Bath audience, gave an extra number and a speech. Sir Adrian, after five recalls gave neither. Sir Thomas brought a brass section, but barely used it; Sir Adrian kept his brass section busy all the evening. Sir Thomas wallowed in music of the eighteenth century; Sir Adrian kept to the nineteenth and twentieth centuries.

Indeed, so little did Beecham use his brass section that three trombonists had made the journey from London simply to play in the National Anthem and a short encore. The rest of the time they did nothing. Neither orchestral concert at the Forum sold out, an indication, perhaps, that the Assembly was not succeeding. Shamefully for the city, nor did a recital by Claudio Arrau, the celebrated Chilean pianist, who also appeared at the Forum. Pooley's review was a glowing tribute to a memorable occasion:

To describe his playing one really needs a new vocabulary: ordinary adjectives seem far too mundane. Arrau likes to work on a big canvas where his powerful technique, emotional intensity and terrific endurance can have full reign... He is an amazing man, a prince of concert pianists if not king.

The city's two main choirs both contributed to the 1954 Assembly. Bath Choral Society directed by William Jackman performed *Judas Maccabeus* by Handel at the Abbey, while at the Forum the City of Bath Bach Choir under Cuthbert Bates sang Mozart's *Requiem*. Musically, this was all standard fare to those who know and love their music, and boring classical dirge to those who do not. Although the Arts Council's grant was raised reluctantly to £600, there was precious little attempt to market the Assembly. The promotional materials for 1948 had been more imaginative than in the following years.

In a letter to *The Bath Chronicle* published on May 29, 1954, Capt. S H Durnford of Sion Hill wrote:

The idea of an Assembly is a good one but it is off the rails – like other things. To be successful surely it must be both popular, without vulgarity, and profitable; otherwise no one will want to assemble again and no one will be able to pay for them to do so. Our Assembly is neither. It is not profitable because the music which predominates is not popular. This year's eight concerts cater exclusively for musical snobs of the Aldeburgh-Wigmore Hall variety. Only some half-dozen works have even a remotely popular appeal. I am told this is because conductors are not allowed to choose their own programmes. This is a double folly because:

1. Conductors themselves prefer to play works which the public enjoy; their London concerts are the reverse of highbrow;

2. The extra rehearsal time taken to perform the unfamiliar works demanded by the Assembly increases the cost of the orchestra.

The 1954 Assembly, the seventh, had other difficulties. The Yugoslav Ballet were engaged, but no one had realised they would require a full orchestra. Even at a squeeze, the pit in the Theatre Royal cannot take many musicians unless a large number of the stall seats are removed, forcing a reduction in income. At the last minute, the performance was cancelled. Their place was taken by Bath Opera Group who revived their recent production of *The Marriage of Figaro*. Unfortunately, many people demanded a refund, and the very shaky opening night played to rows of empty seats.

* * *

After the debacle of 1954, the city council held a heated discussion on the future. Alderman Adrian Hopkins, a staunch defender of the Assembly, conceded that matters could have been better arranged for the 1954 festival. He said:

> *I think the Surveying Committee could have helped by not digging up New Bond Street at that time. There is not a festival in the world that makes a profit, least of all Glyndebourne, which has to be maintained apart from the sale of seats. If you have made up your mind to abolish the Assembly, I think there is a reasonable chance of the press having a laugh at you in the morning. If you stop the Assembly for one year it will mean that it will be finished for all time.*

As the debate continued, Hopkins pointed out that the most successful Assembly, and the one that had given the city the most publicity, had been the very first, which had been directed by an outside impresario, Ian Hunter. Hopkins said:

> *I think it can be fairly said that subsequent Assemblies have not been in the same class as that one. Our sister city of Edinburgh carried on where we left off, and have made an amazing success of their Assembly. It has been said that it has brought £1m of new money into the city during the three weeks' festival, which costs the city in the region of £21,000.*

The realisation was slowly dawning upon the city of Bath that it had missed the boat. Edinburgh, which had been prepared to speculate, was reaping the rewards of a successful festival. And the director of the Edinburgh Festival was none other than Ian Hunter.

The situation in Bath was not helped by the retirement in October 1954 of John Boddington, the spas director, who, if not imaginative in his programming, had nevertheless been thorough in his execution, carrying out the politicians' wishes to the last detail.

A public referendum on the subject was suggested, but the town clerk advised that spending public money in that way would probably be illegal. It was late in the evening before Cllr Arthur Knight began to encourage councillors to think about the city as a whole, and the need to muster enthusiasm if there was to be a festival: 'We must arouse the enthusiasm of the ordinary citizen, the man in the street if you like, who wants something he can take part in.' He suggested a carnival procession and a torchlight tattoo, and said they might even roast an ox on the Recreation Ground: 'If we don't create enthusiasm we won't have an Assembly any longer – public opinion will force us to abandon it.' Cllr Albert Whitcher would have none of it:

I feel the time has come when someone has to make a stand against this waste of public money. We have stuck it for seven years now, hoping that the Assembly committee would improve and show a more enlightened outlook than they have, but they have gone from bad to worse. The only thing we can do is make these people stand on their own legs by withdrawing the support of the City Council. We should not expect the rank and file to subsidise the expensive taste of others.

His view carried the day, and by 24 votes to 22 the council's financial lifeline – a guarantee against loss in 1955 of up to £2500 – was withdrawn. *The Bath Chronicle* was unforgiving in its condemnation: 'the wrong decision... deplorable... detrimental... defeatist... short-sighted...' were all phrases used in the paper's leader column. In another comment it concluded:

Much is made by some critics that the Assemblies should be 'popular', should be for the 'man in the street'. There is substance in the point but it is far from being the whole truth. Everyone would think it silly if a worker at Rolls Royce went on strike because he could not take his wife home a Rolls Royce car. The Bath Assembly may not be to everyone's personal taste locally; but it is equally silly to 'strike' against something that materially helps maintain the city's prosperity and fame throughout the world.

The Chamber of Commerce deplored the council's move, as did the Bath Hotels and Restaurants Association. Behind the scenes, frenetic activity was taking place to engineer a rescue package. Within a week there was a suggestion that the council should run the Assembly directly and not through Bath Assembly Ltd. The only disadvantage was that the Arts Council would not provide funding to a local authority. Indeed, that was the very reason why a separate limited company was established in the first place.

The council met three weeks later when things had calmed down a bit and decided that the Assembly would go on after all, but under city council control, and more specifically under the direction of the Spa Committee. Although no figures were presented, it was clear that to create a worthwhile festival a substantial amount of money would be required. Furthermore, the Spa Committee was empowered to employ an impresario to run the whole affair.

On October 5, 1954, the news broke: Ian Hunter would return and lead the 1955 Bath festival of the arts. The name Assembly would be dropped and instead it would be known as the Bath May Festival. It would, in effect, be a clean sheet. Hunter had driven a hard bargain with the council officials who had visited him in London begging for help. It wasn't to be just his services that the council would engage, but also those of his company, Harold Holt Ltd. There was to be no civic guarantee against loss as in previous years. Instead, Hunter told the authorities that nothing less than an outright grant of a massive £5000 would do the trick. In addition, the use of council rooms should be completely free of charge. Hunter offered the people of Bath his personal assurance that it would all be a great success:

> We are only interested in providing the events which will be superior in quality to anything which has gone before in the city – including the first Bath Assembly. That was only the beginning. We have got to make this festival unique in the world. Bath is unique so there is no reason why this festival should not be unique.

But it was already October 1954, and with the festival set to take place between May 11 and 21, 1955, Hunter had his work cut out. Nothing if not shrewd, Hunter knew that bigger names than his own would be needed if the festival was to have the appeal he had promised. He soon announced that the conductor Sir Thomas Beecham, the designer Oliver Messel, and the theatre impresario Hugh Beaumont, had agreed to serve as artistic directors. Not only would they be taking part in the festival, but their advice and contacts would be at Hunter's disposal.

Hunter was also an expert at making sure the media carried news of his ideas. The *Evening Standard* of December 8, 1954, said:

> Bath is setting up a rival to Edinburgh. This takes the place of the Bath Assembly, which began in 1948 as an annual event, but has dwindled in importance. This time an opera, concerts and recitals, and a 'spectacular outdoor event' are promised; all with an eighteenth century flavour.

The Birmingham Post (December 10, 1954) was quick to point out that:

> ...Yehudi Menuhin was an unexpected visitor to an informal meeting today between the organisers of next year's Bath May Festival and a number of journalists. He is to be one of the soloists at the festival, in which everything to be performed and all the buildings are to be of the eighteenth century, and he told me that he is 'looking forward tremendously' to the occasion.

The stakes were high. Hunter had all but promised the earth and had to deliver: 'The festival will go on from strength to strength, until it establishes Bath as the premier centre for entertainment of a high order in this country not only during the ten days of an annual festival, but for a full season each year, as in its golden period,' he said.

The council were of similar mind. Cllr Miss Kathleen Harper said: 'If we do not make a success of it this time, we shall never have another one.' The council established a Festival Fund, which raised almost £2000 from local businesses and residents keen to demonstrate their support for the revitalised celebrations. Meanwhile, the Chamber of Commerce organised a window-dressing competition, which attracted some 45 entries.

May 11, 1955, the first day of the festival, dawned with brilliant sunshine. Flowers, flags and bunting were draped around the city. In the morning, hundreds of people lined the streets to see the Band of the Royal Marines followed by a naval guard of honour march through the city centre. Milsom Street was an avenue of colour. Shop windows welcomed the festival with flowers and rich drapes, mainly in pastel shades. One of the most attractive was C Milsom & Sons, who had an effective reproduction of Handel's *Water Music* on the River Avon proudly portrayed in their window.

Instead of selling individual programmes at each concert as in previous years, organisers produced a souvenir programme book. A true sense of festival was gradually emerging. The classical music programme was dazzling – Yehudi Menuhin, Gioconda de Vita and Efrem Kurtz were among the line-up of visitors. So too were the flautist Elaine Shaffer, the conductor Josef Krips and the great Austrian soprano Irmgard Seefried accompanied by Gerald Moore. De Vito and Menuhin gave a duet recital at the Guildhall for which seats cost an extraordinarily high £1 each, but they sold out nevertheless. Midway through the recital Menuhin, ever the gentleman, handed his pocket handkerchief to de Vito who was suffering from a heavy cold. Their repertoire included such obscure classics as a pair of duets by Viotti, and Spohr's *Duo for Two Violins (Op.67 No.2)*. They were joined in the second half on the harpsichord by a Bathonian who has since gone on to great musical success, Raymond Leppard.

A couple of days later, Menuhin held a packed Bath Abbey enthralled as he performed unaccompanied music for solo violin by Johann Sebastian Bach – *Sonata No.3 in C major*, *Partita No.3 in E major*, and *Partita No.2 in D minor*. Morley Pooley was there:

A solitary figure, clutching a violin, stood in front of the choir stalls in Bath Abbey on Tuesday evening, and paused while the huge crowd of people who had flocked to hear him settled quietly in their seats. Behind him the newly-restored East Window stood out in bold relief like a beacon of faith, before him a sea of upturned faces waited expectantly.

And as he drew his bow across the strings of his fiddle, magic seemed to fill the air. For 90 minutes he played almost continuously, and throughout that time there was scarce a rustle to break the spell he wove. The player was Yehudi Menuhin, probably the greatest violinist alive today; the instrument he held – almost as old as parts of the beautifully proportioned Abbey Church which formed such a wonderful background to the music of the greatest of all writers of church music, Johann Sebastian Bach – a priceless Strad.

Making his presence felt, Menuhin also gave a performance of Viotti's *Violin Concerto No.22* with the Royal Philharmonic Orchestra conducted by Sir Thomas Beecham at the Guildhall. In an interview for this book, given in

August 1998, Yehudi Menuhin recalled the occasion which was broadcast live on the radio: 'The performance ran a few minutes over time and was duly interrupted by the sports programme. There were quite a few protests.'

At the Theatre Royal, Emlyn Williams appeared seven times reading from the works of Charles Dickens and Dylan Thomas. Dickens's grandson, Admiral Sir Gerald Dickens, was in the audience on one occasion. According to *The Bath Chronicle*, Emlyn Williams 'bowed to an author long dead, and we bowed to this great artist who for the past two hours had made these books live for us. A bare stage, a reading table – impressive in its unobtrusiveness – a spotlight and a pile of books, these made his set.'

Opera returned to the festival in 1955 with several performances of a rare French work, *Zémire et Azor (Beauty and the Beast)*, by André Grétry. Conducted by Sir Thomas Beecham, the scenery was designed by Oliver Messel, who was related through his mother to the eighteenth century Bath composer Thomas Linley. The only previous performances in England had been conducted by Linley himself in 1777. The production, which benefited from extra orchestration by Beecham, was a great success attracting favourable comment from critics and public alike. Unfortunately the conductor was suffering from gout, and his place was taken on two occasions by Denis Vaughan from Melbourne who was on the staff at Glyndebourne. The opera's misfortune was further compounded when the leading lady, Guguette Boulangeot, collapsed at the end of the first act on May 18 suffering from pleurisy. Writing in *The Financial Times* of May 17, 1955, Andrew Porter complained, perhaps a little harshly, that *Zémire et Azore* was the only thing worth coming to see in Bath. He said:

> The other programmes hardly constitute a festival. The bulk of the music chosen is eighteenth century but this is too encyclopaedic a scene to give direction to the whole. Bath will have to find something individual, something which she alone can offer, if her festival is to be established.

Despite the rarity value of the opera, it didn't pack the theatre. At the time Ian Hunter complained bitterly to *The Bath Chronicle* of the apathy and the slow take-up of top price seats: 'With 90,000 people in Bath and half a million in Bristol, I find it difficult to understand why the 1500 seats (300 seats per performance) at 30 shillings have not been sold.' Forty-three years later he recognises where he went wrong: 'If I had called it *Beauty and the Beast*, they would have come, thinking it was a pantomime. It was a wonderful production.'

The magic of Handel's *Water Music* floated across the Avon to thousands of people lining the banks of Parade Gardens. It was performed on a barge, moored mid-stream, by the Bournemouth Symphony Orchestra conducted by Charles Groves, who cut a splendid figure in a turquoise satin coat, white knee breeches, lace cravat and ruffles and brilliant red sash. Afterwards the venerable maestro gave his blessing to the event. He said: 'This is the first time I have performed on a barge and I am well-satisfied with the result. We were given a marvellous reception by the crowd, and I think the costumes and setting were a great help.' Etched in coloured lights, with the beauty of the floodlit Abbey and the half-shadowed colonnade towering in the background, it was a remarkable scene. The crowd stood 15 deep enjoying every minute of it.

To cap it all, the Bath May Festival of 1955 celebrated the 150th anniversary of Nelson's victory at the Battle of Trafalgar with a spectacular re-enactment of that historic occasion in a *son-et-lumière* event. Ten performances were planned; it was expected to make a fortune, and put the festival on a sound financial footing for future years.

Admiral Lord Nelson had been a one-time resident of the city and was honoured with the freedom of Bath in 1797. Hunter's goal was to stimulate a sense of identity and civic pride in Bath as well as offer the greatest outdoor event the city had ever witnessed. He appealed for residents around the Recreation Ground to black out windows that overlooked the ground. Visitors to the pageant – seats ranged from five shillings to ten shillings, and standing space was available for two shillings and sixpence – were able to purchase a full-colour programme book. Moran Caplat, a wartime submarine commander and now general manager of Glyndebourne, was engaged by Hunter for a fee of 200 guineas to create the dramatisation. There was also a corresponding exhibition entitled 'The Navy of Nelson's Day' at the Victoria Art Gallery with Trafalgar silver, costumes, models, letters, plans and portraits.

Narrated by the actor Jack Hawkins, 'The Battle of Trafalgar' took place on three sets with a seascape panorama and involved 600 amateur actors, scene-shifters and technicians. In a little over an hour it told the story of Horatio Nelson's career, culminating in his Trafalgar death and victory through a sequence of twelve scenes. Canon fire and pantomime ice added to the spectacle. At the end of each performance, the salute was taken by a high ranking naval official. The press attention from across the country was remarkable and calculated to be the equivalent of £13,000 in advertising terms. Among those who turned up to view the spectacle was Lord Nelson, the sixth earl and a direct descendent of the Admiral.

The Scotsman of May 18, 1955, summed it up particularly well:

> *The Battle of Trafalgar is neither play, nor pageant, nor tattoo, though it borrows elements from all these media. Written by Captain Broome RN, it consists of a series of episodes,* tableaux vivants, *scattered round a large sports field, each incident being picked out by floodlight. The story is boomed by the recorded voice of Jack Hawkins, and Nelson's words – the famous ones – are spoken by Nigel Patrick. It is all there, plus flashbacks – Lady Hamilton, Napoleon scowling, conferences in the French flagship and in Victory and, of course, the battle itself. (There is previously a reminder of the Battle of Copenhagen, in order to show us Nelson's 'blind eye' gesture.) The climax is an exciting business, with lots of smoke and flashes and manages to look extraordinarily like one of those early nineteenth century prints of naval engagements. Even the grass seems to have a slight swell on it. The ships are life-like, collapsible, slightly mobile, and eventually show convincing signs of damage.*

Sadly the gremlins soon set in. The BBC was to broadcast live coverage to the nation of the third performance on (ironically) Friday, May 13. Unfortunately, ten minutes into transmission the picture was irretrievably lost.

But ultimately it was the cruellest of fates that scuttled Hunter's grand Battle of Trafalgar. No one could have predicted snow in May. Organisers had previously decreed that come rain or shine the show would go on – especially as Earl Mountbatten himself, the First Sea Lord, was coming to take the salute on May 17. Nevertheless, faced with driving blizzards and a mud-drenched Recreation Ground, they had no option but to cancel that prime performance. Earl Mountbatten never managed to see the great re-enactment of Trafalgar.

For Ian Hunter, a greater irritant was finding that public reaction in the provinces was far more apathetic than in London or Edinburgh. Tickets for Trafalgar only began moving in any number towards the end of the 1955 festival. He said: 'I think the novelty of something of this kind in Bath works against the event rather than for it. Think of London or Paris, and the great rush to see something new first, not as it seems in Bath, the last!'

As a piece of theatre the Battle of Trafalgar was an undoubted success – but the bills had yet to be paid.

CHAPTER FOUR

The loss on the 1955 festival was, not surprisingly, substantial.

The outright grant of £5000 given to Ian Hunter by the city council, together with the Arts Council's guarantee of £1000, was clearly not going to be enough to meet all the festival's liabilities. Hunter sensed trouble in the air, and even before the end of the festival launched a major public opinion offensive.

During his final performance at the Theatre Royal, Sir Thomas Beecham gave a speech to the audience reminding them that worthwhile festivals invariably made a loss. Rounding on the festival's critics he thundered:

> *Are you going to be worthy of your great heritage or are you going to be content to be a tenth-rate provincial city? Let those who object to this festival, who object to the pence in the pound on the rates, reflect that the influence of this festival will penetrate to every corner of the globe. This festival does not represent all we can do, nor all we expected to do. We hope this is not the end but the beginning and a good beginning, of many to come. The fate of this festival rests in your hands and in nobody else's. This festival is no oppressive burden on the tax payer. You cannot have a festival which is worthwhile without losing money on music, on opera, or any nonsense like that. You may say this is all vile aristocratic indulgence. Everything worth having, including liberty, is vile aristocratic indulgence.*

The extent of Ian Hunter's overspend soon became known. In addition to the £5000 grant already given to the festival, Bath's ratepayers would have to find an additional £5759 to cover the deficit. And this on a festival with a turnover of less than £26,000. Hunter trotted out his excuses: the bad weather, the General Election, a threatened railway strike – even a newspaper strike – had all conspired against the festival.

When the city council considered the matter the deputy mayor, Cllr William Gallop, tried to defend the festival saying that every performance had been first class and every artist an acknowledged master of his or her own particular art. He said: 'We ought to consider it as part of our duty to spend some money raised from the rates on helping to subsidise forms of art which would not exist unless they had subsidies from somewhere.'

But the critics had a field day – especially as, at the council meeting where the deficit was discussed, there was an attempt to secure funding for a festival in 1956. Cllr Ronald Purdie said he was sure that the citizens of Bath would be shocked when they learned of the enormity of the deficit. He said: 'Mr Hunter referred to general apathy at Bath. I am not conscious of any apathy, I am more conscious of active opposition to the thing.'

Cllr Albert Whitcher was similarly on form:

This thing is not wanted. It is not serving the needs of the city. This opera, which cost nearly £5000, is not wanted by the ordinary person, and the same, apparently, can be said of the Battle of Trafalgar. One wag told me he understood this battle of Trafalgar had cost more than the original.

Alderman Alleyne Berry, hitherto a staunch defender of the festival, admitted that he too was appalled at the financial result:

Can we afford another festival, and can we afford not to have another festival at this stage in our history? Looking at it solely as a piece of representative government I would say no festival at all. But when one lives and moves among those in business life and the hoteliers, one realises that this is a very much wider problem and that the hoteliers of this town are very much worried about the position.

Despite the undoubted artistic merits of the revitalised festival, the city fathers were so appalled at Hunter's financial mismanagement that by 30 votes to 21 the city council removed his financial lifeline, voting through just enough money to clear the deficit and no more. And so, after 1955, Bath's festival was set to end. Still trying to put the best gloss on the catastrophe 43 years later, Ian Hunter blames external events. Speaking in 1998 he said: 'Fortuitously, the Suez crisis gave us a good reason for postponing it.'

Ever tenacious, Hunter was not prepared to accept total abandonment of the project. He immediately set to work trying to raise a private endowment. The problem he encountered working from London was that Bath's festival was considered to be a problem for the West of England. Let the West sort it out. At the time he said:

I am convinced that this idea must not be allowed to die. Equally, I am not prepared to start anything on less money, or without being in a position to give it a run for seven years, otherwise it would stand little chance of success.

When news of Hunter's attempts to keep the festival alive reached the city council in October 1955 they offered a cautious, if unenthusiastic, welcome, providing it did not involve the authority in any financial obligations. Opponents on the council pushed to have the festival completely wound up, suggesting that Hunter would use the window of opportunity to foist a festival on the city by back-door methods. However, protagonists advised caution. Alderman Alleyne Berry said: 'Here we have a reputable lot of people endeavouring to raise money for Bath and we cannot turn it down, we cannot cold-shoulder it.'

Alderman Major Geoffrey Lock insisted that Hunter was doing a grand thing, and if he and others were willing to run a festival at Bath, the city council should give them support. 'For goodness sake give this man some encouragement,' he cried. His plea fell on deaf ears and in 1956 there was no festival.

During the course of that year various ideas for a similar event were floated, including a 'Hollywood Bowl' in front of the Royal Crescent, a military-style tattoo and a 'people's festival', whatever that might be. In September 1956 the indefatigable Ian Hunter returned to the city to meet members of the council. The Chamber of Commerce had been lobbying furiously behind the scenes. It could see the merits of the festival and was anxious that one should take place in 1957. It called on the council to provide a guarantee of up to £2500 to support Hunter's efforts. At a vote, the council was tied 23-23. The mayor declined to use his casting vote but declared the motion not carried, and therefore no money was forthcoming. The chamber refused to be downhearted and decided to raise financial guarantees from businesses in the city. By November 1, 1956, £1900 worth of guarantees were in place. With only ten days to go before their deadline, another £600 was required. By November 5 they had succeeded. *The Bath Chronicle* was generous in its praise:

> *The appeal by the Chamber of Commerce to provide £2500 in guarantee and so make possible a Festival of the Arts at Bath next June has been more than met. This is most gratifying. All those who have recognised the need for such a festival at Bath will be immensely encouraged... What matters now is not the past but the future.*

How would the city fathers react? They were magnanimous, offering the services of equipment, staff and premises free of charge. Overall there was a sense of relief at being able to claim the kudos for a festival without having to take responsibility for the financial side of it.

On November 14, 1956, Ian Hunter presented his theme for 1957: 'Elegance, wit, caricature, humour and light-heartedness.' Behind those fine words he was lining up a spectacular array of internationally renowned classical musicians, the likes of which Bath had never seen before. They included the brother and sister violin and piano duo Yehudi and Hephzibah Menuhin, the pianist Claudio Arrau, the soprano Elisabeth Schwarzkopf and the keyboard player Rosalyn Tureck.

Unfortunately, early in 1957 an outside influence scuppered his grand plans: petrol rationing. It simply was not possible to guarantee either artists or audiences the fuel they would need to journey to Bath. Even Ian Hunter's extensive and influential contacts could not solve this problem. The idea of holding a more limited festival or delaying it until the autumn was considered, but eventually Hunter and the Guarantors' Executive Committee, which had been set up to protect the guarantors' interests, felt that it would be better to postpone until the following year.

* * *

The announcement of plans for the 1958 festival attracted uproar. Twenty deer were to be paraded through the streets of Bath before being roasted at a barbecue on the Recreation Ground. The ensuing outcry – 'barbarous', 'inhuman', 'a disgusting orgy reminiscent of the pagan Romans' – brought swift denials and claims of misunderstanding. Within hours the plans for such an exhibition were scotched. The idea behind the barbecue was to widen the scope of the festival and make it attractive to a greater section of the community. The outdoor event did go ahead, without the macabre parade, but due to torrential rain had to be postponed until the following day.

The Bath Chronicle's headline captured the spirit: 'Bath Festival for All' and for the first time the paper printed a special festival supplement. It also had a daily festival page devoted to news, views, reviews and previews. British Railways joined in the spirit by offering half-price excursions from Paddington Station to Bath Spa – each train had an advertising board on the front bearing the city's coat of arms and the dates of the festival. In London, Ibbs & Tillett Ltd had been selling tickets from their office at Wigmore Street.

In keeping with the ambition to widen the festival's appeal, jazz made its first appearance on the programme. The unknown quantity of the swinging sixties may still have been a couple of years away, but Bath was leading the way in offering community entertainment and a festival for everyone. The Bath Festival of Jazz took place in the Regency Ballroom between June 2 and June 7. Writing in the introduction to the jazz festival programme, Duncan Harrison, managing director of the ballroom, said: 'Jazz now plays such an important part in our life that to ignore it would be indeed churlish, and that jazz is an art form most certainly cannot be denied.'

There was dancing to Johnny Dankworth and his orchestra while almost 1000 people turned up to hear Chris Barber and his band. Humphrey Littleton not only gave his scheduled performance, but also lit up the festival with an impromptu jam session in the city centre afterwards.

Both in jazz and classical music the list of artists was impressive for a ten-day festival, including many of those whom Hunter had intended for the aborted 1957 festival. Not the least of these was Yehudi Menuhin, who received a standing ovation for his performance of Beethoven's *Violin Concerto* in the Abbey with the London Philharmonic Orchestra conducted by a 29-year-old rising star, Colin Davis.

The 21-year-old pianist Ingrid Haebler also played with Davis and the London Philharmonic Orchestra (Beethoven's *Piano Concerto No.1*) as well as giving a recital. She had taken a dislike to the Steinway piano provided for her concerto at the Guildhall, and a Blüthner piano had to be hastily rushed over from the Pavilion for her. When it was returned to the Pavilion, the irascible and diminutive Russian pianist Shura Cherkassky played Gershwin – the *Piano Concerto* and *Rhapsody in Blue* – with George Boyd and his orchestra.

Isaac Stern appeared with the Goldsborough Orchestra led by Emmanuel Hurwitz; Rosalyn Tureck performed an all-Bach programme twice on the same day to satisfy demand; John Gielgud performed a Shakespeare monologue at the Theatre Royal; Harry Blech brought the London Mozart Players; local boy made good Raymond Leppard brought the Leppard Orchestra together with soprano Jacqueline Delman for a programme that included a performance of Mozart's *Exsultate Jubilate*; Yehudi Menuhin returned with his sister Hephzibah for a recital featuring Beethoven's *Spring Sonata*; and the City of Bath Bach Choir once again turned their attentions to Bach's *B minor Mass*.

One of the 1958 festival's greatest moments came with an appearance by the 42-year-old German soprano Elisabeth Schwarzkopf at the Guildhall. Schwarzkopf was one of the greatest – *The New Grove Dictionary of Music and Musicians* suggests *the* greatest – of post-war women lieder singers. Writing in *The Bath Chronicle* (June 4, 1958), Morley Pooley summed up the reaction to her performance:

> *They clapped, they cheered, they even stamped in their enthusiasm to pay tribute to Elisabeth Schwarzkopf at the close of her song recital with Gerald Moore, accompanist, in the Guildhall Banqueting Room on Tuesday evening. It was the biggest, the warmest and the most spontaneous demonstration of enthusiastic delight which any soloist has yet received at this very successful Bath Festival. And she deserved every bit of it, for not only did she thrill us with the magic of a magnificent voice, but she brought the songs to life with her mature artistry and vivid personality.*

Regular open-air performances from the Band of the Life Guards and no fewer than three dress balls, all added to the festival spirit. Bath Drama Club gave an anthology of poetry, prose and plays portraying Bath from the fifth to the twentieth centuries, including writing by Chaucer, Shakespeare, Austen, Pepys and Dickens, called 'In Praise of Bath'. Meanwhile, the Arts Council's 'Three Modern British Masters' exhibition was on display at the Victoria Art Gallery featuring works by Matthew Smith, Victor Passmore and Francis Bacon. Who could deny the attraction of such a compact but spectacularly star-studded programme?

The festival was formally opened during a televised ceremony in Abbey Church Yard performed by the archaeologist Sir Mortimer Wheeler. In his speech, Sir Mortimer hit on a familiar theme when he warned that it would be easy for Bath to become a museum, 'a mere archaeological specimen.'

He continued: 'I am going to be quite frank with you about this. If there's one thing in the world I dislike more than another, it is archaeology. The moment you think of a place as mere archaeology, you may be sure that the place is dead. But Bath, you'll agree with me, is not dead. It is a Roman city; it is a Georgian city; but Bath is also a modern city.' He added that for every new nuclear reactor built, the country should invest in a new festival such as Bath's.

The final result of the 1958 festival was an artistic triumph and only the smallest demand was made on guarantors. 'Festival: all pleased' ran *The Bath Chronicle's* front page headline on the final day, June 7, 1958.

* * *

The news that would ultimately make, and later almost break, the Bath Festival came on March 5, 1959: Yehudi Menuhin was to be the artistic director. It was a stroke of absolute genius on the part of Ian Hunter. Speaking in 1998 he said: 'I was his agent and the great thing with Yehudi was that it kept him interested with new ideas. He had fallen in love with Bath in 1955 when he appeared with Beecham.'

Few had not heard of Menuhin and his appointment opened up contacts to just about every artist on the planet. The appointment also confirmed, should there have been any doubt, the festival's direction as first and foremost a festival of classical music. Speaking in August 1998, Yehudi Menuhin explained why he agreed to take up the position:

> *I was looking for the opportunity of being able to invite colleagues, young and old, people from other arts. The choice of venues was so wonderful in Bath, so many beautiful buildings, and nothing too big. It was a beautiful city. It was a real temptation and worth all the trouble.*

Announcing Menuhin's role in the festival, Hunter said:

> *Of all my dealings with artists I feel there are very few indeed who command his diversity, interests and tastes and human understanding, and about whom a successful festival could be woven.*

Giving details of the 1959 festival, Hunter explained that although Menuhin would not perform in every concert, he would appear in four differing roles: that of speaker in a discussion, violinist, viola player, and conductor of a hand-picked Festival Chamber Orchestra. Banished were the big symphony orchestras which had hitherto dominated the festival's orchestral programme.

The Festival Chamber Orchestra already existed in all but name. It was a London-based band consisting of many of the top chamber music players of the day and was used by the record company EMI as a backing group for Menuhin, their top-selling classical star. His producers at EMI immediately saw the advantages of hijacking the city's name, and over the coming years the array of classical programmes presented at the Bath Festival would often be dictated by recording schedules.

The Daily Telegraph of June 6, 1959, welcomed Menuhin's appointment:

> *It is his artistry that dominates the programmes, his taste that is reflected in their choice. So wide and distinctive are his sympathies that a sense of unity is provided without the accompanying danger of an exercise of personal whim. Not the least of Menuhin's gifts is his ability to create a special atmosphere of music-making. Virtuosity combined with personal modesty is but part of it; his contact with music is one of unshakeable integrity.*

There was also good news on the finance front. The local ITV company TWW, forerunner of HTV, was to come on board as a major sponsor with a donation of £1000. Their association with the festival was to last for many years providing not only a substantial financial base, but also added publicity and an important archive of festival footage. The Arts Council's grant shot up to £1750 including £1000 ring-fenced for opera.

With the austerity of the war years now 14 years distant, and basking in the success of 1958, the Bath Festival decided to spread its wings. The music programme was larger and more comprehensive than ever before. Menuhin was joined by his piano-playing sisters Hephzibah and Yaltah. The ladies performed Mozart's *Concerto for Two Pianos* while Menuhin himself directed the Bath Festival Chamber Orchestra in a complete cycle of the *Brandenburg Concertos* by Bach. Eschewing the Pavilion, the festival made use of Christ Church in Julian Road, where the sixth *Brandenburg Concerto* was performed twice – ostensibly as an encore, but in all probability because the concert would otherwise have finished embarrassingly early. Menuhin also took three of the *Brandenburg Concertos* to Wells Cathedral.

Although well out of the Bath area in terms of political and funding considerations, Wells – and particularly Wells Cathedral through the ancient diocesan links – has a strong relationship with Bath. In festival terms it is a link that has survived where many others faltered, not least because Bath concert-goers have rarely failed to patronise events in such elegant surroundings.

At the Guildhall, Yehudi Menuhin was joined by Hephzibah on the piano and the clarinettist Reginald Kell for a programme that included a relatively modern work called *Contrasts* by the Hungarian composer Béla Bartók. Announcing his intention of giving a repeat performance Menuhin added, with a twinkle in his eye, that anyone who wished to do so could, of course, leave. According to *The Bath Chronicle* there was a burst of ironic applause when one well-known, but unnamed, Bath resident got up from his seat near the front and solemnly walked out.

The 1959 programme included ballet with soloists from the Royal Swedish Ballet. The accompanying Goldsborough Orchestra spilt over from the pit of the Theatre Royal into the stalls while the group's harpist was forced to sit in a box. Children from the Spa School of Dancing formed part of the show. As the festival progressed, opera took over from the dance at the theatre in the form of Bizet's *Dr Miracle* and Purcell's *Dido and Aeneas* with Joan Hammond singing Dido. Also in the cast were such famous names as Janet Baker, Jacqueline Delman and Heather Harper.

That year also saw the first appearance of music from a foreign culture. Menuhin personally introduced a sarod recital by Indian musicians which took place at the Guildhall on June 8, 1959. Ever since then, Indian music has been a regular and popular feature of the festival. Other events in 1959 included an afternoon recital at the Guildhall by the tenor Peter Pears accompanied by the composer Benjamin Britten, and a dramatic recital at the Theatre Royal featuring Dame Peggy Ashcroft with Marius Goring and the harpist Osian Ellis. Hunter had originally invited Michael Redgrave and his wife Rachel Kempson to perform a dramatised version of Christopher Anstey's *New Bath Guide* at the theatre, but to his embarrassment had omitted to check their availability before publicising the event.

At the request of TWW, the festival introduced a violin competition to be judged by Menuhin and another well-known violinist, Manoug Parikian. The 100 guineas first prize was won by 14-year-old Peter Thomas from Aberdare, the youngest entrant.

Bath with Menuhin could certainly attract some big names in the classical field, and the jazz side fared no differently. Throughout the 1960s the name of Johnny Dankworth would become as closely associated with Bath as Menuhin's. The success of the 1958 jazz programme had been overwhelming and in 1959 it was extended to the full ten days of the festival, bringing great names not just from this country but from all over Europe. Led by Dankworth, the line-up included Monica Zetterlund, Hans Koller, the Ted Heath Band, Stephane Grappelli and Acker Bilk (who was born at Pensford), as well as the memorable Old Etonian, Humphrey Littleton. But with the exception of Dankworth and Heath, the size of the audiences was disappointing. Nobody quite worked out why. Possibly it was a case of simply too much at once.

To complement the music and theatre there was an outstanding exhibition of 46 Turner watercolours at the Holburne Museum, the first time the collection had left its home at Farnley Hall in Yorkshire. There was a Wedgwood display at the Victoria Art Gallery, and a flower exhibition by the Bath Floral Decoration Society at Abbey Church House. Departing from the world of the arts, the festival began a tentative alignment with sport: runner Chris Brasher inaugurated the new cinder running track at Norwood, where the programme included the Somerset AAA championships in field and track events. Other events included a pigeon race, a golf tournament and a scooter race.

These, together with the emergence of a strong Ladies Committee, which provided helpers at many events as well as catering and domestic assistance, were the forerunner of the fringe. The Ladies Committee took on responsibility for all types of entertainment as well as offering hospitality to visiting artists. With their tea-parties, open houses and hospitality, Bath's reputation as a friendly and welcoming festival began to grow, and was much remarked upon in the press.

A fanfare by trumpeters of the Royal Corps of Signals on the roof of the colonnade facing the Abbey formally opened the celebrations on June 3, 1959. Brilliant sunshine accompanied the ceremony by Lord Wilmot of Selmeston, a governor of the Old Vic and a director of the Glyndebourne Opera Trust. *The Daily Telegraph* captured the mood:

> *Perhaps encouraged by the kindness of the weather, Bath this week has truly caught the festival spirit. There is a continental atmosphere in the city's streets, where striped shop awnings and banks of flowers make a colourful scene.*

Two days after the festival finished Ian Hunter was declaring it an unqualified success. Owing to the numbers visiting from nearby Bristol, the suggestion was raised of staging events there as part of future festivals. The festival chairman, Cllr Hugh Roberts, said: 'There is quite a strong feeling that we should put something on in Bristol next year as an integral part of the Bath Festival.'

Despite his enthusiasm for expansion, Cllr Roberts was still anxious to put the festival onto a more secure financial footing. The existing arrangements were for a guarantee fund, underwritten by local businesses and patrons, amounting to £2500. Any loss above that figure was borne by the Orchestral Concerts Society, an organisation set up by Ian Hunter's company, Harold Holt Ltd, to administer the festival. 'I don't think the Orchestral Concerts Society can any longer be asked to carry on under that liability,' said Cllr Roberts. 'And I do not believe that we can go on scratching around for £2500 every year.'

The reasons for his anxiety became clear in September 1959 when that year's figures were released: either Hunter had returned to the old days of over-stretching himself, or his luck – often a variable feast – had turned once again. '1959 Bath Festival: substantial loss shock' ran the front page headline in *The Bath Chronicle*. Guarantors, possibly lulled into a false sense of security by the easy ride in 1958, were obliged to dig deep into their pockets and pay 75 per cent of their guarantees. The extent of the Orchestral Concerts Society's total liabilities were not revealed, but were undoubtedly substantial.

* * *

Miraculously the ever-resilient Ian Hunter, as impervious to criticism as ever, bounced back and before long plans were in place for a 1960 festival, once again with Menuhin as figurehead. This time Menuhin's brother-in-law, the pianist Louis Kentner, would be joining the party. TWW were back on board increasing their sponsorship from £1000 to £1500.

The 1960 Bath Festival was opened by the conductor Sir Adrian Boult, who had been conductor of the BBC Symphony Orchestra from 1930 to 1950. The orchestra had spent the war years based in nearby Bristol. At the midday Abbey Church Yard ceremony on May 18, 1960, Sir Adrian said:

> *I think 'staggering' is not too strong a word to describe the programme you have before you. It contains really everything that anyone can possibly want in the way of artistic pleasure and privilege. I am quite sure that anyone who comes to any of the programmes will go away richer in spirit from what they are going to hear.*

The musical programme was greatly expanded but still largely focused around Yehudi Menuhin and his family. Menuhin and the cellist Gaspar Cassado opened the programme with a concert in the Abbey of solo violin and cello music; the pianist Gina Bachauer was called upon to replace an indisposed Claudio Arrau in a Guildhall performance of Mozart's *Piano Concerto K491* – the concert also included Stravinsky's *Dumbarton Oakes*; the composer Nadia Boulanger came to conduct the Ensemble Vocal Paris; and a special *Homage à Chopin*, conceived to celebrate the 150th anniversary of the great pianist's birth, studiously avoided any of his piano music. The festival also saw the world première of Manuel de Falla's *Balada de Mallorca* and a specially commissioned work by Arnold Cooke, *Concerto for Orchestra*. Meanwhile Britten and Pears returned to perform Schubert's great song cycle, *Die Schöne Müllerin* at the Guildhall.

For the second time *The Bath Chronicle* provided a special festival supplement as well as a dedicated daily festival page. The paper was also attracting music writers who simply wanted to be in Bath for the festival. Kenneth Loveland, a prominent national critic, was co-opted onto the paper's staff for the duration.

The festival featured a formal public debate, which included a look at what a festival should be. Some 600 people turned up at the Festival Forum, which was held in the Pavilion, to hear Professor Thomas Bodkin, Fr Angellus Andrew, Christopher Hollis and Hugh Ross-Williamson answer questions on a variety of subjects, including how to arrange a festival of the arts and music in order to make it appeal to as wide a section of the public as possible. Professor Bodkin said it was an unanswerable question. To show every kind of art in every period and of every technique, and to cover the range of literature and music, would require 25 enormous halls, seven symphony orchestras, exhibitions of pictures, lectures, literary discussions and debates, and even then, in his opinion, it could not be done if all tastes were to be pleased. Hugh Ross-Williamson made the point that a committee should not organise a festival. It should be a man of taste, or perhaps two or three; they should arrange for nothing that they themselves did not like.

But not everything worked out the way Ian Hunter had hoped it might, as *The Bath Chronicle* pointed out on May 19, 1960:

A dismayed Ian Hunter looked out of his Festival office window into Bath's Abbey Church Yard this morning and sighed, 'Where in the world is there a setting such as this for a festival of the arts?' But it was a sigh of pleasure tinged with disgust. There was pleasure at being able to present fine music, fine plays and fine artists in the city with which he is obviously so much in love; disgust at the shocking first-night attendance at Dear Liar *at the Theatre Royal on Wednesday. Jerome Kilty and Cavada Humphrey played to a near-empty theatre. Fewer than 150 of the 1000 seats were filled and those that were taken contained a good number of critics who (by and large) applauded the production. 'I am appalled and disgusted,' said impresario Mr Hunter. 'We have brought all that is best to this festival and this is the kind of response which we get. It makes you wonder if it is all worthwhile.' A moment later he was told that the only two stalls seats sold for this afternoon's 'half-day-closing' performance had been cancelled.*

If the jazz had been impressive in 1958 and 1959, 1960 brought a whole new concept: an all-night Carnival of Jazz at the Regency Ballroom from 10.30pm to 7am for just 15 shillings (75p). Names like Ken Colye, Alex Welsh, Mick Mulligan, the Bob Wallis Storyville Group and the Clyde Valley Stompers were all on the same programme. Being the best in jazz, the festival brought out the strangest fashions among supporters with sloppy sweaters, grubby jeans, black stockings and floppy hats very much in evidence. One eccentric fan lost himself behind an outsize pair of sunglasses, and another girl enthusiast 'got with it' in a snazzy leopardskin costume. For those that stayed the all-night course, George Melly had an answer. At 6am he was sympathetically warbling: 'T'ain't no sin to take off your skin and dance around in your bones.'

Jazz wasn't the only all-night activity that evening. The festival ball moved to a new level. Entitled 'La Ronde', the 587 guests drove to one of four local manor houses – Combe Hay Manor, Freshford Manor, Widcombe Manor and Widcombe Hall. Each had different music and different food. A small fleet of buses – again equipped with music and food – ferried them to another manor when they wished to move on. It was a wondrous whirl through the countryside and ended with a cooked breakfast at the Octagon on Milsom Street. This was the first in a decade-long series of flamboyant events, which both raised much needed funds for the festival and provided an exciting social focus for festival supporters. Behind them all, and aided by a willing army of ladies, was Barbara Robertson, wife of Charles Robertson of the jam-making firm. They lived at Combe Hay and revelled in the livelier side of festival life.

Another dimension to the festival came with a carnival complete with a Carnival Queen, 22-year-old nurse Una Husbands from St Martin's Hospital. Organised by Bath Round Table, it ran for three days throughout the city and raised a substantial amount of money for the building of a Cheshire Home at Timsbury. There was also a list of fringe events organised by local societies, including plays, floral arrangements and an Old Time Ball, as well as a Festival Club in the Pump Room. The great talking point was the presence of the 29-year-old Crown Prince of Bahrain, Sheik Isa Bin Sulman Al Kalifa, who gained notoriety for handing out pearls and diamonds to several of the ladies associated with the festival.

As Sir Adrian Boult had said at the beginning of the festival, the programme was 'staggering'. And remember this was only 1960.

With no liabilities beyond providing rooms and a £1000 grant, the city council was basking in the success of the festival, but by 1961 the event's two main financiers, TWW and the Arts Council, wanted greater commitment from the city. The proposal was to make everything above board. A grant of £1500 would be made available to the festival, but the festival would in turn pay for the hire of buildings, rooms, and so on. Despite the memories of the 1955 disaster, the proposal was carried with only four dissenters opposing the plan. *The Bath Chronicle* (May 6, 1961) welcomed the news:

> *This change in atmosphere is most welcome. It is wholly right that the city council should contribute in a direct fashion to the support of the festival, a major undertaking for the benefit of the city. A very practical point is that those outside bodies who have supported the festival so generously could not be expected to continue doing so unless it received the open support of the city council. In the past the city council's difficulty in running the festival was that their liability was unlimited. By the present decision a direct but limited contribution is to be made.*

The new financing arrangement came in the wake of the establishment of a proper, businesslike structure. The Bath Festival Society Ltd, a company limited by guarantee, was set up in the autumn of 1960. Ian Hunter and Cllr Hugh Roberts, formerly chairman of the guarantors, were among the board members. The chairman was Edwin Leather, member of parliament for North

Somerset. To complement the Society, a 'Supporters Club' was started to raise money and organise fringe events.

And so by the early 1960s the festival was riding on the crest of a wave. Although never completely secure financially, it was bringing great names, organising big events and involving local people. After the success of 1960, the highbrow/lowbrow critics were mostly silenced. However, in an interview with *The Bath Chronicle*, Ian Hunter couldn't resist a pre-emptive swipe at anyone who might accuse the 1961 festival of being too highbrow:

> *I can put on a festival with a much wider appeal and pack it to the doors but it would do nothing for the prestige of Bath. I am not prepared to lower my sights artistically. Let us face it, the festival is, from the national point of view, for the connoisseur of the arts. But that does not mean that during the period that it takes place in the city it should not be made an event which should draw wide civic interest.*

The general direction of the festival for the next few years was set. Menuhin and Hunter were drawing in big names, performances were, in the main, solidly classical with a sprinkling of contemporary masterpieces, and the social side of the festival was well established. There were dissenters, such as the occasional letter-writers to *The Bath Chronicle*. A Mr Croxford from Weston wrote: 'A great many people I have talked to have expressed the view that the festival is put on for the sake of the few at the expense of the many, and will never achieve local popularity in its present form.' However, a Mr E M Guiness from Lime Grove Gardens wrote: 'How can the citizens of Bath express their gratitude to Mr Menuhin? Again he has poured out his genius and his energy to put Bath on the map – the musical map.'

Despite the relative stability, organisers continued to be in need of secure financial support, and once again begging letters were circulated. Cllr Hugh Roberts wrote to hundreds of people in November 1960 explaining that the Bath Festival Society needed them as guarantors. He had some success: by the time the 1961 festival got under way it had nine life benefactors, 68 benefactors for that year, and 350 guarantors.

That year's festival saw the return of Nadia Boulanger conducting Fauré's *Requiem* in the Abbey; Menuhin commissioned a violin concerto from Lennox Berkeley; and the Spanish guitarist Segovia came to give a recital. The Festival Chamber Orchestra was a veritable who's who of the music world of the time and included, for example, Suzanne Rozsa and Rodney Friend in the violins and Nannie Jamieson on viola. Another member of the orchestra was a young cellist who also appeared in a chamber music concert previewed by *The Bath Chronicle* on May 19, 1961:

> *A 16-years-old Oxford-born girl, Jacqueline du Pré, who is something of a musical prodigy, will be heard by Bath audiences during the festival. This fair-haired young girl is rapidly making a national musical reputation for herself as a cellist of outstanding merit.*

The paper's review of that concert, by A Chislett on June 12, described what came after Schubert's *Trout Quintet*:

> *For the second work, the* Quintet in C major *(by Schubert) for two violins, a viola and two cellos, which is much more dramatic and is imbued with deep melancholy, the piano and double-bass were replaced by Robert Masters (violin) and Jacqueline du Pré as additional cellist. And young as she is, the latter at once showed the fine quality of her musicianship as well as technique in the cello duet, which occurs early in the first movement and in the second movement with the first violin in which the violin is bowed and the cello plucked, she played with rare judgement and beautiful sensitivity. She matched, indeed, the perfection of Mr Menuhin himself.*

Reaching further into the community, the festival staged three sell-out concerts involving festival artists, including Menuhin himself, with the organisation Youth & Music, for which tickets were made available only through schools. Artistically, at least, the love affair with Bath was blossoming. At the end of the festival the chairman, Edwin Leather MP, presented Menuhin with a silver dish saying: 'Yehudi, you are incomparable in the world of music, and incomparable in all our hearts.' Menuhin's response was similarly gushing: 'With me are those I love the most. To make music with them – the music I love best – is a dream that only comes to life at Bath.'

Socially, the festival carried on where 'La Ronde' of 1960 had left off. Fringe events in the 1960s were largely aimed at the same audiences as the musical and theatrical programmes, and armies – usually of ladies – moved heaven and earth to make them happen. The 1961 festival ball was an infamous 'Roman Orgy', which took place at the Roman baths. Guests, each paying a little over £4, were issued with togas. Those sporting formal evening dress were to be refused admission. Carefully researched, the food was designed to be not dissimilar to a Roman diet, including boar and roast swan. There was also a 'horror food' table of fried dormice, nightingales' tongues, sows' udders and thrushes. The full title was 'A Roman Feast of Ludi Sulis', and it attracted publicity all over the world, including newspaper comments in Japan and Argentina. It was the first time in living memory that people had officially been allowed to swim in the famous bath and was the precursor to the 'Roman Rendezvous', which in subsequent years opened the baths for bathing only during the festival. Across the waters floated a boat with slave girls bearing guests' meals while above, the statue of a centurion guard stood perfectly still and stone-faced listening to a specially composed Latin hymn praising the goddess Sul Minerva. On the terrace and in the waters the revellers danced the night away. When the last bathers refused to depart at 4am, the city authorities pulled the plug out. But as *The Bath Chronicle* noted, 'some swam on down to the last puddle.'

As riotous pictures of the 'Roman Orgy' began circulating, Menuhin's patience began to wear thin. He threatened to resign, claiming that the serious side of the festival was being undermined, a point he made again in 1998:

I must say I was not particularly pleased about the 'Roman Orgy'. I thought this was a music festival. If we'd gone deeply into the subject and found out what kind of music the Romans were listening to, and followed up the archaeology and the history, that would have interested me enormously. I love frivolity, I love gaiety, I love abandonment. But to see a lot of rich people get together and find some excuse for getting drunk – that attitude to the festival was at odds with my own feeling about it.

Alternative festival entertainment came in the form of 'The 11 O'Clock Special', a party at Green Park Station, which started after the last scheduled train had left at 11pm, and continued all night with a shuttle train between Green Park and Wellow. Entertainment, food and drink was provided both in the carriages and on the platforms. At Wellow there was a giant barbecue while in Bath, Humphrey Lyttleton performed at the station.

'Jambeano', a circulating outdoor music festival that appeared on different streets on different days, became well-established and popular with young dancers, while during another all-night jazz festival Edwin Leather tried his hand on the drums. For the second year the Round Table held a carnival for the Cheshire Home at Timsbury, and this time they were honoured by the attendance of Group Captain Leonard Cheshire VC.

But when the final curtain came down the financial result was disappointing – a loss of £1000. The critics were out again. In an ill-advised comment, Lord Harewood described the city council's support for the festival as 'mouldy'. In an effort to keep the corporation sweet, Duncan Harrison, now secretary of the Festival Society, fired off his retort: 'We do not think that the contributions made by the corporation to the festival are mouldy.' Ian Hunter, meanwhile, was in London, pushing for better funding and threatening to take 'his' festival away from Bath: 'If we do not get more, the ultimate future of the festival might be in doubt. The council should give an amount of money which corresponds to the prestige they gain.'

The festival had already enjoyed corporate support from TWW. Now other local businesses were beginning to see the value of alignment with the arts and Wessex Associated Newspapers, publishers of *The Bath Chronicle*, became sponsors, as did Ushers' Brewery and Harvey's in Bristol. The Calouste Gulbenkian Foundation, which has a long track record of supporting the arts, paid £500 early in 1962 for a mobile stage to be used in both Bath Abbey and Wells Cathedral.

The 1962 New Year's honours brought a knighthood for the chairman, Edwin Leather MP, and the festival itself found a permanent home, acquired and given by the former mayor, festival chairman and local architect, Cllr Hugh Roberts. Linley House had been the eighteenth century home of Thomas Linley, Bath's most famous composer, and it was particularly apt that the festival should be there for the next 35 years. The festival also managed to staff and equip the office. It was the first time the festival had enjoyed a permanent home in the city since it had been run by the city council's Spa Committee. To signify its permanence, the festival adopted a Wife of Bath logo based on Chaucer's *Canterbury Tales* and designed by Osbert Lancaster.

While artists from overseas were not uncommon in the festival, visits from the Soviet bloc were distinctly rare. The Moscow Chamber Orchestra's 1962 concert in the Abbey, with their conductor Rudolf Barshai, was a joint affair with the Festival Chamber Orchestra, and appropriately enough featured Michael Tippett's *Concerto* written for double string orchestra.

The festival included Handel's *Water Music* and *Fireworks Music* performed from a barge on the River Avon; a soirée at Dyrham Park; the popular 'Roman Rendezvous' at the baths; 'Jambeano' dancing in the streets; a medieval drama, *The Raising of Lazurus*, at the Abbey; the British première of a film version of *Der Rosenkavalier* starring Elisabeth Schwarzkopf and conducted by Herbert von Karajan; and concerts featuring the guitarist John Williams and the London Symphony Orchestra conducted by their 87-year-old chief conductor Pierre Monteux.

The artistic highlight of 1962 was a visit by Dame Margot Fonteyn to the Theatre Royal. Speaking in 1998, Yehudi Menuhin said that including dance in the festival programme had been one of the highlights of his tenure: 'Ever since I saw [Anna] Pavlova at the age of six in San Francisco I've always loved ballerinas. They are an expression of human beauty and sound.' With Menuhin playing the taxing violin solos in the pit, Dame Margot took to the platform for a performance of the famous Act Two of Tchaikovsky's *Swan Lake*; a unique fusion of their two unique talents. *The Bath Chronicle's* John White described the scene: 'What the audience neither knew nor expected was that they would see and hear this spectacle twice. But that is precisely what happened. With her partner David Blair, Dame Margot danced the *pas-de-deux* again. It was a triumph.'

Joining in the festival atmosphere with her husband Viscount Snowdon was Princess Margaret, who had visited the very first Bath Assembly back in 1948. The couple stayed for three days and were among the 500 guests at 'La Serenissima', a Venetian carnival organised by Barbara Robertson. Robertson commandeered, had built, and otherwise acquired some 35 river craft to sail near Parade Gardens in true Venetian style. On the banks there was food and other entertainment. Captain Freddie Hayden, stationed with the Admiralty in Bath, gave her plenty of help and advice, while the city of Venice itself sent over two gondoliers, and invited Robertson on a fact-finding visit. But there was discontent in the city after police prevented locals watching the spectacular from the banks of Parade Gardens. The magistrates were similarly dour in refusing to grant late licences to nearby public houses wishing to cash in on the event's popularity.

The other great social highlight of 1962 was the 'Cave Rave', a night of jazz in Cheddar Caves, which began at 9.30pm and lasted through until 3.30am. Over 1000 people, many in stone-age costumes, went to hear Mick Mulligan and his band, George Melly, and the Avon Cities Band. As *The Bath Chronicle* said the following day: 'Staggering stalagmites! The Cave Rave is over. The Ancient Britons who descended on Cheddar for the carefree night have gone home, and today the caverns were back to normal. They rocked, rolled, jived and twisted and did everything else that a caveman never dreamed of.' It wasn't all plain sailing. Fears of teddy-boys gate-crashing the Cave Rave led to a strong police presence, not all in costume, and the Avon Cities Band found themselves short of one member when it transpired that he suffered from claustrophobia and needed medical attention.

After years of discussion, the festival tentatively spread its wings to Bristol with a concert at St Mary Redcliffe, where Menuhin and friends performed Brahms's *Sextet* and Schubert's *Octet*. At Wells Cathedral, Nadia Boulanger conducted the Festival Chorus and Chamber Orchestra in Stravinsky's *Mass*, while Menuhin was the soloist on that occasion in Mozart's *Violin Concerto in D major*.

Amid some excellent music and a first-rate social/fringe programme, an entertaining collection of rows flared up. The sculptor Henry Moore loaned the festival a bronze entitled *Seated Figure Against Curved Wall* to which Sir Edwin Leather took a dislike. He said: 'The day that women look like that I shall commit suicide. I have great taste in women as God made them, but not as Henry Moore makes them.'

The main battle of 1962 was over applause inside church buildings. Without official guidance there had been great embarrassment. On the one hand church buildings in general and the Abbey in particular were considered to be the House of God; on the other hand, as buildings, they had been prostituted out as concert halls to an organisation willing to pay the going rate for use of the space. Prebendary Geoffrey Lester, the rector of Bath Abbey – which was sporting a canopy 23 feet by 19 feet and suspended 24 feet off the ground to encourage the sound to be projected forward – originally said he felt there were only two ways of showing appreciation: one was with applause, the other by saying Alleluia. And he thought that the former came more naturally. He was backed by no less a figure than the Bishop of Bath and Wells himself – but not by everybody, as a furious correspondence on *The Bath Chronicle's* letters page showed. The Hon. Mrs Holmes à Court wrote:

> *I, and many there, were horrified at the applause in the Abbey on Friday night and Saturday afternoon. The music is so great and our appreciation so profound, that the performers feel, I know, that they do not need to look for cheap vulgar applause. In the Abbey and our churches hitherto the rector has especially asked for none to be given. Mr Menuhin, the conductor and the orchestra behaved with great dignity – they were obviously embarrassed by the applause and walked out without acknowledging it.*

One wonders how such a correspondent might have coped with the ripple of applause that spread around Westminster Abbey during a royal funeral 35 years later. Another letter writer took a lighter approach. Mr R J Wall said:

> *What nonsense some people talk. Why is it irreverent to applaud a performance of fine music by gifted musicians because it is given in a church? It wouldn't surprise me if God welcomed a popular entertainment in His House as a relief from the eternal sombre devotions. If your readers had contained their indignation, they might have heard some celestial clapping.*

* * *

The city council's financial support of the festival in 1962 had remained at a paltry £1500, bringing a scathing rebuke from Aubrey Jackman, chairman of the Bath Hotels and Restaurants Association. He said such a low level of support was 'utterly unrealistic and almost incredibly unenterprising.' Meanwhile the Arts Council and TWW had put up £1750 each. Despite these contributions, when the final figures for 1962 were known there was a loss of £2792, bringing the accumulated deficit up to £3789.

In 1963 the festival began to make more serious overtures towards the Bristol authorities. Seen from a London standpoint, the two cities seem very close; why not capitalise on their proximity? The first suggestion was for a jointly hosted open-air production of *Anthony and Cleopatra* at Dyrham Park. The National Trust, the Drama Department at Bristol University and the Fringe Committee were all keen, but the Entertainments Committee of Bristol City Council vetoed any financial support for the project.

Even without Bristol's backing, things began looking up financially in 1963. Bath City Council, the Arts Council and TWW increased their contributions to £2500 each. The festival was also blessed with a new venue: the Assembly Rooms. Still intimate in scale, it could nevertheless accommodate more people – and hence raise more revenue – than the Guildhall. Consequently, box office takings hit a record £14,500. Despite the extra accommodation, popular events began selling out quickly, and festival membership, with its priority booking period, became a sought after commodity. The festival was clearly settling into what would later be seen as something of a golden era.

John Betjeman, long a fan of the city of Bath, wrote an extensive introduction to the festival programme book in 1963 comparing Bath to Rome. But he concluded with a warning:

> *It remains to be seen what more our own indecisive age of internal combustion and nuclear physics will do to Bath. The slabs of new flats off the London Road, the sprawling suburbs, the new technical college are all signs of the times. No one can look at Royal Crescent and Lansdown Crescent and the Pump Room without realising we once were civilised.*

The applause in churches argument of 1962 was resolved with a sentence in the programme for each concert held in such a venue: 'If they so wish, members of the public is *(sic)* invited to show its appreciation by standing in silence while the artists leave the church.'

Although there was no danger of forfeiting its highly regarded classical music heritage, the festival was reaching out more than ever into the community and involving local people and young people. Bath Cantata Group under the baton of David Lloyd-Jones sang cantatas by Buxtehude; Roger Norrington conducted the Springhead Ring Choir; the Essex Youth Orchestra with their Bathonian conductor Raymond Leppard appeared at the Pavilion; Menuhin conducted the City of Bath Bach Choir, and also took time out to rehearse an orchestra made up of pupils from several local senior schools including Bath

High, Kingswood, Monkton Combe and the City of Bath Girls' and City of Bath Boys' schools.

In an attempt to break down barriers between followers of classical music and jazz, Yehudi Menuhin and Johnny Dankworth united for an event called 'Musical Encounter', which was only moderately successful, as Morley Pooley recalled in *The Bath Chronicle* (June 13):

> *Did this programme of new music improvisation and jazz bridge the gap between classical music and jazz? That, after all, was its avowed intention. I believe that the gap between the two types of music stood as widely apart as ever at the end of an overlong programme which was heavily weighted in favour of jazz. But I doubt if any jazz fan will agree.*

Notable visitors in 1963 included the Zurich Chamber Orchestra with Edmond de Stoutz; the cellist Maurice Gendron performing all six Bach solo cello suites in two concerts; Peter Pears singing Schubert's *Die Winterreise* accompanied by Benjamin Britten; the Smetana Quartet; and Claudio Arrau in an all-Chopin programme at the Assembly Rooms. But the acoustics of the Assembly Rooms gave cause for concern to some critics. *The Daily Telegraph* said: 'It turned out that this hall will not take well to collective string scales.'

The Daily Mail was particularly sarcastic in its verdict:

> *One thing Bath lacks, surprisingly, is a first-class swimming bath. After returning to hear Arrau's recital last night I suggest that by putting a few feet of water in the ballroom of the newly rebuilt Assembly Rooms the corporation could provide the city with the handsomest indoor pool in the country. For a piano recital the acoustics are intolerable.*

As an emergency measure, velvet drapes measuring 40 feet by 25 feet were installed behind the platform in a moderately successful attempt to deaden the resonance.

The final figures, although in the red, were no more depressing than previously. On a turnover of more than £27,000, the 1963 festival lost £1373 bringing the accumulated deficit to around £5000. Sir Edwin Leather MP, chairman of the Festival Society, said at the end of the 1963 festival:

> *It has been a happy festival this year. I think the reason is that the artistic world at large and the people of Bath have finally accepted the festival. The people of Bath are beginning to feel proud of, and inter- ested in, the festival. We don't want to grow bigger, but we do want to become better, at the same time keeping the intimate family atmosphere and maintaining the present high quality.*

* * *

After her successful and widely acclaimed appearance in 1962, Dame Margot Fonteyn pitched up again in 1964, this time with Rudolf Nureyev. She was scheduled to appear in two gala performances with him at the Theatre Royal, the first on Tuesday, June 9. The previous evening she had been rehearsing before dining at the Hole in the Wall restaurant when, unknown to Dame Margot, her husband, Dr Roberto Arias, the former Panamanian ambassador to Britain, had been shot and critically injured in Panama City. Shortly before midnight she returned to the Lansdown Grove Hotel to be greeted with the news by Diana Menuhin. A night of frantic telephone calls followed. The following morning she declared to her anxious and expectant audience that, as Dr Arias was out of danger, for that night at least the show must go on. She said: 'Naturally I want to go and see my husband but I don't like rushing off today and letting down the festival.'

And on the show went, culminating in a stunning and highly charged performance by Fonteyn and Nureyev of Bartók's *Sonata for solo violin*, played by Menuhin. Speaking in 1998, Menuhin recalled the occasion: 'I played in a kind of sentry box on the left hand side of the stage and they danced. I loved it – just the feeling of seeing people dance to your music, whether in rhythm or inspired by the mood.' Immediately the curtain came down, Dame Margot was whisked away to London to begin a 6000-mile flight to the bedside of her wounded husband. Her declared intention had been to return to Bath for a second performance just four days later on Saturday. Alas, she found her husband's condition to be worse than expected, and Lynn Seymour stood in to dance with Nureyev.

There was an element of humour in the tragedy. Dame Margot was waiting at the Lansdown Grove Hotel for an important telephone call from Buenos Airies to tell her if Dr Arias was sufficiently out of danger for her to give her performance that night and leave the following day. The world's media and press had been gathering in the hotel's lobby, where the elderly head porter was in his element organising the camera crews and journalists who were milling around. In the middle of the kerfuffle the old-fashioned switchboard, which was open to everyone, started ringing. In the absence of the switchboard operator the porter picked up the phone, and silence fell over the assembled company. A distant voice said 'Allo. Allo, this is Buenos Airies.' To which the porter replied: 'This is no time for practical jokes, we've got a crisis on' and pulled out the plug, creating uproar among the gathered media.

While the Fonteyn episode dominated the festival – and the appearance with Nureyev undoubtedly ranks in the festival's top ten achievements – there was plenty more besides. In Bristol, a church opera by the conductor Gian Carlo Menotti was given its world première in the cathedral, and Yehudi Menuhin gave an all-Bach recital of solo violin music at the church of St Mary Redcliffe. If the programmes looked much the same as previous years, that was because the format was, in essence, unchanging: Bach, Mozart, Haydn and Beethoven played by Menuhin, members of his family – Hephzibah Menuhin and Fou T'song for example – and a collection of regular friends such as Raymond Leppard, Janet Baker and the Festival Chamber Orchestra.

But as long as Menuhin and Hunter could find a few surprises for the audience, they could paddle in the same direction. After having their fingers burnt with the classical-jazz crossover of 1963, Menuhin and Dankworth were more cautious in their partnership this time around. At a concert in the Assembly Rooms, Dankworth, a clarinettist by profession, took part in a performance of Bartók's *Contrasts* with Menuhin on the violin. As the wind part had originally been written for Benny Goodman, the whole thing was a more natural collaboration than the 1963 attempt at fusion.

This was the year that brought the composer Michael Tippett, resident near Corsham, a few miles east of Bath, into the festival fold. He conducted a performance of his new secular cantata, *Crown of the Year*, with the Bath Cantata Group and Janet Baker. It was the beginning of an important association between the festival and one of the greatest British composers of the second half of the century. The other great gem of that year was a trio of appearances by the soprano Victoria de los Angeles, including a performance of Mahler's *Symphony No.4* at the Abbey with the London Symphony Orchestra under the baton of István Kertész.

The 'Roman Rendezvous' and 'Jambeano' continued with a vengeance, and Barbara Robertson organised a Festival Ball at Combe Hay Manor which was disrupted by rain but nevertheless continued indoors until breakfast. The jazz programme continued largely unaltered, and at the Holburne Museum an exhibition looked at the history of baths and bathing through the ages. But it was in repeating previously successful events that, in the author's view, the Bath Festival began making mistakes, just as it had when under the control of the city council in the early 1950s. Assuming that what worked one year will work again the next year is a false premise. Although only just over halfway through Menuhin's tenure as artistic director, the signs of stagnation – only ever visible with the benefit of hindsight – were slowly beginning to creep in.

The loss in 1964 was £848, a figure shrugged off not unreasonably by Sir Edwin Leather as 'a thoroughly manageable figure'. He insisted that the finances of the festival were 'in good heart'. But in January 1965 the festival was approaching financial crisis, and asked the city to double its annual grant from £2500 to £5000, the amount given ten years earlier. The council declined. Leather declared that, despite the rebuff, the festival would go on. However, he warned that Yehudi Menuhin had received an approach from elsewhere. He said: 'Personally, while I would do anything to bring Menuhin's music to the British people, if we move outside Bath, the whole character of the operation will have completely changed and this would be a thousand pities.' Although there was no extra cash forthcoming from the city or from TWW, the Arts Council upped their contribution to £2750 and also agreed to cover some of the rehearsal costs for visiting orchestras.

In February 1965 Aubrey Jackman, long an outspoken supporter of the festival and chairman of the Bath Hotels and Restaurants Association, called on the city council to have a wider vision towards the festival. He said: 'Those in a position of responsibility in the Guildhall know full well that the festival is worth at least £30,000 a year.' He added that it was the duty of councillors to put the good of the city first and to explain to opponents in their wards the wider implications of its abandonment. He said: 'The ramifications and indirect benefit of the festival is enormous. The city council must have wider vision. If the festival is lost to Bath there will be nothing to take its place.'

Nevertheless, the increasingly highbrow feel of the festival's musical programme – particularly in the midst of the swinging sixties – was clearly causing rancour. Sir Edwin recognised this point. In March 1965 he said: 'We are working on the question of a wider appeal, because some people contend that our festival is terribly highbrow. But it is inevitable in the business in which we are concerned. Producing excellent music and producing popular music at the same time is a paradox and we are acutely conscious of it and are doing our best to deal with the matter.' It was statements such as this that, in the long run, probably did the festival more harm than good. It reflected a long suspected view that the festival was out to convert the people rather than reach them.

The crossfire continued. On April 27, Sir Edwin lashed out at the festival's critics during a Bath Rotary Club event claiming the city was 'perilously close' to losing the festival as it had done the annual military tattoo, once a major part of the city's social calendar. He said:

> *If the city and the city fathers say they do not want the festival, that is okay by me. I've nothing more to say. But if they do want it, then it is neither sense nor fair to think you can go on like this leaving enormous burdens of effort and responsibility to a handful of enthusiasts to do it all in their own time and very often at considerable expense to themselves. Some of the enthusiasts are now getting very tired. I am heartily sick and tired of the silly, ignorant sniping that goes on, particularly from those people whose criticisms have been answered over and over again.*

He then went on to reveal that Menuhin, in response to the festival's financial plight, had waived all his fees for 1963 and 1964. Appealing for more support from everyone in Bath, Sir Edwin said: 'If you are going to have a genius like Menuhin, you have got to provide him with proper facilities or you just don't have him at all.'

Sir Edwin was right. The world's greatest violinist deserved to be paid for the work he was doing. However the MP's approach – once again fostering a 'you must help us' direction rather than a 'how can we work together' angle did nothing to endear him to the city nor the city fathers.

Sir Edwin had reason to be worried. The cost of mounting the 12-day extravaganza was continuing to rise, and in 1965 was estimated to be £37,000. Something had to be done to widen its scope and raise greater funds. A member of the Festival Society's board, George Comer, established a Festival Association. It was intended to be an organisation to run and develop fringe events that would complement the main festival. It was in essence the forerunner of today's fringe as a separate organisation, two differences being that, firstly, its relationship with the main festival was one of close co-operation, and secondly it would – despite the organisers' best intentions – end up appealing largely to existing festival supporters and others in the socio-economic group that the festival reached, rather than drawing in those whom the festival did not normally attract. Sport, tennis, five-a-side football, golf and skittles were suggested. Despite being a member of the Festival Society's board, George Comer had to vigorously defend himself from charges that he was undermining the Society and criticising its running. He said:

> *There has been a feeling abroad for some years that the festival should broaden its scope and encourage fringe activities during the festival period which are attractive to the general public to help to identify the citizens of Bath with their Festival of the Arts. I shall leave no stone unturned in my endeavour to make next year's festival a gay and happy time for Bathonians of all ages, but I must state frankly, that to succeed it is vital to have wholehearted co-operation, not least from our city council, police and licensing justices. I sincerely believe that events must be organised to embrace and involve all Bathonians.*

Sir Edwin welcomed the move but Lord Strathcona, the deputy chairman, was condescending: 'I don't think it is fair to suggest it will help the festival's finances, but it would help to silence the knockers.' In its first full year, to July 1966, the Festival Association itself made a loss of just under £200, largely on a week of old-time music-hall that had been expected to reach those to whom the festival didn't appeal, but which turned out to be poorly attended.

An Olympic-style relay of athletes opened the 1965 festival, running through the city's streets to Abbey Church Yard where a flame – which was supposed to burn in a circular stone dais for the duration of the festival – was lit by Arnold Goodman, chairman of the Arts Council of Great Britain. Trumpeters in colourful blue outfits sounded a fanfare and the drums rolled as the final runner approached. Designed by architect, former mayor and ex-chairman of the festival, Hugh Roberts, the structure was about ten feet in diameter enclosing a tiered flowerbed. The circle of stone surrounding the flame-producing apparatus was engraved 'Bath Festival Floreat Bathon' (Bath Festival: long may Bath flourish). Unfortunately the flame proved somewhat temperamental and had to be regularly checked and relit. There was also suspicion of sabotage or vandalism, and eventually police with guard dogs were brought in to watch the flame.

Building on the successful window display competition of 1964, Milsom Street won the Best Decorated Street Award and Jollys department store won the festival rose bowl for a spectacular depiction of the Agincourt Ball. How sad that in the 1990s Jollys, now part of the House of Frazer, no longer take part in this annual event. The city probably looked its best ever in 1965, with window displays and flowers everywhere. Ian Hunter took time out to write a rare letter of thanks to *The Bath Chronicle*, saying: 'Having been connected with the Bath Festival since its inception in 1948... I have never seen Bath more beautifully decorated or looking more festive than during the present Festival.'

The introduction to *The Bath Chronicle's* four page supplement in 1965 unintentionally gives another clue as to the stagnation that was subtly grabbing hold:

The Bath Festival of the Arts, a festival known throughout the world nowadays as Menuhin's English Festival, opened today. Musically, its programme is on the lines we have come to expect since Yehudi Menuhin has been its artistic director.

The major musical development in 1965 was the première of a violin concerto by the Australian composer Malcolm Williamson for Yehudi Menuhin. There was also a welcome return of the Moscow Chamber Orchestra who, with their conductor Rudolf Barshai, had appeared in 1962. This time they gave four concerts. George Malcolm performed Bach's *Goldberg Variations*, the Smetana Quartet returned to the city and so too did the London Symphony Orchestra with programmes that included Elgar's *Cello Concerto* (soloist: Maurice Gendron), Tchaikovsky's *Symphony No.6* and Liszt's *Piano Concerto No.2* (soloist: Louis Kentner). But essentially Yehudi Menuhin, his family, and the Bath Festival Orchestra (the word Chamber had surreptitiously been dropped from its title this year) remained at the heart of proceedings.

The 1965 Festival also saw the spectacular Agincourt Ball at Farleigh Castle, organised by the fringe committee. Together with other fringe events the ball contributed £200 to festival finances. These themed social evenings were now a well-established part of the festival calendar. And while their content, design and price would clearly appeal to a limited sector of the public, this was a group of society that gave the festival solid support both morally and financially. No matter how rarefied they might seem to the man or woman on the Twerton omnibus, such events provided a backbone for the festival, not to mention much-needed income. The story of King Henry V's victory over the French at the Battle of Agincourt in 1415 was told by 60 costumed characters within the ruined wall of Farleigh Hungerford Castle from 10pm to 3am, and at a price of four guineas per head. Among the 400 guests was Prince William of Gloucester, who played the part of Humphrey Plantagenet. Leaflets advising on costume were issued well in advance (including a section entitled Hints for Helpless Men) and descendants of the Hungerford family came from as far as Tanganyika (now Tanzania) and New Zealand to participate.

Kenneth Goodman described the scene for *The Bath Chronicle* (June 19):

The costumes were gay, and the variety such that one wondered whether there could possibly have been so many fashions at the same time. And, for once, the men outshone the ladies, who looked charming in their fifteenth century court attire, but could not match the brilliance of the men's outfits. They came as knights, cardinals, bishops, friars and courtiers, a galaxy of characters the like of which not even the ancient castle had ever seen before. It is said that no ghost haunts the ruins, but last night many must have been there in spirit. People, well known in the public and professional life of Bath and district, who are normally seen in immaculate conventional dress, took on new and convincing personalities of an age centuries old.

However, much to the festival's embarrassment, tickets had to be given away to three concerts at the Assembly Rooms as well as to Johnny Dankworth's concert with his wife Cleo Laine, performing Kurt Weill's *Seven Deadly Sins* with the Bournemouth Symphony Orchestra at the Colston Hall in Bristol. The festival's image of reaching into the community wasn't helped by the ending of the 'Jambeano' street dancing, on the grounds that numbers had been down the previous year. To add to the festival's woes, two speakers – Lord Gladwyn and Lord Snow – both cancelled their engagements. *The Bath Chronicle's* diary columnist hinted at troubles ahead:

> *After this diary is in print there will be a Council of Management meeting in private, when an 'inquest' is held on this year's festival, which had more than a few snags and several disappointments. I should not be surprised at the loss financially being rather heavier than it has been in the last few years. If I were on the council I should cut out the non-popular items for a year or two, and I would try to get speakers who could and would turn up. What has happened to the Festival Club incidentally? This 1965 festival has seemed rather a remote affair, though it has had plenty of good things.*

Despite these problems, Sir Edwin vigorously defended the festival: 'It is not because the Bath Festival is losing its appeal. We have not dropped behind in our claim that we are one of the world's great music festivals.' Nevertheless, alarm was caused by an article in *The Observer* claiming that 'the festival itself may go out when the event ends on Sunday.' Sir Edwin was furious. He said: 'It is harmful and quite untrue. We are not in deep financial trouble... I have no idea where they got the story from.'

July 1965 brought about the end of the MP's chairmanship. At the closing concert of the 1965 festival he had been presented with a bronze bust of Yehudi Menuhin. He was replaced at the helm of the Bath Festival Society Ltd by the deputy chairman Lord Strathcona, who lived in Lansdown Crescent. Strathcona immediately declared a desire to widen the festival's appeal:

> *We shall retain the essential musical character of the festival, based on Mr Yehudi Menuhin, but we are hoping to spread the type of events rather wider and make a greater awareness of the popular appeal of the festival.*

In the summer of 1965 there came a surprise move by the city. Acknowledging their debt to Yehudi Menuhin for putting Bath so firmly on the international map – an indisputable fact, regardless of how one views the day-to-day organisational details – Bath City Council offered Menuhin the freedom of the city, an honour previously reserved for sovereigns, outstanding statesmen or forces of the Crown.

Continuing their desperate bid to make the festival more attractive as well as better financed, plans were mooted to hold a festival casino in the Assembly Rooms. This was not as absurd as it might sound. Beau Nash, the man who had brought the city music, entertainment and dancing, had financed his lifestyle through the gaming tables. Nevertheless, the city's Spas Committee was po-faced about the proposal and rejected the concept outright in September 1965.

Whether it would have bridged the growing gulf – whether anything would ever bridge the gulf – is debatable. But an increasing inability to reach the ordinary people of Bath at a time when accessibility was all-important was a dangerous position to be in, and storm clouds were gathering ahead.

CHAPTER FIVE

After seven years of a rarely varied diet – Yehudi Menuhin plus family and friends – the Bath Festival was probably ready for a change. Menuhin wanted to develop it from within, building on his own reputation, expanding the classical side and introducing opera. Meanwhile, the city and its residents continued to call for the festival to be less elitist and more accessible.

In their pursuit of funds, the festival approached neighbouring councils for support. Shepton Mallet sent £25, while Bradford-on-Avon and Melksham each donated £15. Others were less generous. If it was a desperate move, it was a necessary one. By early 1966, the Festival Society's overdraft had exceeded £7500. There was some respite when Bath City Council agreed in March of that year to increase its contribution from £2500 to £3500, and there was further good fortune in June when TWW threw in an extra £1000 to help reduce the burden.

It was during the mid-sixties that another key player in the history of the Bath Festival arrived on the scene. Naomi Page (later to be Naomi Buchanan) had worked at a public relations company in Bristol in 1962, which at that time had the contract for the festival. In 1966 she was appointed festival administrator and enjoyed an insider's view of Menuhin's role. To her mind, he was a figurehead: 'I do not think Menuhin had much to do with planning, but he did attract a great many stars, especially chamber musicians.'

But, she said, Menuhin was prone to sweep in and sweep out again: 'He descended from the 4.15pm from Paddington, stayed in a suite at the Lansdown Grove Hotel, and returned to London again.' However, Buchanan defends Menuhin's artistic prowess within the festival: 'It was because of Menuhin that we were able to do things like Margot Fonteyn, and he gave magical performances.'

During the 1960s summer music in London, the Proms excepted, was scarce: 'Critics were happy to come to Bath. We ran a full-time press office. Even the *Daily Mail, The Daily Express* and *Evening Standard* had critics.'

Despite the large overdraft, with extra funding coming in for 1966 the festival loosened its belt. It had long been Yehudi Menuhin's dream to conduct opera and now, having styled himself for the first time 'artistic director', he was to see that dream become a reality. Speaking in 1998, Menuhin said: 'Bath was my training ground for opera. Thanks to Bath I went on to [conduct opera in] Bonn and Leipzig.'

In 1966 Phoenix Opera was booked to perform Mozart's *Così Fan Tutte* and Menuhin himself was in the pit. *The Daily Telegraph* was unkind, although probably accurate, in its assessment of his prowess: 'We learned hardly more about Mr Menuhin's ideas than we would have about Herbert von Karajan's if this conductor were to decide tomorrow to play the solo part in Beethoven's *Violin Concerto*.'

Menuhin had a warm regard for Phoenix Opera:

I don't begrudge Covent Garden their money, but my own personal loyalty is with the people for whom it means a new dimension, for whom it means a new world of art, of song, of theatre, of dance. Phoenix used to go to the smallest little villages with an upright piano and put on opera, which was invaluable. Of course that had to flounder. When you think what they needed was peanuts, it's very tragic.

Another first for Menuhin in 1966 was sharing the stage with the great Indian sitar player Ravi Shankar. In an interview before the festival Menuhin said: 'It is the first time a Western violinist has squatted on the floor to play. But I have had some experience of this sort because I have often had to practice squatting in train corridors.' More than 30 years later, the encounter remained one of his favourite memories:

Since we first met in 1952 in India, Ravi Shankar had said 'why can't we work together', but I was terribly hesitant because, after all, I know nothing about performing Indian music. I've never been more nervous than walking onto the stage with him. We had worked together for about two or three days non-stop, night and day, just resting when we felt we couldn't go on. It was a great success.

Among the other musical highlights of 1966 were a return visit by Elisabeth Schwarzkopf, this time accompanied by Geoffrey Parsons; a run of one-man shows by Larry Adler (which drew a disappointing response); a couple of concerts by the Czech Chamber Orchestra; a recital by the guitarist Julian Bream; and an appearance with Bream by Peter Pears.

Days before the 1966 festival was due to begin, Bristol City Council announced that, despite two of the major festival events taking place in the Colston Hall, it would be making no financial contribution to the festival's coffers. It underlined Bristol's (not unreasonable) lack of serious commitment to a festival that didn't bear its name. But it left the Bath Festival exposed. Lord Strathcona put a brave face on the snub: 'We were not expecting any money from Bristol, though we hoped they might help. We don't want to sulk. If anyone can help we are very pleased. If not, it is regrettable but we don't hold it against them.'

William Beckford, who ended a long, strenuous and largely useless life (save for his ability to erect follies) in Bath in 1844, was remembered during the 1966 festival with 'Mr Beckford's Arabian Banquet'. Held at the Assembly Rooms, it was Barbara Robertson and her ladies' contribution to the proceedings. Based on Beckford's eighteenth century novel *Vathek*, it ran from 10pm to 3am, cost four guineas a head, and specialities included sheeps' eyes. No doubt the extravagance of the event would have appealed to Beckford. Interestingly, the festival's chairman, Lord Strathcona, was at that time living in Beckford's former house in Lansdown Crescent. The Beckford theme was taken up by the Holburne Museum, which mounted an exhibition of the author's memorabilia.

Barbara Robertson also devised a popular *son-et-lumière* event entitled 'The Building of Bath Abbey', which was enacted on scaffolding in the shadow of the great centre of worship, and involved the blasting of 500 watts of sound into Abbey Church Yard.

By the end of 1966, unease was mounting. Yehudi Menuhin was growing increasingly irritated with the dilution of the classical side of the festival and was anxious to insulate the Bath Festival from the danger of becoming what he called 'a kind of variety programme with no specific character or homogeneous quality.'

Lt-Col N J Gell of Sion Hill wrote to *The Bath Chronicle* pointing out what a bargain the festival was compared with other civic provision such as library books, swimming and adult literacy classes:

> *The admirable festival and fringe events diary, now on sale at only 1s [5p], certainly shows that entertainment has been provided this year to suit all tastes. Are we not, however, being given something for very nearly nothing? The city council's contribution is around £3000 – under 9d per year per head of population... The city's financial future must be largely dependent on the tourist. The festival brings tourists. We say our children must have educational opportunities: the festival supplies these in the fields of music, drama, opera and ballet and reduced [subsidised] admission prices.*

But Mr B L Jacot from Shepton Mallet bemoaned the lack of appreciation from the young:

> *Is it not symptomatic that we can have, in what is surely one of the loveliest cities in the world, the world's most deeply moving music, suffused with the genius of the greatest of this age, if not of all time, and nine out of ten could not care less? What, it may be asked, has happened to culture and that out-reaching aesthetic appreciation that gave this country its Shakespeares and Miltons? The culture is still with us, but it seems to have turned to shoulder-length hair in males, electric guitars and hysterical females with eyes like holes burnt in a blanket.*

And for the first time, 1966 saw active opposition to the festival. It came in the form of a rival festival organised by the Bath Co-operative Society, which arranged a series of its own community events. Its president, Edgar Evans, said:

> *The Festival of the Arts does not represent or capture the imagination of the city as a whole. There are various functions attended by the elite; few in which everyone can take part. We believe that the city should be positively encouraged to make a contribution so that the citizens feel a greater sense of involvement in events. We would substitute for guinea concerts at the Guildhall, half a crown events on the Recreation Ground.*

The Bath Chronicle gave its own reaction to Mr Evans's ideas:

> *Mr Evans might care to explain one fact that puzzles the Festival Society – it is always the expensive seats that are filled, while the cheaper seats are slow to sell. He might also indicate how distinguished artists such as Yehudi Menuhin and Elisabeth Schwarzkopf could be expected to perform in the open air on the Recreation Ground at 2s 6d a head admittance; this is not artistic snobbery – it is merely an impracticable suggestion, physically and financially.*

Given that, for example, the only festival club in 1966 was a private affair – entrance by invitation only – held at the Lansdown Crescent home of Lady Strathcona, did Mr Evans indeed have a point? Nevertheless, the festival's own fringe diary was bigger than ever. The Bath Festival Queen, 19-year-old Shirley Phillips, flagged off the 75 entrants in the Festival Motor Rally. A festival cycle race, a festival medal golf competition, festival cruises, a festival carnival with a procession a mile-and-a-half long watched in the rain by 60,000 people, and a festival beer garden in Parade Gardens, which some wanted made into a permanent attraction, all added to the ambience. Nor was the festival completely divided into the haves and the have-nots. Yehudi Menuhin himself took time out of his schedule to work in the community and rehearse members of the Bath Schools' Orchestra, an awe-inspiring and unforgettable experience for those who took part.

Whatever its rights and wrongs, the 1966 festival attracted a good collection of distinguished visitors, including the Conservative party leader Edward Heath, the dancer Dame Marie Rambert, and the arts minister Jennie Lee who handed over to the city a 1:500 scale model of Bath commissioned by the Bath Preservation Trust worth £5,500. Measuring 165 square feet, it was largely financed by the Bath Portland Group Ltd and now sits in the Building of Bath Museum.

Confusion reigned later in 1966 as to what the theme for the following year would be. More than once, festival chairman Lord Strathcona promised an American theme, but at the end of July a French flavour was settled upon. Small as it may seem, with hindsight the confusion appears symptomatic of the problems that were just beginning to mount.

The start of the 1967 festival was to be an inter-denominational service in Bath Abbey including a string quartet led by Yehudi Menuhin, playing the accompaniment to a Purcell anthem, conducted by Michael Tippett. It was, instead, the source of the first in a series of rows, as *The Daily Telegraph* explained:

> *The first teacup storm of the 1967 Bath Festival began bubbling over the brim today when Yehudi Menuhin, the artistic director, gave the reasons for not attending the opening service at the Abbey yesterday. The row between the festival authorities and Prebendary Geoffrey Lester, the rector, centres on Purcell's* My Beloved Spake, *a 12-minute anthem which was to have been conducted by Sir Michael Tippett. The festival wanted to bring in a quartet of outside solo singers, including*

the well-known counter tenor Mark Deller, to take part in the anthem. The rector said this was a 'slur' on the Newton Park College of Education choir which could have given the work without outsiders.

The anthem was eventually dropped and Sir Michael Tippett also absented himself from the service. Menuhin later said:

I wanted to play, and I wanted to join the others as a contribution to the service. When this contribution was made impossible, there was no reason for me to be there. I am not a member of any of the churches represented and I am not by nature a gate-crasher.

Among the stars of the 1967 festival was Mattiwilda Dobbs, the American coloratura soprano who sang in four performances of Mozart's *Die Entführung aus dem Serail* produced by Phoenix Opera. After the previous year's visit by arts minister Jennie Lee, an extra £2000 was found from the Arts Council's coffers specifically for the opera. However, it also took an unprecedented donation of £3000 by Menuhin to ensure the production went ahead. Speaking in 1998 he explained why:

I thought it might give an example. I'm always interested in giving examples. I was devoted both to the operatic work and to the theatre. It was a great experience and we recorded Die Entführung.

The city's contribution in 1967 was £3500. While balancing the books was, as always, a problem, the new regional television consortium Harlech TV (later HTV) suggested that if the festival were to become a more regional event it might be more active. Tempting as the offer might have been, it was wisely rejected by the festival. But the change of television companies did create a financial headache. It caused the city, now more sympathetic than ever before, to increase its subsidy to £4000 in 1968, and to guarantee a further loss of up to £1250 if television did not contribute to the festival – providing that the Arts Council gave a similar undertaking.

Meanwhile, back in 1967, the programme was initially hailed as broader than in previous years. Maybe it was, but it differed more in style than in substance. In some respects it was little more than a carbon copy of 1966 and the year before that. Writing in *The Bath Chronicle* (June 7), Morley Pooley was ambivalent:

Basically it is the same formula – the Menuhin family, intimate concerts in lovely halls, small orchestras, recitals: well-worn festival paths so far as the Bath Festival is concerned. Yet it is just these very things that have given it the place it occupies as an international festival; its recognition as a world musical event... Yehudi Menuhin's English festival. It is that and that alone on which its importance nationally and internationally rests.

Familiarity, however, breeds contempt. And the festival format was certainly by now very familiar. Nevertheless, it still promised many treats. A highlight of 1967 was to have been a visit by the cellist Jacqueline du Pré who, in 1961, had made a great impression. Unfortunately war broke out in Israel and she raced there to play for the troops. Even though hostilities were technically over at the time of her Bath concert, du Pré remained in the Jewish homeland and her accompanist Fou T'song gave their recital on his own. Her other appearances were covered by the cellist Maurice Gendron. Lord Strathcona was scathing of the musician's deliberate flouting of her contractual obligation. He said:

> It seems to be accepted in the artistic world that people can rule out of commitments. She ran out on a contract and left a lot of people feeling cross. Artists should not be allowed to get away with this sort of thing unless there is a legitimate excuse.

Mrs Mary Lee, a letter writer to *The Bath Chronicle*, felt this criticism was unfair:

> The fact is this warm-hearted young Englishwoman – she is only 22 – decided to be at the side of her fiancé, Israeli pianist and composer Daniel Barenboim, in his country's hour of peril. Perhaps this is the spirit which makes Miss du Pré's playing so outstanding.

The 1967 fringe grew in its eclectic nature with the music shop Duck, Son & Pinker giving twelve instruments to be destroyed in Royal Victoria Park during a piano-smashing competition. It formed part of a day of events in the park for all the family. But was piano-smashing simply part of the festival's gaiety or, as some correspondents claimed, organised vandalism? George Brown, a member of the fringe committee, defended the idea – albeit slightly incredulously: 'This is an exercise in time and motion study, strict discipline, and a knowledge of applied mechanics.'

What was claimed as the largest Bath Festival fringe event ever was a 'King Arthur Pageant' staged in Abbey Church Yard and written, as always, by Barbara Robertson. 'Mrs Beeton's Supper Party' at Hinton Priory caused a lot of laughs as diners adopted dress and recipes of the 1880s, while at the Roman baths the 'Roman Rendezvous' sprang to life once more.

The Menuhin diet, as already discussed, was predictable – a broadly classical repertoire with a couple of new pieces thrown in each year for good measure. World premières in 1967 came from the composer Nicholas Maw and his American counterpart Easley Blackwood. Among the notable appearances were those by the harpist Marisa Robles and the conductor Nadia Boulanger. The soprano Elly Ameling joined Thomas Hemsley, the Festival Orchestra and Menuhin (conducted by Boulanger), together with Bath Cantata Group, for a concert at Christ Church in Julian Road that included Fauré's *Requiem*.

At the Colston Hall in Bristol, a scoreless and batonless Pierre Boulez conducted the BBC Symphony Orchestra in a concert that featured Berg's

Left: The brochure for the first Bath Assembly held from April 21 to May 1, 1948 *(kindly lent by Glyndebourne Festival Opera).*

Below: Morley Pooley - otherwise known as Monty or AMP - began covering the Bath Festival for *The Bath Chronicle* in 1949. He retired from the paper's staff as news editor in 1969, but continued to contribute his musical columns until 1983. He died in 1994. Without his enormous output, enthusiasm for music and words, and erudite opinions, this book would have been both thinner and poorer. Thank you Monty.

Left: A rare informal picture of Yehudi Menuhin with his children, taken at the Bath May Festival in 1955.

Below: Yehudi Menuhin in discussion with Gioconda de Vita. The pair gave a duo recital at the Guildhall in 1955.

Menuhin's musical family were regular guests at the Bath Festival such as in this concert in 1961. Left to right, Yehudi Menuhin, Fou Ts'ong, Louis Kentner and Hephzibah Menuhin, with the Bath Festival Orchestra.

Princess Margaret visited the festival in 1962 with her husband Viscount Snowdon. During her visit she took part in 'La Serenissima'.

'La Serenissima', a Venetian carnival, was the social highlight of the 1962 festival and attracted support from the city of Venice. Depicted is work in progress on the superstructure of one of the barges. Barbara Robertson, the brains behind the party and who visited Venice to undertake research for the event, is second from left.

The great Czech string quartet, the Smetana, visited the festival in 1963, 1965 and 1974.

Fonteyn and Nureyev dancing at the Theatre Royal, with Menuhin playing in the wings.

Yehudi Menuhin, Margot Fonteyn and Rudolf Nureyev on the stage of the Theatre Royal on June 9, 1964, after a specially choreographed performance of Bartok's *Divertimento*. Hours earlier Fonteyn had heard of her husband's critical condition after an assassination attempt in Panama, but insisted that the show must go on.

Above: In addition to his heavy concert schedule each festival, Yehudi Menuhin often took time to work with local school children. In this picture from 1963 he is rehearsing the Bath Schools' Orchestra at the Guildhall.

Left: The festival often strayed into Bristol and in 1964 Menuhin gave a recital of solo violin music by J S Bach at the church of St Mary, Redcliffe.

Above: A special dais containing a festival flame was built for the 1965 festival. In the background, trumpeters serenade the formal opening.

Left: Captain Freddie and Mrs Ruth Hayden in full dress for the 'Battle of Agincourt', the social highlight of the 1965 festival. Throughout the sixties, costume parties, often continuing until dawn, attracted hundreds of people and raised large sums to support the festival. *(Reprinted by kind permission of Mrs Ruth Hayden)*

Janet Baker rehearsing at St Mary's Church, Bathwick, in 1966.

Yehudi Menuhin accepting the freedom of the city of Bath in Janaury 1966 from the mayor, Cllr Elsie Hanna.

Yehudi Menuhin, Ravi Shankar and Alla Rakha rehearsing at the Lansdown Grove Hotel in 1966. It was the first time that a western violinist had appeared on stage with Indian musicians, and Menuhin performed in the lotus (crossed-leg) position.

Above: Yehudi Menuhin rehearsing the Bath Festival Orchestra with the harpist Marisa Robles at the Assembly Rooms in 1967.

Above: In the eyes of many Johnny Dankworth was as important to the festivals of the sixties as Menuhin. Although a mainstay of the festival programme for many years, jazz gradually slipped in profile and did not return until the 1980s.

Below: Menuhin's farewell: pictured on the last night of Yehudi Menuhin's final festival in 1968 are (l-r) Lord Strathcona (chairman of the festival who had the unenviable task of severing the festival's links with Menuhin), Diana Menuhin, Yehudi Menuhin, Princess Irene of Greece (sister of King Constantine), Alderman Roy Hiscocks (mayor), Mrs Hiscocks (mayoress) and Lady Strathcona.

Above: Administrators Luke Rittner and Naomi Page took delivery of the festival's first vehicle in 1968.

Below: Under Sir Michael Tippett's aegis, the festival began having motifs or themes for its publicity. In 1971 thousands of butterflies were in evidence. Unfortunately, some felt they symbolised a lightweight programme. In this picture administrator Luke Rittner is pictured with one of the larger butterflies.

Above and below: The annual Roman Rendezvous was the only time in the year when residents could swim in the city's historic baths. It originated from the 1961 'Roman Orgy' which was denounced by Yehudi Menuhin as being 'at odds' with his view of how the festival should be. The 'Roman Rendezvous', pictured below in 1972, continued until the mid-seventies with a band playing each night – their platform, extending over the water, is to the right of the picture.

Sir Michael Tippett introduced many younger artists to the Bath Festival. In this picture he is talking with Bernard Gregor-Smith and Peter Cropper of the Lindsay Quartet in 1971.

Sir Michael Tippett rehearses soloists Pamela Bowden, Clifford Grant and Ronald Dowd at the Guildhall in preparation for a memorable performance of the composer's oratorio *A Child of Our Time* at Wells Cathedral in 1968. The following year Tippett became joint artistic director before becoming sole director in 1970.

Sir Michael Tippett with the programme for the 1974 festival, the last of five programmed solely by the composer who lived near Corsham, Wilts. He remains the only artistic director to have left entirely voluntarily.

Sir Michael Tippett rarely conducted at the Bath Festival, but when he did his performances were inspiring. *(Reprinted by kind permission of B&NES Record Office.)*

Sir William Glock was artistic director of the Bath Festival for ten festivals from 1975 - 1984 during which time the present length - two weeks and three weekends - was established.

The theme of Sir William Glock's last festival in 1984 was 'maze and labyrinth' and a lasting momento of that year is the Beazer maze which stands near Pulteney Bridge in the centre of Bath.

William Mann, festival director in 1985. He was ousted before his first festival had taken place.

Amelia Freedman, founder of the Nash Enemble, who were regular visitors to the festival under Sir William Glock's regime. She became artistic director in 1986 and now directs the Mozartfest.

The violinist Anne Sophie Mutter appeared in the festival in 1987 – but at the Colston Hall in Bristol. *(Photo courtesy of Bath Festivals Trust)*

Artist David Mach aroused the wrath of many with his nuclear submarine built from car tyres outside the Assembly Rooms in 1986. It was at a time when the nuclear arms race was high on the international political agenda.

It's not music. But is it art? These two copulating horses outside Green Park Station caused controversy as part of the visual art element of the 1988 Bath Festival.

The Contemporary Art Fair became an internationally renowned institution and attracted some unusual installations. *(Photo courtesy of Bath Festivals Trust)*

A public meeting was called on February 11, 1992, to air local people's views that the festival was out of touch and had lost its way. The ultimate outcome was the establishment of Bath Festivals Trust to provide a much wider ranging festival than had hitherto been the case.

Tim Joss, who was appointed chief executive of Bath Festivals Trust in 1993 and subsequently artistic director. He had the task of removing the "elitist" image of the festival, while still maintaining its high international standing.
(Photo courtesy of Bath Festivals Trust)

The ever-growing jazz programme, which now includes the Clerical Medical Jazz Weekend, is the responsibility of Nod Knowles. During the difficult years of 1992 and 1993, he also kept the administration together. *(Photo courtesy of Bath Festivals Trust)*

The first five literature festivals (1995-1999) were directed by children's author Laurence Staig. *(Photo courtesy of Bath Festivals Trust)*

The Burning Angel was intended as an exciting work of art on opening night in 1995, but there was controversy when some Christian groups accused the festival of blasphemy. The "fire sculpture" went ahead, although it caused a scare when the burning head toppled to the ground and stopped just short of the crowds of spectators.
(Photo courtesy of Bath Festivals Trust)

*(Left: photo courtesy of
Bath Festivals Trust)*

The theme of the 1995 festival was 'utopias' and local school children were encouraged to
create banners and posters reflecting this ideal.

One of the most remarkable visits of recent years was that by the Val Reef Choristers from the newly-liberated South Africa, who were a highlight of the 1995 festival. Here, they are performing on the opening night stage. *(Photo courtesy of Bath Festivals Trust)*

The opening night celebrations include hundreds of children dressed in costume, such as these from Weston All Saints Primary School who took part in 1996.
(Reproduced by kind permission of Weston All Saints Primary School).

Thousands of people gather in Royal Victoria Park, in front of the Royal Crescent, for the opening night celebrations each year. (*Photo courtesy of Bath Festivals Trust*)

Although the opening night celebrations are a relatively recent addition to the Bath Festival, and the fireworks even more so, they have rapidly become an annual institution. With candles in the windows and street lights extinguished, the silhouette of the Royal Crescent takes on a magical appearance. *(Photo courtesy of Bath Festivals Trust)*

Violin Concerto, with Menuhin as soloist. At first glance the combination of Boulez and Menuhin might seem like an unusual one. But writing in his biography of Yehudi Menuhin, Henry Raynor says:

> *Their differences seemed to complement each other. To Menuhin, the work is richly and almost over-ripely emotional, to Boulez it is sternly architectural, but what might have been a disjointed and unsatisfactory compromise became a fine, strong performance in which each of the collaborators affected the other.*[1]

The final result of the 1967 festival was one of the best ever – a loss of a mere £267 on a turnover of over £37,000. Nevertheless, the substantial accumulated deficit remained. By now, even the traditionally supportive *Bath Chronicle* was beginning to have its doubts. Yes, the paper worried about the financial position of the festival, as it always did. But its main concern lay in the festival's direction and appeal. The headline on June 14, 'Festival? It's not much fun for us, say the young', must have sent a chill through the festival office. The article was a vox pop of eight 16-21 year olds, and suggested widespread apathy. When even the local jazz hero Acker Bilk, making his first festival appearance for several years, failed to draw a crowd, it was further evidence that something was seriously amiss.

On June 20, 1967, *The Bath Chronicle* finally spoke the unspeakable: 'Bath may have to learn to live without Menuhin.' It was a chilling prospect. *The Bath Chronicle's* well-connected 'special correspondent' wrote:

> *In recent years the festival has followed a rather anonymous pattern, with scarcely a distinctive ripple from one June to another, to stir the musical waters. A largely undiluted musical recipe of eighteenth century works, offering less and less of Menuhin as a solo performer, has ceased to attract the close attention of major musical critics. It has also – let's face it – failed to pierce the thick skin of local apathy, to convince the man in the street that this isn't just culture for the visiting rich.*

The author continued with a shocking suggestion:

> *There is one major change the festival could make. It concerns the artistic director Menuhin himself. Now this, I am aware, may seem like heresy. To the musical world Menuhin is the Bath Festival. Next year will be his tenth as the man in charge. Most of the artists are attracted by his magnetism or friendship and the Bath Festival Orchestra is largely his creation. The danger lies in over-dependence on Menuhin's personality and influence. The festival needs more than one man's brilliance at its head. But before Bath could do without Menuhin altogether, it must know exactly what it wants in its place. Somewhere*

---

[1] From *Yehudi Menuhin* by Robert Magidoff and Henry Raynor, published by Robert Hale & Co, 1973, p.296.

there has to be found another personality, who can both rejuvenate the event artistically and permit a broader spread of interest.

Clearly the author had hit the nail on the head. The Bath Festival, which had made its name with Menuhin, would have to consider living without him. The paper's speculation brought howls of protest – as well as further complaints about elitism, inaccessibility, high prices and highbrow programmes. Tempe Fenton and Vera Lindey of Devonshire Buildings wrote:

All of us who have the welfare of the festival at heart cannot be too grateful to Mr Menuhin for all he has done. Apart from the contribution made by his outstanding genius, he has generously given free concerts to school children and a gift of £3000 towards the delightful production of Il Seraglio [Die Entführung]. *What other citizen of Bath has done so much for the festival?'*

Adrian Pegg, leader of one of the piano-smashing teams, waded into the debate:

Menuhin has become too large for Bath, or Bath too small for Menuhin. With all due respect to this brilliant musician and United Nations' leader, Menuhin is *Bath Festival. Perhaps this is basically why the average person in Bath has become apathetic towards their festival. Menuhin's music does not appeal to the average person; he's not a Flash Harry or a Sir Adrian Boult. He has, however, within the last ten years given Bath a much needed injection and can certainly rate on a par with Beau Nash for the amount of good work he has done for Bath generally. But the festival must change.*

The original newspaper article quickly found its way to America where Menuhin was on tour, arousing his suspicion that it had been planted by members of the Festival Society. A file note in the festival council's minutes by Naomi Page reads:

A letter from Mr Menuhin in America to the chairman saying 'don't count on my participation after 1968, my tenth festival' crossed with a personal letter from the chairman to Mr Menuhin saying 'I can't envisage the festival without you and that article wasn't planted by us'.

A month before the 1968 festival was due to start, the news of Menuhin's departure was made official, as *The Bath Chronicle's* front page of May 13 reported:

Yehudi Menuhin and Bath Festival Society are to part company. The ten years' partnership will end after this year's festival. This afternoon's surprise announcement came just over a month before the 1968 festival starts. Principal reason for the parting of the ways: money.

The official communiqué from the festival said:

In the present economic situation the society feels it is unable to keep pace with the financial requirements which Mr Menuhin considers necessary for the future rate of achievement and growth of a festival under his direction.

Speaking in 1998, Naomi Buchanan said:

Yehudi Menuhin was fairly well past the middle of his performing career and he wanted to do opera. The festival simply could not afford it. Some musicians worked on the 'God will provide' principle, and were amazed when He did not. It came to a major crunch. Menuhin said, either you provide the money or I go.

The festival chairman Lord Strathcona, concerned about the impact of such brinkmanship, asked Buchanan what she thought they should do. She replied: 'If he puts a pistol to our head we pull the trigger.' Menuhin did. And they fired.

In the same way as they had a festival orchestra, Menuhin and Hunter now wanted a festival opera company as well. No longer were they prepared to buy in outside productions. The cost of such an enterprise would have been astronomical. Opera had been the undoing of Beecham's brief reign in 1955. So too it was to be the undoing of Menuhin's long incumbency.

Speaking in 1998, Menuhin insists it was his decision to part company with Bath:

I had prepared Mozart's Magic Flute, *chosen the singers and was looking forward to it, and then the [festival] council decided that they could not afford it. So I had a feeling that it was probably time for me to leave. As soon as they said they were not prepared to pay for the* Magic Flute, *I decided to leave immediately with no hesitation.*

Morley Pooley, *The Bath Chronicle's* veteran music critic, said:

People forget that Sir Thomas Beecham, long before Menuhin took over, always advocated pretty much the same type of festival for Bath as Menuhin produced. And even as far back as 1938 that great showman C B Cochran had his eye on Bath as a festival centre where elegant surroundings would frame fine music. All through those years there have been squabbles because those responsible for the art side wanted more money to spend to make it a better festival. It happened in Beecham's time, but unfortunately the maestro was too strong for the opposition and always won. I say unfortunately because Sir Thomas was far too expensive for Bath but the results were always superb.

Pooley had a great deal of sympathy for Menuhin, and wouldn't let his achievements go unremarked upon:

> *Menuhin often played at Bath for peanuts – according to his standards – and certainly succeeded in establishing an intimate family festival essentially suited to Bath. And his family helped enormously. People from abroad came to Menuhin's English festival, for that is the reputation it had achieved in the world of music.*

Another witness to the end of the Menuhin era was Luke Rittner, later to become Secretary General of the Arts Council. He had been studying at the London Academy of Music and Dramatic Art. Jobless, he had returned to the family home at Wellow near Bath in 1966. After a temporary post at the Theatre Royal, he joined the festival staff in 1968:

> *My first festival was Menuhin's last, and because of all the shenanigans with Menuhin they were trying to see how they could survive in the post-Menuhin era. The rows about his departure were enormous. It all went very sour. Euan Strathcona was chairman and decided, in effect, to sack Menuhin.*

But what, in Rittner's view, had gone wrong? Looking back after 30 years as a professional arts administrator he sees a number of problems:

> *Menuhin had been doing it for ten years. It had got to the point where he was really just approving a programme that was put together by his agent, Ian Hunter. The Festival Society council were increasingly feeling that Menuhin had less and less really to do with it. That he was taking all this glory and the festival programme was losing a bit of lustre and getting more and more esoteric. And because it was getting more esoteric it meant the box office wasn't doing what it should be doing.*

There were other warning bells as well, says Rittner:

> *It had got this sort of very elitist feel about it, and there were lots of dinner jackets around. This was in the sixties when everything was being thrown upside down and students were rioting all around Europe. And here was this now slightly ageing, aged, elitist event which seemed to be less and less part of Bath and simply imposed on Bath. Bath was a beautiful place and a useful place to have a festival.*

In just ten short years, the festival – with its all-night jazz, 'Roman Rendezvous' around the baths, and decorated streets – had become out-dated, starchy and elitist. With the benefit of hindsight, it is easy to see that the festival had not moved with the times. And during the 1960s the times moved very quickly indeed. The blame cannot be laid wholly at the feet of Yehudi Menuhin or Ian Hunter. As local festival supporters took on family and work commitments, those who were prepared for all-night jamborees in the late 1950s were unlikely to be so eager a decade later. New blood had not come in, and now the festival was in crisis.

From the BBC's point of view, the Bath Festival was no longer very exciting either. Sir William Glock, at that time head of Radio 3 and later to become director of the festival himself, explained in an interview for this book why he as a broadcaster had paid scant attention to the later festivals of Menuhin's era. He said: 'Menuhin's festivals were too unadventurous, too much of a family affair for the BBC. But there was a great following.'

Amelia Freedman, who became artistic director in 1985, says that with Menuhin it was very much Yehudi and friends. She said:

> It was a lovely, vivacious festival and he was a great man, but I think his festival was very focused around the baroque repertoire, his Bath Festival Orchestra and his musical friends, whereas Sir Michael Tippett [1969-73] and Sir William Glock [1974-83] broadened it out, broadened the repertoire and broadened the artists whom they invited to the festival.

David Pratley, who engineered the rescue of the festival in 1993-94, said: 'Without Menuhin we wouldn't be here. I suspect he was arrogant, as many gifted people are.'

In April 1968, Yehudi Menuhin gave his own perspective on his imminent departure:

> I feel I have brought my festival to Bath and made it into a very success-ful and internationally known festival. My conception of the purpose and function of my festival has perhaps outgrown that of the festival council. So many things have remained static in Bath. I had hoped there would have been that much more that I could have implanted in Bath; that there could have been a little more of my own enthusiasm.

Was Menuhin's festival being snatched away from him? Or was the city of Bath reclaiming its own heritage? On one point during that interview Menuhin was certainly correct: 'A ten year tenure of public office presents a maximum span of obligatory mutual tolerance.' Ian Hunter said:

> Mr Menuhin and I would wish to have gone on for another ten years... We felt our only course was to withdraw because neither he nor I can afford to be concerned with an interest which, owing to a financial condition, may have to stand still.

There was to be no graceful departure, recalls Rittner:

> He left in a very dramatic way, making an extremely emotional speech on the last day of the festival at the start of a recital. It was a very bitter speech, and lots of the old faithful were very upset and very angry. All sorts of people were writing in and cancelling their subscriptions and saying they would never come to the festival again.

In a long and bitter polemic, Hunter took his point of view to *The Bath Chronicle* (June 28):

> *It is quite true that lack of financial provision to keep pace with Mr Menuhin's vision for the future development of the festival was the prime cause of his and my withdrawal. Our pressing for the means to achieve our ends created a situation of 'we' and 'they' and, when it became apparent to us that 'they' had neither the acumen, the drive, nor the courage either to find the money or to hand over the task to others better qualified, there seemed no point in continuing to build a festival which had already achieved so much on so little.*

Like Aldeburgh, with its personality cult built around Britten and to a lesser extent Pears, Bath had become Menuhin-centric. There was the family, the inner circle, the outer circle and the rest. Hunter went on to praise the family atmosphere Menuhin had built up but added disingenuously:

> *This family atmosphere has never been allowed to let the festival develop into a clique and it is due to Yehudi Menuhin that the variety of great and world-famous artists has been so wide and covered so many fields.*

Hunter was in no doubt where the blame for the end of the era lay: '...if in the future there are regrets at the premature ending of an era the responsibility lies mainly with the city corporation and the Bath Festival Society.'

Lord Strathcona was quick to rebuke Hunter, telling *The Bath Chronicle*: 'Statements such as these are necessarily personal opinions and reflect more on the people who make them than on those they are made about.'

But quite simply it was time for a change, as eventually it always must be. The Menuhin era had personified the 1960s. The 1970s were now looming. Luke Rittner could see that:

> *The sadness was that Menuhin took it so personally, whereas I think: if only he had been able to rejoice in the fact that he had put it on the map, done ten years, and now it was time to move on. But that didn't happen.*

Taking his grievances to *The Daily Telegraph*, Yehudi Menuhin said:

> *I don't think it is chiefly a question of money. Either there would have to be a new Society or the present one would have to change its attitude completely. I wanted Bath eventually to become something like Tanglewood in Massachusetts with its own concert hall and providing something large for the region and particularly its youth. But this was not taken up, partly of course because of the silly jealousies between Bath and Bristol.*

In *The Times*, Lord Strathcona, confirming that the festival would continue, suggested that it was they and not Menuhin who had been constrained: 'We have depended on his artistic initiative and this will now mean unleashing many of the ideas we have ourselves.'

To the *Bristol Evening Post*, Menuhin again suggested that money wasn't the only source of disagreement:

> *I would say that the trouble at Bath is a lack of vision. Bath is such a beautiful jewel of a city. It lulls people into a self-contentment. That does not at this moment rhyme with my own awareness of world news and problems, the terrifying situations that exist artistically, politically, financially, and most importantly humanly. A festival should bring these things to the fore and give expressions to the ills of the century and possible cures and solutions. I would not make it a political forum, but I do want people to see art more as a part of life. We fell apart on this matter. The financial angle was more a symptom than a cause.*

With the benefit of 30 years hindsight, Menuhin added in 1998:

> *I don't think that directors should remain in their position much more than ten years, because there's always a little sediment. At that time there was the feeling that Ian Hunter was putting his own artists in, which was not true. Any artist I wanted I could have. I chose the whole programme, but in consultation with the people of Bath. I never like to impose unduly.*

* * *

Amongst all this conflict, the 1968 festival went ahead. The new television company HTV did not offer a straight-forward subsidy. Instead they paid for the rights to broadcast certain events, including a 'Viennese Evening' which ended the festival. The council's grant, meanwhile, quietly slipped up to £4000.

The biggest theatre event of the entire festival was the first appearance in Britain of the Batsheva Modern Dance Company from Israel. Among the audience were the Israeli Ambassador and Jennie Lee, the arts minister. That event wasn't without trouble either. The dancers had been touring all around Europe with a tape recording for backing. Here in England, the Musicians' Union were having none of it and demanded an orchestra. The festival simply did not have the resources and, faced with the prospect of blood on their hands, the Musicians' Union declared it to be merely a point of principle and promptly paid for a 27-piece orchestra itself.

Musically the menu may have been not dissimilar to previous years, nevertheless it remained of the highest calibre. Menuhin was accompanied in recital by the pianist Clifford Curzon; another violinist, Igor Oistrakh, also appeared. He later joined Menuhin for an exhilarating account of Bartók's *Duo for two violins*. The young pianist Rafael Orozco, winner of the fledgling Leeds Piano Competition, offered a recital and a concerto. In the Abbey, the Newton

Park College Choir with organist Dudley Holroyd tackled Bernstein's newly written *Chichester Psalms*, and gave the première of *Concertante Music for Orchestra* by John McCabe. At the Assembly Rooms, the soprano Elisabeth Schwarzkopf returned to the city and was accompanied in recital by Martin Isepp. But probably the most radical musical event of 1968 came in Wells Cathedral, with a performance of Michael Tippett's *A Child of Our Time* by the Bournemouth Symphony Orchestra with the City of Bath Bach Choir. Among the soloists were Pamela Bowden, Clifford Grant and Ronald Dowd.

On the social side, the suffragettes were remembered in the recreation of a 'Suffragettes Supper' marking the fiftieth anniversary of women's votes. 'Pot Luck Dinners', involving paying for a meal but only finding out on the day where you were dining, proved popular. In Abbey Church Yard a play remembering King Richard the Lionheart by Barbara Robertson was performed. (It was King Richard who granted Bath its city charter in 1189, established the pageantry of coronations and instigated the tradition that the Bishop of Bath and Wells should stand at the sovereign's left hand.) Poetry had rarely enjoyed a profile in the festival, but an appearance by Dame Peggy Ashcroft at the Theatre Royal rectified that in a programme of words and music entitled 'Homage to Purcell'. With her was the harpsichordist Raymond Leppard.

Opera, the great divide between the Menuhin camp and the city camp, consisted of a double bill: Mozart's *The Impresario* and Stravinsky's *The Soldier's Tale*. For the former, Robert Morley wrote a set of new lyrics in just two days, full of topical allusions and modern innuendo, including a part for one Diana Gould – also known as Mrs Menuhin.

But on the tip of everyone's tongue and in the front of everyone's mind, was the departure of Menuhin. For the statistically minded, during his ten years at the helm of the festival Yehudi Menuhin appeared in 105 concerts and performed in 320 musical and theatrical items. Looking back 30 years later, Ian Hunter eventually concedes that the festival had stagnated and, even without the operatic agenda which brought matters to a head, his and Menuhin's time was running out. Nevertheless, he felt the festival committee led by Lord Strathcona could have been more supportive. Speaking in 1998 Hunter said:

> *He lacked the drive to match Menuhin's and my vision for the festival. We felt we had to have opera in the Theatre Royal annually. Yehudi Menuhin and I both felt a little bit depressed that the committee and the city were not prepared to support us. They lacked a lot of imagination.*

Beginning to dip its toes into new waters, the traditional festival souvenir programme was replaced by a souvenir folder containing all the bits of paper a devoted festival-goer could ever need. In a tribute to Menuhin included in the folder, the critic Kenneth Loveland wrote:

> *He has, of course, made Bath an international festival. I wonder if the city which honoured him appropriately by making him a freeman has ever stopped to work out just what Menuhin has been worth to it in terms of publicity? All those record sleeves for example. Every musical capital in*

the world has displays in the shop windows. From Tokyo to Buenos Aires they know that Bath is a festival city where Menuhin feeds the pigeons outside the Abbey, and wherever a single record of the Bath Festival Orchestra is sold, the city gets a handsome advertisement.

At an invitation-only extra event on the Sunday after the festival had officially finished, gifts were exchanged and farewell speeches made, notably by the chairman of the Arts Council, Lord Goodman. Naomi Buchanan recalls: 'The departure was not as graceful as it could have been. Lord Goodman's farewell speech papered up the cracks.'

Lord Goodman told the audience that Menuhin was 'a great man, and not only because he has bestowed his great musical talent on this city.' He did not think it would ever be possible to assess the generosity of Menuhin's gift to Bath, which he believed was:

...almost unequalled in musical history. He has given so much without any thought of return. The best reward you can give him is to ensure what he has built remains. Honours – and he has had many bestowed upon him including the freedom of the city – mean little to Mr Menuhin, but I know this festival has a very special significance for him and means more than perhaps anything else he has created.

The public end of this most extraordinary and successful era in the history of the festival came in a peaceful and relaxed way. In what was probably the least formal event of his decade-long tenure, Menuhin and his orchestra gathered at the Assembly Rooms in an evening of Viennese waltzes and polkas, food and wine, conversations and reminiscences. Recalling the occasion 30 years later, Menuhin said it was an emotional evening:

My send off in Bath was a lovely one. I was presented with a wonderful set of white porcelain and a violin case made by one of the great English cabinet-makers. They had an evening when everyone dressed in nineteenth century costume and I was the Strauss of the evening leading my orchestra – Bath Festival Orchestra – in waltzes and polkas. Just to see the people dancing to the music was a great, great experience. It gave the visual proof of what people may feel when they listen to music and are seated in serried ranks in the concert hall. This was the liberation of an audience. I loved it.

Menuhin insists that, despite his disappointment over the opera, he felt no lasting resentment: 'None at all. I felt it was their right to accept or refuse. After all, I wasn't providing the money. There was no bitterness. Only gratitude for ten lovely years which I thought was a good term.'

HTV broadcast 30 minutes of the Viennese event live and at midnight no one wanted to leave. For one last time at the Bath Festival, Yehudi Menuhin placed his violin beneath his chin. The great virtuoso's final contribution to the Bath Festival was Johann Strauss's famous waltz, *The Blue Danube*.

CHAPTER SIX

After 1968 Yehudi Menuhin flatly refused to have anything further to do with the Bath Festival. There would be no honorary or advisory role. He wanted a clean break. With Menuhin's departure, Bath also lost the services of Ian Hunter and his company, Harold Holt Ltd. They left behind them the biggest loss since 1955 – £3200. But once again, rather than call in guarantees, the chairman, Lord Strathcona, allowed the Society's overdraft – now secured against Linley House – to continue growing.

The names of a three-man team were announced in June 1968 as joint artistic directors – the conductor Colin Davis; Ian Hunter's former colleague at Harold Holt and the festival's artistic administrator since 1955, Jack Phipps; and the local composer Sir Michael Tippett. But clearly there was a need for the local administration team to be built up into something more substantial. For Luke Rittner, it was to be his lucky break. He became Naomi Page's assistant as part of the new look festival.

The team's first thoughts were about what to do in 1969. If it was to be a clean sheet, it had to be a radically clean sheet. Luke Rittner saw the new regime as a positive thing, particularly after the stuffiness which characterised the closing years of the Menuhin era. Speaking in 1998 he said:

> *Of course there's always a new dawn, and the great thing was that Michael Tippett, who then was not the sort of household name that he is now, was immensely youthful and enthusiastic. The combination of him and Colin Davis was a great force for change. We all got together and began to think about how we could change the festival. In the post-Yehudi era things went to our heads a little bit. The festival went from ten days to three weeks.*

Within five months the changes were being felt. In an attempt to distance itself from the Menuhin era, the festival's Wife of Bath symbol (based on the character in Chaucer's *Canterbury Tales*) was discarded in favour of a modern trumpet-like motif, designed by Nicholas Jenkin, a lecturer at the Royal College of Art, and still in use today.

When the first details of the programme were announced, *The Bath Chronicle's* John Donaldson offered this comment:

> *Enthusiasm; drive; energy; tolerance; understanding; acute profes- sionalism. They are communicated by three men of widely differing temperaments – Sir Michael Tippett, Colin Davis and Jack Phipps. It is on this triumvirate that the success or failure of this year's Bath Festival depends. And there will be more than usual interest in their success or failure. The eyes and minds and ears of the professional*

musicians and the critics will be keen. For this is the year of change in the Bath Festival – in style, scope, presentation, outlook, approach and aims. And Bath does not care for change; there are groups who do not like to break out of their twittering cages.

But in the main, goodwill was behind the threesome, as Sir Michael Tippett said: 'All the hatchets of the past have been buried.' On the opening day of the festival, Yehudi Menuhin sent a telegram to *The Bath Chronicle* offering his 'heartfelt wishes to Bath and to my friends there. May the festival continue successfully and happily and bring them great joy.'

The change in mood brought about a change in sartorial style. Evening dress was no longer required. Naomi Page told *The Bath Chronicle* (June 12, 1969): 'We are de-pomping everything this year. Dinner jackets are certainly being discouraged even at the major events.' Visual art was at last given what many hoped might become a permanent home, in an old basement garage in Railway Place. But although much effort went into preparing it, once the festival was over, the venue reverted to being an old garage.

Amid the change there was some important continuity. Barbara Robertson's contribution to the social side of the festival was as remarkable as ever. She hosted *Supper with Michelangelo* at Combe Hay Manor, a play based on the summer of 1546 and presented against the façade of her manor house, with guests eating picnics and sitting on cushions on the grass bank.

Pot luck suppers contributed handsomely to the festival coffers, while the Festival Association, which hitherto had not had much success as a fringe promoter and fund-raising body, took on a new look. Ken Aldred took over the chairmanship from Cllr George Comer and changed its *modus operandi* from being the organiser of events to being the umbrella under which city organisations could contribute to the festival.

Financially, of course, things had not particularly improved. The brave new world of the Bath Festival was faced with an attempt to reduce the city council's contribution from £4000 to £3500. It was easily defeated, but with an annual budget in the region of £40,000 there was still much fund-raising work to be done. A Gallup poll suggested that up to £150,000 was spent at festival time in shops at Bath which would not otherwise have been spent – proof that the city's investment in the festival over the years really had been worthwhile. HTV, although declining to broadcast from the 1969 festival, gave £2000, while Westward Television came onboard and handed over £750.

Hundreds of people crowded into Abbey Church Yard for an open-air concert by the Philip Jones Brass Ensemble to mark the formal opening of the festival. It included a specially commissioned fanfare by the composer Stefan de Haan. Philip Jones himself was born at Wellsway, Bath, and enjoys a pre-eminent position in the brass world. His father, Jack Jones, had been a trombonist in the Pump Room Orchestra from 1927-31 and his grandfather, Leonard Copestake, played drums with the same orchestra.

The new look festival was quickly being seen. A series of concerts at the Little Theatre cinema, entitled 'Composer's Choice', brought contemporary and revolutionary artists such as Richard Rodney Bennett and

Peter Maxwell Davies performing modern music. Maxwell Davies even dared to dress informally and chat with his audience. The radical new approach was encouraged by the arts minister Jennie Lee, who spoke at the festival lunch. She said: 'People generally do expect only the best but it does not preclude leaving a place for the new, the experimental and the dangerous.'

The Forum was also pressed into use. Morley Pooley, who had officially retired but was to offer his words of wisdom at festival time for many more years to come, wrote:

> What a joy to rediscover Bath's 1700-seater concert hall with its comfortable seats and its freedom from the vice of acoustical trouble to which every other Bath hall seems so subject.

One event in the Forum is recalled with glee by Luke Rittner:

> We spent two days and nights building an enormous stage for a performance by the New Philharmonia Orchestra and Chorus, with Carlo Maria Giulini conducting Beethoven's Missa Solemnis. Even though it was scaffolding, we managed to get the chorus tiered on three levels. The orchestra and chorus came on and then Giulini arrived with his agent. He strode onto the platform and stood on the rostrum surveying the scene in front of him before turning to his agent and saying 'I would like the entire chorus raised three inches.' We only had two hours between the end of the rehearsal and the start of the performance. I knew it was physically impossible so we all went out into the corridor and said, 'What are we going to do?' I said, 'Nothing, absolutely nothing.' That night Giulini drove up in his limousine. He walked into the wings, peered through the curtains, and looked at the orchestra and chorus and turned to his agent and said, 'Perfect'.

The concert, one of the classical highlights of 1969, included four well-known soloists: Margaret Price, Janet Baker, Robert Tear and Clifford Grant.

The 1969 festival had events all over the place, even as far afield as Salisbury Cathedral. Rittner recalls:

> To be honest, we probably bit off more than we could chew. But it sort of blew the cobwebs away. Here was Tippett, this great radical guy, saying he doesn't want his festival full of people in dinner jackets. If they want to wear dinner jackets then fine, but equally if they want to wear jeans they are very welcome.

Overstretch themselves they did. Never since has the Festival attempted to venture as far as Salisbury, but in stretching its wings the festival divorced itself from the Menuhin era and set its sights to the future. The expansion was also an attempt to court further money from the television companies, and Salisbury came under the remit of Western Television. In point of fact, the Salisbury venture, a concert by the Northern Sinfonia conducted by George Malcolm, was a step too far, and only 160 of 1800 tickets were sold. At the last minute, it was switched to the Forum in Bath where it attracted an audience of 412. The loss on this escapade alone was £1000.

Introducing the festival in that year's *Bath Chronicle* festival supplement, Morley Pooley wrote: 'The violin has been ousted by the composer-pianist, and the intimate chamber concert by big-scale orchestral works.'

In their attempts to widen the scale of the festival, organisers decided to create a new Festival Chorus of 140 voices to sing Berlioz's *Damnation of Faust* at the Forum with the BBC Symphony Orchestra and Colin Davis. It was directed by John Alldis and included top amateur singers from Bath and the surrounding area, and was boosted by amateur and professional singers from London. Local choirs immediately saw it as an insult. Cuthbert Bates, from the City of Bath Bach Choir, said the Festival Chorus was 'an oblique invitation to the cream of my choir to divide their loyalties in the midst of crucial Bach rehearsals.' He added: 'You could call it a snub. It would have been less of a shock if we had been consulted.' It was an allegation the festival denied, but it created an air of bad feeling with a choir that had once been a central plank of the festival.

Other classical music events included two concerts by the Academy of St Martin in the Fields, one in the Abbey conducted by Sir Michael Tippett, with music ranging from Bach to Charles Ives, the other with Sir Neville Marriner at the Assembly Rooms. The soprano Elly Ameling appeared in recital at the Guildhall, Bath's Silver Ring Choir were at the Assembly Rooms with their conductor Kelvin Thomas, and the harpist Osian Ellis joined Janet Baker for a recital accompanied by George Malcolm at the Assembly Rooms.

Although there was no opera in the 1969 festival, true to form there was a storm in a teacup over the issue. A company called Opera Piccola wanted to establish a Glyndebourne in the west at Chipping Sodbury, which would run at the same time as the festival. They approached festival organisers with a view to being billed as a fringe attraction. Jack Phipps saw this as a potential threat to his audiences, and refused to include them, writing to the organisers: 'I ought to warn you that the festival is mounting performances throughout Somerset and Wiltshire and in Gloucestershire and I feel we could well prove a considerable threat to your performances if you maintain them during the festival.' Jill Watt of Opera Piccola was decidedly put out and told the press: 'We are clearly getting the cold shoulder from Bath and we regard Mr Phipps's letter as an attempt to warn us off during the festival.'

There was also a disagreement with the Theatre Royal. Hitherto, the owner, Frank Maddox, had charged £1000 for a week's rent, and with this in mind organisers had intended inviting the English Stage Company to be part of the festival. Suddenly, the rent shot up to £1400. Unable to afford such an enormous rise in charges, the festival withdrew. Maddox duly brought in the Oxford Playhouse Company to perform Chekhov's *Uncle Vanya*, advertising their appearance as a 'festival attraction'.

Writing in *The Guardian*, Edward Greenfield's assessment of the new festival arrangements was encouraging: 'As you would expect with Tippett around, there is a new wildness, an unpredictability in the air, well removed from the civilised eighteenth century manners encouraged by Menuhin.'

Morley Pooley's verdict in *The Bath Chronicle* (June 30) came after Claudio Arrau's closing piano recital:

> *Unlike previous years, the 1969 Bath Festival ended on Sunday afternoon without a single word being spoken, without presentations, tributes and without pomp or ceremony. But Claudio Arrau saw to it that musically the ending was an occasion of great pianistic display. It has been said of him that while other pianists are famed for their Chopin, Bach or Beethoven, Arrau always impresses as the outstanding interpreter of whatever composer he's playing at the moment. He is always so assured and convincing.*

However, before that final concert came the festival's most extraordinary project ever. Responding to criticism of elitism and snobbishness, the festival called a meeting with young peoples' groups to find out what they would like in the festival. Naomi Buchanan said: 'They wanted a Blues Festival and we had no idea how to run one.'

The first was held at the Recreation Ground, normally the home of the city's rugby club, in the centre of Bath. The stars included Led Zeppelin, John Mayall, Fleetwood Mac, Chicken Shack and Keef Hartley. The compère was John Peel. 'You could smell the marijuana,' reminisces Naomi Buchanan. The festival approached Fred Bannister, a pop promoter, who put the two-day event together. Rittner said: 'It was the most phenomenal success to the extent that we budgeted on about 6000 people buying tickets and printed 7000 tickets. In the end, 30,000 people descended on Bath and brought the entire city to a standstill.' For two days and two nights the Recreation Ground, and indeed the whole of the city of Bath, resounded to the thump and thud of folk and rock.

Writing in *The Bath Chronicle*, Tom Browne predicted the size of the event – but also predicted, accurately, the ultimate reaction:

> *Are you ready world? Because just about the largest single bill of names from the blues scene ever to appear in one place on one day is about to descend. The hand of destiny has chosen Bath. Just how many people are going to make the pilgrimage from Wales, the Midlands, London, all points West and South is a matter of some speculation. My guess is that the number of blanket rolls being tied in preparation for an all-night stop in Bath and rural districts has been underestimated. Whatever happens, it is sure that letters will be rolling in on Monday protesting about noise, damage to floral displays, appearance of hairy visitors, lack of police supervision, and wild games of tiddlywinks on North Parade. But then you could say the same for Broad Street at chucking-out time any Saturday night.*

The Blues Festival's insurance cover alone ran to a staggering £500,000. Bath was transformed into a shanty town. Along river banks, under hedgerows and in fields people bivouacked. Public benches became a rare luxury and ancient buildings propped up many a tired body. It was the first truly inclusive outdoor event the festival had seen since the abandoning of the 'Jambeano' street dancing of the early 1960s.

The festival chairman Lord Strathcona called for more: 'I think it was a good thing for the festival and for Bath. It was a thoroughly worthwhile venture.' Promoter Fred Bannister, who had personally underwritten the whole event and no doubt made a fortune from it, simply said it was 'incredibly successful.' The police were equally happy. Superintendent Don Waite said: 'We are well satisfied.' Looking back 30 years later, Luke Rittner has fond memories. He says:

> *You could not walk down Brock Street or around the Recreation Ground because people were simply standing, sitting, lying, sleeping. There was not a single pint of milk that was left on any doorstep anywhere.*

Eventually, as the city ground to a standstill in the worst traffic chaos it had ever witnessed in its entire history, the decision was taken to leave the Recreation Ground open all night for those who needed somewhere to sleep. The original intention had been that all drinks and food would be sold in plastic containers. However, as the numbers rose, supplies had to be brought to the Recreation Ground from anywhere and everywhere. It meant the rugby ground was littered with glass and a major clean-up exercise followed. Fred Daws, the city's parks director, was not best pleased: 'It ruined the weekend of a lot of men in my department and also in the health department. If another such event is held we must see that it is properly organised.'

Although in terms of serious law and order the Blues Festival had run as smoothly as anyone could hope for, there was outrage in the city. Cllr Laurie Coombs told the council's public safety committee that there had been a complete breakdown of public behaviour: 'I would accept there was no rioting, but I had reports of petty larceny such as stolen milk.' Cllr Graham Mower thought the complaints were unnecessary: 'I thought the young people behaved in very great wisdom.' But Cllr Mary Rawlings said: 'I am 100 per cent against it ever being held there again.'

The letters to *The Bath Chronicle* came flooding in. Miss Goldey from Pulteney Street wrote:

> *Those responsible for allowing it to take place showed, in my opinion, a complete lack of understanding of what is appropriate to the dignity of our beautiful town, and no consideration whatever for the residents.*

Another correspondent said:

> *Quite apart from the appalling din, there was the obstruction caused to citizens who had literally to step over prone bodies to enter shops,*

and the long-haired fraternity (male, I believe) who slept in unauthor-
ised places – e.g. Orange Grove. If we must have this deplorable type
of event, may I suggest we ask the noble Marquis to accommodate it at
Longleat? No doubt the lions would clean up some of the leftovers.

But Miss V A Hewitt of Trowbridge wrote: 'Please let us have more of this 'deplorable' event which was enjoyed by myriads and despised by the bigoted few.' Mr Raddon of Devizes agreed: 'On Saturday, Bath looked for the first time for at least seven years as if it was staging a festival.'

Still revelling in his memories of the event, Luke Rittner recalls with great amusement that the city council was so inundated with calls of outrage from Pulteney Street and the surrounding houses that a meeting was called. 'The result was that they adopted a decision that the thing would never, ever, ever, be allowed to happen in Bath again.'

The final word on the 1969 Blues Festival should perhaps go to Mr A Swaton, a correspondent to *The Bath Chronicle*: 'Correct me if I am wrong, but I believe the orgies of Beau Nash and his friends make the Blues Festival look like tea on the vicarage lawn.'

* * *

As with the previous holy trinity of musical directors in 1955, the new triumvirate of Jack Phipps, Sir Michael Tippett and Colin Davis was not a success. As Naomi Buchanan observed, 'it was great fun, but a working nightmare. It was impossible to get them together often enough.' The festival's financial controller of the time, Robin Buchanan, says they simply had no focus: 'Individually they were lovely people, but it was not the right answer.'

In September 1969, Jack Phipps told *The Bath Chronicle* that the arrange-ment was coming to an end and that the festival should now be run locally. He said: 'I don't think there was any disagreement over the content of the programme. The three of us put it together and were equally responsible for what it was.'

The termination of Jack Phipps's and Colin Davis's contracts set the festival back £1000, a sum it could ill afford. By the autumn of 1969 the overdraft had topped £10,000, and a major fund-raising drive had to be launched. Not only was money needed for the ever-rising costs of the early 1970s, but the debt simply had to be cleared. There were attic sales, gala dinners and other special events. The Festival Club, long since the preserve of the few and held at 16 George Street, above the Hole in the Wall restaurant, was opened on Thursdays and Fridays from November until Christmas 1969. The council chipped in an extra £500 for 1970 bringing their total to £4500 – still less than they had given in 1955. However, there was a setback when neither Harlech nor Westward television companies would offer any funding for 1970.

At a festival meeting late in 1969, the chairman Lord Strathcona abruptly turned to Naomi Buchanan and Michael Tippett and told them that they were to take over the day-to-day running of the festival. According to Buchanan, when it came to the selection of artists, Tippett's London agent, Howard Hartog, selected many of the programmes and undertook the time-consuming task of booking and negotiating fees with the visiting artists. Tippett, says Robin Buchanan, was wonderful: 'He had never done anything like this before and threw his heart and soul into it, as did everyone. He was prepared to use his muscle to get people to come.'

In the autumn of 1969 Roy Strong, the radical 33-year-old director of the National Portrait Gallery, joined the festival's council of management. It was widely hoped that by having someone associated with the visual arts on the board for the first time, there might be more of a look in for exhibitions. However, over the ensuing 24 months, Strong only managed to attend one meeting. He also had ideas beyond the festival's means, which was evident from the outset, when he said: 'I've had enough of scratching around with imagination and a ball of string.'

At the end of January 1970, Lord Strathcona announced that he would be resigning both as chairman and from the festival's council of management after the 1970 festival. His successor was Barbara Robertson, who had been heavily involved with the festival's social scene for a decade, but who had little time for the musical side of things. Her mission was straightforward: 'I would like to get the financial situation really tidied up and put the festival on a even keel.'

As well as pop music, the festivals of the newly emerging Tippett era saw the advent of the Contemporary Art Fair. The basement of Linley House was opened as a permanent gallery; something the festival had long sought to achieve. With harmony and goodwill in the air, *The Bath Chronicle* of June 4, 1970, looked forward to the imminent opening of the festival with greater enthusiasm than ever:

> *The night of the long knives is over. For once the people who run the Bath Festival... are counting on a crisis-free fortnight. They're so happy they've even invited Yehudi Menuhin to take part next year (He can't come. He's booked up). After the power struggles that followed his departure and a few quieter, more recent resignations, three local people are in the driving seat.*

Indeed 1970 was the first time that the festival had been both conceived and executed locally. Lord Strathcona welcomed the development:

> *Only a strong feeling of local involvement can stamp a festival with a particular character which distinguishes it from the myriad festivals which have sprung up in recent years all over the country.*

As if to prove its populist appeal, the festival's cocktail party in 1970 took place on the top deck of the Avon Street multi-storey car park – and there wasn't a black tie in sight.

Amidst all the years of change, the 'Roman Rendezvous', which had started with the 'Roman Orgy' a decade earlier and was still the only time of the year when members of the public could swim in the Roman baths, continued to prove immensely popular, with tickets for the entire period selling out within a matter of hours.

Musically, the 1970 festival opened in the Abbey with the Academy of St Martin in the Fields directed by Neville Marriner performing Tallis's 40-part motet *Spem in Alium*, Vaughan Williams's *Fantasia on a theme of Thomas Tallis* and Tippett's *Plebs Angelica*. Morley Pooley's daughter Hilary Coates, by now an established concert pianist, gave a recital of her own at the Guildhall, while at the Forum, Men O'Brass appeared under the baton of Harry Mortimer together with the Bath Cantata Group. The Julliard Quartet appeared in the festival – and when they heard that Lord Strathcona had been hospitalised with back problems, gave an impromptu performance at his bedside.

Although the over-stretching of 1969 was cut down to more manageable goals, the festival continued to use venues in both Bristol and Wells. At the Colston Hall in Bristol, Joan Sutherland gave a recital which was attended by the Prince of Wales. It was His Royal Highness's first visit to the Bath Festival, and the beginning of an association which was to continue until the present day.

But there were hiccups. At Strode Theatre, the horn player Barry Tuckwell, appearing with the violinist Brenton Langbein and the pianist Maureen Jones, startled his audience by announcing from the platform that the piano, the theatre's own Bechstein instrument, was not up to scratch. He said: 'The piano is a disgrace to the Bath Festival. It is also mechanically defective. The soft pedal does not work. Miss Jones says it is the worst piano she has played on – with the possible exception of one in Indonesia.' The theatre agreed with his remarks and said they had advised the festival to hire a decent instrument for the occasion. Ruefully, the festival's assistant administrator Anthony Tootal conceded to the press: 'It's something to learn.'

The festival team's lack of experience and steep upward learning curve continued to show, as was demonstrated at a concert featuring the choir of Newton Park College at the Abbey. In pouring rain the doors were not opened, there were no stewards to show patrons to their seats, and the programmes had disappeared. The episode prompted an apology and a tightening up of the festival's operations.

Barry Tuckwell was in action later in the festival at the Colston Hall with the London Symphony Orchestra and André Previn performing Mozart's *Horn Concerto in E flat K447*. The programme also included Ravel's *Le Tombeau de Couperin* and Schubert's *Great Symphony*. A few days later at the same venue Colin Davis led the London Symphony Orchestra and Chorus in a performance of Beethoven's *Choral Symphony*, one of several events that marked the bicentenary of the composer's birth.

Barbara Robertson's new role as chairman-elect meant she played a lower-key role in the festival's festivities, but she still found time to write and produce a Greek mythological play at Combe Hay Manor, *The Golden Fleece*.

A 'Friends' organisation was established which continues to this day. With four categories of membership and preferential booking rights, it provided an opportunity for local people to support their festival for a modest sum.

The festival, meanwhile, was determined that after the success of the 1969 Blues Festival it should happen again – somehow, somewhere. Following the city's ban on the use of the Recreation Ground for any similar event, a desperate search was mounted. It looked as if Lansdown racecourse might be the answer, but the owners were unhappy. It was a difficult dilemma. On the one hand, the city council fretted about being seen as 'anti-youth'. But at the same time they were unable to solve the problem. Norwood playing fields near the newly established University of Bath was considered, but the council's parks committee objected.

Eventually Luke Rittner found a way forward: 'We held it on the then new permanent site of the Bath & West Show. At the time the manager happened to be my brother.'

There was a blanket ban on alcohol at the ground, with the notable exception of the artists and members of the press, who had a bar erected behind a doubly-enclosed and heavily guarded compound, surrounded by a 20-foot high fence. The festival did another deal with Fred Bannister and this time the festival brought virtually the whole of Somerset, Dorset and Gloucestershire to a standstill. The roads were so congested that even the musicians had problems reaching the site. Queues for the 580 temporary toilets stretched at times to over 200 people per lavatory. Rittner said:

This was pre-Glastonbury. The police ... reckoned there were half a million there. [One day] it was impossible to get to Cornwall because every road for fifty miles in each direction was blocked. Trains were laid on, buses, coaches, everything, to get people there.

It took months to get the showground back to something that looked respectable and normal. Rittner said: 'It was actually bigger than the Isle of Wight, and it was probably the genesis of Glastonbury.'

Although it was the last event of this scale organised under the auspices of the festival, with these two outdoor events Tippett's purpose had been achieved. 'What all that did,' says Rittner, 'was blow away the cobwebs of the previous ten years.' After two successful years, the festival decided not to risk the exposure again. As Naomi Buchanan explained at the time, future outdoor events looked set to have incredible regulations slapped on them. Chairman Barbara Robertson said: 'I think now is the time to get out; we have done two without getting our fingers burned.'

Tippett's first two years changed many other things at the Bath Festival. He encouraged many young performers to play, including unknowns like the Lindsay Quartet. The 'Friends' organisation began to develop in that time, as did fringe events like the garden tours which were immensely popular. Rittner said: 'The main festival didn't lose any of its standards and programmes became much more interesting.'

Early in 1971, Naomi Buchanan was employed by the city council to run the Edgar Celebrations for 1973, marking the 1000th anniversary of the coronation of King Edgar on the site of Bath Abbey – but not before she had told *The Bath Chronicle* (December 9, 1970) of the festival's vision for that year:

We are de-gimmicking the festival. Times have changed and the style of the festival too. We used to have costume balls with tickets at £4 and £5 to raise money for the musical programme, but I don't think that fits the pattern of the festival now. It used to be said the festival was a snob social event and to a large extent that criticism was justified. But there was far less interest in the arts in the early days and you had to do mad things that made the news to promote the name of the festival.

Her departure put the festival into the hands of her 23-year-old assistant Luke Rittner and his 23-year-old friend Anthony Tootal, both ambitious and enthusiastic and, particularly in Rittner's case, well-known in the city. They made a habit of proselytising for the festival. Travelling all over the west of England they spoke to women's groups, luncheon clubs and anyone else who would listen. They wrote articles, letters and comments. In short, they shouted the virtues of the festival from the hilltops to anyone and everyone who would listen. Rittner recalls:

All through the winter, Anthony and I used to go and speak to every Townswomen's Guild and every Round Table and Rotary and Young Farmers Clubs. From Exeter to Gloucester we were out night after night after night talking about the festival and drumming up local support. I think that in that time we built a huge affection for the festival which some people had become rather separated from in Yehudi's time.

Although he only lived up the road at Corsham in Wiltshire, Sir Michael Tippett was a busy man and much in demand as a composer. Like his predecessor Yehudi Menuhin, how much attention he was able to give to the festival has been the subject of some debate. Sir William Glock, his successor, has his doubts about Tippett's commitment. In an interview in 1998, he said: 'There was one programme each year called the Director's Choice. I wondered if it was the only one he programmed.'

Tippett defended his programming in an interview with *The Bath Chronicle*:

It seems to me that festivals like Bath can only make very limited use of the vast amount of contemporary music and therefore some choice has to be made. It is essential that the choice of work should be as good as possible and that no false compromise to the box office is made otherwise it will falsify the value.

False compromise or not, Tippett was excellent at keeping within his agreed budget, a pattern which over his tenure helped stabilise the festival's financial position enormously.

Tippett, Luke Rittner and his colleague Anthony Tootal, also benefited from a degree of enlightenment in the city council when David Eastman was its chief executive. Eastman was in his thirties and, according to Rittner, the first city council official who saw the festival's opportunities and possibilities:

'He became a terribly important bridge with the council and a great proselytiser for the festival within the council.'

That didn't stop the elected members of the council from attempting to undermine the festival's financial standing. With the festival enjoying a declining overdraft, Cllr Frederick Gilbert proposed reducing the city's support from £4500 to £2500 in 1971, saying he felt the amount was disproportionate to that given to other arts organisations. Cllr Lydia Ashman agreed, saying: 'It is time this lame duck got out of splints.' Cllr Will Johns was no help either, arguing that the festival did not help the ratepayers 'by one penny'. Mercifully there were enough wise old sages on the council who had heard it all before. Cllr George Comer pointed out that the city's investment generated some £100,000 of national and international publicity. Alderman Alleyne Berry told members that if the city removed £2000 worth of support, the Arts Council would follow suit and the whole thing would collapse. The proposal was ultimately defeated.

Tippett's financial approach was a breath of fresh air for the festival's administrators, who had previously been accustomed to walking on egg-shells as Rittner recalls:

It was as financially secure as anything ever is in the arts. Of course we had endless financial problems, we were constantly having to raise money, constantly having shortfalls. But where the great change came with the Tippett administration was that if the festival council said to Michael when he proposed his programme: 'Look, the box office just isn't going to add up on all these programmes, can we drop a couple of the slightly more difficult concerts and put in something that is going to get an 80 per cent box office rather than a 20 per cent,' he would say, 'Absolutely, yes of course'. It was a real change.

In 1971 the festival adopted the first in a series of annual motifs and chose butterflies. The colourful insects were everywhere – in shops, in windows and on posters. It was part of a concerted approach to make the festival more visible. More than 170 shops, building societies, banks and hotels entered the reorganised festival display competition, ensuring that there were brightly coloured butterfly-themed displays everywhere. Across the city, an estimated 40,000 of them fluttered. Having won the display competition every year since 1964, Jollys department store gracefully bowed out. In time, however, the butterflies came to be seen as a suitable emblem for a lightweight festival that was unable to afford any new commissions and that used college bands and members of the BBC Training Orchestra rather than the real thing.

Musically there were excellent performances, but the criticism that the festival lacked gravitas and was a great deal smaller than previously was undoubtedly justified. Nevertheless, among the concerts were visits by the Amadeus Quartet, the Academy of St Martin in the Fields, and the City of Bath Bach Choir with Cuthbert Bates at the Abbey. The Royal Opera gave a performance of *The Barber of Seville* at the Colston Hall, Bristol; Opera Rara sang unusual arias and ensembles from long-forgotten operas at the Guildhall; and the Lindsay Quartet, with the help of the 22-year-old pianist Imogen Cooper, appeared in a young performers' series.

The editor of *The Times*, William Rees-Mogg, loaned his nearby house for a concert by Marisa Robles (harp) and Christopher Hyde-Smith (flute), while the Beau Nash Room at the Lansdown Grove Hotel was the setting for a theatrical and musical entertainment about Richard Brinsley Sheridan and Elizabeth Linley. However, serious attempts to bring the ageing pianist Artur Rubinstein to Bath came to nought, and a scheduled visit by Gennadi Rozhdestvensky to conduct the New Philharmonia Orchestra fell through after he was injured in a road accident in Moscow. His place in the concert at the Colston Hall was taken by Lawrence Foster.

Although the 1971 festival was lightweight, the Tippett era was very different, as *The Bath Chronicle* noted in an article on June 2, 1971:

> *No crisis. No rows. It's hard to believe that it's Bath Festival time. Gone are the tensions and twitchiness of previous years. For once it is possible to walk into the festival office at Linley House without feeling that the organisers are in the middle of the biggest drama since the last one. This is because everything is going their way. Customers are rolling up to enjoy the sold-out concerts in a sun-kissed Bath swarming with butterflies. But the big news – hooray, at last, at last – is that Bath Festival will be rid of its 12-year overdraft next year if not this.*

By the end of the year, the Festival Society's financial controller, Robin Buchanan, was proudly announcing that the deficit – which at one point had topped £11,700 – had been whittled away to a mere £411. But there were other threats. Although the festival had long enjoyed a fund-raising and supportive 'fringe' of its own, it amounted to little more than a social club for those who enjoyed the main music festival. Bath Arts Workshop now came along with 'The Other Festival' which did what it liked, when it liked. A spokesperson for The Other Festival justified its existence to *The Bath Chronicle*: 'I cannot help but feel disappointed that once again the festival will cater to only a very small proportion of the Bath community. What about the other nine-tenths who have no interest in classical music? Are they once again to be ignored?' *The Bath Chronicle's* retort to this remark was that it was 'about as logical as criticising a blues festival for ignoring Beethoven.'

The festival benefitted from the philanthropy of the Carnegie Trust which sponsored a scheme, both in Bath and at other festivals around the country, whereby local people who contributed to local music – for example the director or secretary of a local choir – could be given free tickets for festival events.

Elsewhere in the 1971 festival, 'Roman Rendezvous' tickets were selling out almost as soon as they went on sale, and the Round Table ran a Mardi Gras carnival which spread out across the city bringing in thousands to enjoy the floats.

As well as Tippett's careful housekeeping, the festival's finances benefited from sales of *Food of Love*, a book of favourite recipes by well-known classical musicians. However, with her responsibilities as chairman, Barbara

Robertson's social side to the festival was wearing thin. There was no pageant or *son et lumière*, although she did write the cabaret for a low-key end of festival party, held at the University of Bath.

The 70th birthday of Tippett's contemporary, Sir William Walton, was marked in style during the 1972 festival and the composer was in the city to receive its congratulations. In an all-Walton programme at the Assembly Rooms, the Academy of St Martin in the Fields, directed by Neville Marriner, gave the first European performance of his *Sonata for String Orchestra*, the world première of *Five Bagatelles,* and the first festival performance since 1930 of *Façade*, this time with Eleanor Bron and John Amis instead of Constant Lambert.

The festival of 1972 – with funding of £6500 from the Arts Council and still only £4500 from the city – opened with a march past by the band of the Royal Engineers outside the Guildhall. After the success of the *Food of Love* recipe book, the festival published another fund-raising publication, *Yesterday in Bath*, which contained some 200 pictures of the city taken between 1849 and 1949. Despite the financial limitations imposed on him, Tippett insisted that he did not find it frustrating:

> *The job of artistic director is to create an interesting festival within the budget he is given. I find it challenging and absorbing. Certainly there are things we would like to do if the money were unlimited, but we have to be realistic. This is one of the best managed festivals in the country and, as a local festival, is rightly grounded in the local community.*

Parasols replaced butterflies as the festival motif in 1972. The 'Roman Rendezvous' continued as ever, and such was the demand for tickets that a thriving black market built up, and there were reports that some were changing hands for double their 75p face value. Nevertheless, the council's Spa Committee refused to cash in by opening the baths at other times of the year.

Following the thinness of the 1971 festival, there was decidedly more meat on the musical programme. The pianist Alfred Brendel, well on his way to becoming an elder-statesman of the keyboard, played a programme of Haydn, Schubert and Liszt, bringing the elder-statesman of *The Bath Chronicle*, Morley Pooley, out of retirement to wonder at it all:

> *He plays Liszt like no other, putting in so much finesse which is all too often missing, but sparing nothing when it comes to the big moments. And yet every note is heard. It was the most magical Liszt I have heard for many a day. I was fascinated, and judging by the reaction, so too was the audience.*

At Wells Cathedral the Royal Philharmonic Orchestra and Norman del Mar performed Beethoven's *Violin Concerto* with Iona Brown. Pierre Boulez returned to the festival for the first time since 1967, this time with the BBC Symphony Orchestra, performing a challenging programme of Berg, Webern, Bartók and Stravinsky. Another festival returnee appearing at the Colston Hall was Sir Charles Groves who, in 1955, had conducted the Bournemouth Symphony Orchestra on a barge on the River Avon. He brought with him the Royal Liverpool Philharmonic Orchestra, the alto Bernadette Greevy and the tenor Ronald Dowd, for a concert of Beethoven's *Seventh Symphony* and Mahler's *Das Lied von der Erde*. Alas, both Bristol concerts had row upon row of empty seats. In the case of the former, the repertoire was undoubtedly bold; but in the case of the latter, the only explanation can be the venue – Bristol.

The Other Festival reappeared, this time with a base in the form of the empty Cleveland Hotel in Pulteney Street loaned by its owner, Charles Ware. But when the organisers of The Other Festival announced that their security guards would be drawn from a group of Hells Angels, Mr Ware drew the line and insisted on more conventional protection for his property. Their activities included a party at Widcombe Manor (loaned by Jeremy Fry) and a Gay Lib Ball. In an attempt to point out his belief that the two festivals should complement rather than rival each other, Sir Michael Tippett took himself along to the Cleveland Hotel and offered his blessing: 'It's a glorious jamboree. Just what it ought to be.'

With 1973 marking the 1000th anniversary of the coronation of King Edgar on the site where now stands Bath Abbey, it was not surprising that the festival should revert to the royal theme it had adopted in coronation year, 1953. Where previously butterflies and parasols had filled the shop windows, this year there were crowns in all shapes and sizes, as 200 entries flooded in for the display competition, demonstrating once again the city traders' backing for an event that brought people into the city. The Amadeus Quartet, the Academy of St Martin in the Fields (who included Schoenberg's *Verkläte Nacht* in their Abbey concert) and the pianists Paul Crossley and Murray Perahia were typical visitors.

After several years of negotiation, Tippett had secured the services of the National Arts Centre Orchestra of Canada with their conductor Mario Bernardi. They appeared firstly in the Abbey with the violinist György Pauk, in a performance filmed by Canadian television. Unfortunately modern television lighting proved too hot for many, and provoked a rash of complaints. The orchestra then travelled to the Colston Hall in Bristol, where they performed Beethoven's *Piano Concerto No.4* with the British pianist John Ogdon. Finally, and strangely, given that it was under the auspices of the Bath Festival, the orchestra gave a concert at the Queen Elizabeth Hall in London. Billed as a festival concert, it was the furthest the festival had ever strayed from home.

At Wells, the London Symphony Orchestra appeared with David Atherton in a performance of Tippett's *Third Symphony*. Two days later the orchestra, this time with Riccardo Muti, were at the Colston Hall performing Verdi's *Requiem*, with a list of soloists that included Jessye Norman, Anne Reynolds, Veriano Luchetti and Bonaldo Giaiotti. *The Bath Chronicle's* Martin Wainwright was there and wrote that:

Jessye Norman has a majestic presence, increased last night by a voluminous gold and scarlet gown. This final concert was one of the most ambitious Bath Festival has ever staged. A measure of its success was the thunder of clapping, stamping and calls for more which echoed round the hall at the end of the evening.

Although a film festival (including *Elvira Madigan* and *Death in Venice*), the regular round of festival art exhibitions, and of course the 'Roman Rendezvous' were in evidence, the festival, while by no means all Bach and Beethoven, was distinctly cerebral. The social side had dwindled and rather than using the venues available in Bath, Michael Tippett was tending to go to whichever venue would take his chosen musicians, no matter how far away that might be.

A steadily growing army of sponsors were now contributing to the festival's finances. Some, such as Wessex Newspapers, had been supportive from the beginning. The net result was, for the first time in living memory, a surplus in 1973 of more than £1000. The money was used to contribute to the cost of a conference of European festival leaders, which took place in the city in October 1973, with delegates from 20 countries including representatives of the festivals at Bayreuth and Salzburg.

Where Sir Michael Tippett differed from any of his predecessors or successors is that he is, so far, the only director of the festival to voluntarily relinquish the reigns of office. More to the point, he did so when in many respects he was on a high. Under his tenure the very classical, very elite, very dinner-jacketed Menuhin regime had been replaced by a completely different feel. Big orchestras and special occasions had succeeded the family affair. However, Tippett had said from the outset that he would do no more than five years at the helm, and he was true to his word. Five years in a job, says Robin Buchanan, is long enough '...and Tippett did not want to stay any longer than that.' Luke Rittner agrees that Tippett was someone who would never hang around: 'He was terrified of becoming stale and always wanting to move on to new pastures.'

Tippett's departure earned him great respect, while the nostalgia for his programmes – not to mention the perceived contrast with the Menuhin years – means his tenure is today regarded as one of the best yet. David Pratley, who engineered the rescue of the festival in 1993/4, says: 'For me, the five Tippett years were the great years of the old festival. You came knowing you would hear new works, many of which were commissions. There was a real sense of artistic purpose.'

At the start of the 1974 festival, Tippett penned this comment in the programme:

When I took over the artistic directorship of the Bath Festival five festivals ago there was a double challenge. One, to get us out of debt and prepare a sound financial base. Two, to broaden the festival towards more variety and a wider public. But the second challenge did not really wait upon the first. With the dedication and tenacity of those Bathonians to whom the festival means a lot, and through the generosity of patrons, the finance was strengthened. With more adventurous events and programmes and reasonably low priced tickets the new public was found and grew. So I can hand over to my successor (to whom I wish every good fortune) with some assurance, and (dare I say it?) with a modicum of pride.

In bidding farewell to Sir Michael Tippett, the festival presented him with five bottles of vintage wine, one for each year he had served, together with an ash walking-stick bearing an engraving from Goethe, the composer's favourite poet, on a silver band. He in turn again delivered a festival where, miraculously, the books balanced.

By 1974 the income from sponsorship – and there were 14 major sponsors in total – was in the region of £6000. Bath City Council's contribution still stood at £4500, while Bristol paid £1000, as well as offering free use of the Colston Hall. That year's festival brought some excellent music, not least in the form of a return visit by Jessye Norman. She packed the Assembly Rooms for a recital with Irwin Gage of leider by Schubert and Wolf. Morley Pooley appreciated her performance:

It was an inspiration to include four nonsense songs by Erik Satie, the whimsical French composer, who always said he slept in a round bed with a hole in the middle, in between two hefty chunks of Wolf leider. It not only broke the tension but also showed us another side to this fine dramatic soprano – her ability to turn from the serious business of German lieder to comedy at the drop of a hat. Jessye Norman is as big in voice as she is in stature – a second Rita Hunter. Her voice has the same big range, the same Wagnerian quality. Although she had sung 21 songs, the audience clapped and stamped until Miss Norman not only had to give one encore, but also a second one. And even then they clamoured for more.

The festival opened with a military band marching past the Guildhall, while inside the Pump Room the arts minister Hugh Jenkins was the guest of honour at a VIP-only official festival lunch. However, Tippett was absent. Having cut his schedule too tight in Glasgow the previous night, he had missed a flight and was making his way to Bath by train and car.

The festival once again brought an orchestra from the New World. This time it was Neville Marriner's Los Angeles Chamber Orchestra making their European début. However, when they advertised a programme at the Abbey which included *Symphony for Strings* by Schumann, many of the audience failed to realise that it was not a work of the romantic Robert Schumann, but of the twentieth century American composer William Schumann. Coupled with the ultra-modern *Study in Sonority* by another American, W Reigger, the concert brought several complaints to the festival. Again dabbling beyond their territory, the festival promoted the orchestra in a concert at the Queen Elizabeth Hall in London. After hearing the orchestra, *The Bath Chronicle's* nostalgic diarist wrote: 'Under Sir Michael there has been a marked trend towards 'difficult' music. I can't help agreeing with those who would prefer Bath Festival to achieve a distinctive identity as classical as its setting.'

To add to his woes, Tippett found himself having to apologise to the orchestra for the Abbey's acoustics, which failed to suit their repertoire (which in addition to the aforementioned works also included Strauss's *Capriccio* and Mozart's *Divertimento K247*). The problems of 1974 continued as Michael Tippett, the festival chairman Barbara Robertson, the mayoress Anne Johns, and some members of the Los Angeles Chamber Orchestra were taken ill with food poisoning, later identified as *Colostridium Welchii*, after a buffet reception. At the festival club, a small blaze in the kitchen while Jessye Norman was in attendance caused consternation and alarm.

Elsewhere in the music programme the Smetana Quartet, who in 1965 had performed their compatriot Janácek's first quartet, the *Kreutzer Sonata*, returned for two concerts at the Assembly Rooms, the second of which included the composer's only other work for this medium, *Intimate Letters*. Morley Pooley wrote:

> *The Smetana hadn't a note of music in front of them. To them every note was engraved on their hearts. And their playing was of such magnificence that the whole work was also engraved in the hearts of the audience which packed the Assembly Rooms. It was sheer magic.*

The Spanish pianist, Alicia de Larrocha, gave a recital of music by Soler, Granados, Albéniz and Ravel; the Chilingirian Quartet played at the Holburne Museum; the Ensemble Instrumental de France appeared with the flautist Jean-Pierre Rampal; the Richard Hickox Singers and Orchestra pitched up at the Abbey with an all Handel programme; and both the BBC Northern Symphony Orchestra (with Bathonian Raymond Leppard reappearing for the first time in some years) and the London Symphony Orchestra and Chorus were at the Colston Hall in Bristol.

Two new festival venues appeared: The Hermann Miller Theatre on Lower Bristol Road was pressed into action as the venue for a sell-out multi-media, audio-visual entertainment, which was way ahead of its time; meanwhile the Midland Bank in Milsom Street hosted an exhibition telling the story of the Royal Opera House, Covent Garden – accessible during banking hours only. The hot air balloon motif of the festival proved a popular theme, and a balloon meeting, complete with cooked English breakfast, took place in Royal Victoria Park on the first weekend of the festival. The Holburne Museum chipped in by offering an exhibition entitled 'A girdle round about the earth – astronomical and geographical discovery 1490-1630', which was put together by the curator Mary Holbrook, assisted by Barbara Robertson. The window display competition, however, slipped to a disappointing 98 entries, as traders concerned themselves with weathering the harsh economic climate that was gradually befalling the country. Naomi Buchanan was persuaded out of retirement to mount an exhibition to celebrate the 25th festival. To questions about a lack of fun in the festivals of the 1970s, she replied: 'The festival is still fun but it's a different sort of fun.' Luke Rittner, reflecting perhaps more of the uncertainty of the times, said: 'People's attitudes to fun have changed, and they are much more wary about having fun.'

Certainly the carefree days of 'Jambeano', 'La Serenissima', 'Agincourt' and the like were long gone. Also long gone were the formal Menuhin-family events. In throwing out the bath water, had the Bath Festival also thrown out the baby? Tippett's departure after the 1974 festival cleared the way for another well-established figure to try his hand at running the Bath Festival.

CHAPTER SEVEN

William Glock's reign at Bath had long been in the planning. During an interview given in May 1998 for this book he said:

> *In April 1970 Michael Tippett came to London to see me and said 'Would you like to take over Bath as my successor?' But I was committed to the BBC for three years and especially to Boulez [at the BBC Symphony Orchestra]. So instead of getting anyone else, he decided to wait for me, even though he did not want to go on [running the festival].*

Three years later, Tippett, this time accompanied by the festival chairman Barbara Robertson, approached Glock once again. Eventually Glock agreed to carry the mantle from 1975 for five years. Glock enjoyed working with Robertson for two reasons. He said: 'She was a very cultivated person. And she did not interfere.'

Robertson, the brains behind many of the festival's spectacular fund-raising and outdoor events of the past, maintains that in the chairman's seat an interest in music is unnecessary: 'When I was chairman I had to pretend to be interested,' she says with a wicked grin.

Under William Glock, Luke Rittner became sole administrator. He said:

> *I was quite nervous with William because he had a reputation for having absolutely transformed the Proms and BBC music generally, as well as really encouraging new music, new works and young performers. I remember his first press conference at Bath when a reporter asked, 'What's your aim for the Bath Festival?' And William replied, 'My aim is to give the people of Bath today what they will like tomorrow.' I thought 'Oh my God, this year's going to be really interesting.' But what was so fantastic is that by then there was such a groundswell of support and a following for the festival that actually they largely took it, and they were buying tickets for things which were tough. OK, we were being cautious and we were tending to put them into small venues.*

Compared to his predecessors, Glock was completely different to work with, as Rittner remembers:

> *He was quite daunting in the sheer encyclopaedic knowledge he had of music and musicians. It was extraordinary. You would sit down to a programme planning session and you would be looking at a concert or a recital or something and there would be three pieces that he wanted in the concert. He would say 'that is about 21 minutes 40 seconds, so*

we can have the Beethoven; that's 32 minutes, 12 seconds', and he would be absolutely right. He knew the precise length of every single piece of music from his BBC days.

With both the Menuhin and the Tippett legacies still ringing in his ears and around the world, Glock had to find a novel way of programming the festival. He said:

I was influenced by being in the BBC, for which one planned repertory of many centuries, lots of contemporary music, and trying to make programmes eventful if possible. I was still running Dartington which also influenced me. I combined early and new music. It was tricky, but they enhanced each other if they came off.

Luke Rittner remains full of admiration for the way Glock sandwiched established and contemporary music:

The reason for the sandwich with William was never to sugar the pill, but always because there was an artistic and a musical reason for doing so, and he was completely uncompromising in that.

Naomi Buchanan believes Glock was an inspired choice as artistic director. Speaking in 1998 she said:

He was the absolute professional. His predecessors were not pro-gramme directors. He was the first we had with a track record.

Over the subsequent ten years, Glock was to involve his regular circle of favourite composers: Elliot Carter, Harrison Birtwhistle and Michael Tippett, to name but three. But it wasn't all to be modern music, as he explained in 1998:

Away from contemporary music the most telling thing was the amount of seventeenth and eighteenth century music such as Purcell, Handel and Bach. We performed all Haydn's quartets and all his trios, a very rare event in a festival. We also had a lot of Monteverdi.

Glock brought many favourite artists back time and time again:

Some of the best concerts were in Wells Cathedral. There were many splendid concerts in Bath Abbey, but not as thrilling as Wells. The most wonderful evening in Wells was Monteverdi's Vespers *(1610).*

Sir William Glock's first festival in 1975 opened with a performance of Bach's *B minor Mass* in the Abbey with the English Chamber Orchestra conducted by Charles Mackerras. They were joined by the soloists Felicity Palmer, Helen Watts, Robert Tear and John Shirley-Quirk, and the Taverner Choir.

Later that evening came the first hint of what would eventually evolve into the massive opening night celebrations. To celebrate European Architectural Heritage Year, residents of the Circus were invited – cajoled, even, once Barbara Robertson and her friend Freda Shellard began knocking on doors – to place lighted candles in their windows between 10pm and midnight. The city council turned out the street lights. Under the full moon which shone that evening, the effect was a magical one, a display not witnessed since the advent of domestic electricity supplies. At midnight the crowd burst into a spontaneous rendition of *Auld Lang Syne*. The only slight hiccup was the number of motorists driving slowly round and round the Circus admiring the spectacle. There were several minor bumps. In future festivals the road would be closed to traffic on opening night.

Thirty years after the end of the Second World War, which had delayed the very first festival by a decade, Vera Lynn was in Bath for a 'Dig This For Victory Dance' at the Pavilion, with Sydney Lipton and his orchestra. Black market wine, ration boxes and 1940s dress were the order of the evening, as Miss Lynn led the hundreds who turned out through wartime favourites such as 'We'll Meet Again' and 'A Nightingale Sang in Berkeley Square'.

Plans to mount a performance of *Dido and Aeneas* at the Theatre Royal by students from the Royal Northern College of Music were abandoned after the Musicians' Union complained it would be depriving their members of work. Rather than face a showdown or risk any of the contracted professional musicians pulling out, the festival cancelled the production altogether.

Nevertheless, relations with the Theatre Royal, long since somewhat frosty, were back on course – an achievement in which Glock today takes particular pride. Glock used the venue for several concerts in 1975, including a performance by Alfred Brendel of three Beethoven piano sonatas, a visit by the chamber ensemble Fires of London who played music by Peter Maxwell Davies and Bartók, a concert by I Musici of Bach and Vivaldi, and a performance by the King's Singers in their original line-up, including the future radio presenter Brian Kay and the future Bath conductor Nigel Perrin.

Speaking in 1998, Sir William Glock said: 'The Theatre Royal was a great part of the festival.' But, he added, only for the right event: 'For recitals, it wasn't very good for sound. We had Alfred Brendel. It was too dry.'

Influenced by a new member of the board, Lady (Dione) Digby, who had run a series of concerts in stately homes, the 1975 festival took music out to country churches – there was music from the French Middle Ages at St Julian's Church, Wellow, early music at St Leonard's Church, Farleigh Hungerford and a performance at Holy Trinity Church, Bradford-on-Avon. Glock deftly paid tribute to his predecessor with a 70th birthday tribute to Sir Michael Tippett at the Colston Hall where the BBC Symphony Orchestra and Chorus directed by Colin Davis performed the composer's oratorio *A Child of Our Time* preceded by Mozart's *Oboe Concerto* (with the soloist Heinz Holliger). The Lindsay Quartet added their voice to the Tippett tribute with an account of his second quartet at the Assembly Rooms. In an earlier concert in the festival they had given the first performance of a clarinet quintet by Iain Hamilton, with the clarinettist Janet Hilton.

Of the international visitors in 1975, one of the greatest was the violinist and pedagogue Sándor Végh. He gave a recital of music by Bach and Bartók at the Assembly Rooms accompanied by Peter Pettinger, and a masterclass at the Technical College (now the City of Bath College). One of the seven promising students he coached was Nigel Kennedy, then a relative unknown, whom Glock described as 'one of the most brilliant young violinists of today.'

But inflation was catching up with the Bath Festival prompting a jumble sale in Pierrepont Street which brought in £600. Although the Arts Council gave £10,000, Bath City Council £4500, Bristol £1000, sponsors £7500, and ticket sales pulled in £3500, a single concert in Wells – the Monteverdi Choir and Orchestra conducted by John Eliot Gardiner – cost a staggering £5300 to stage. Recalling that Wells concert, which sold out within two weeks and later was opened to people sitting on cushions and rugs on the floor or standing for 60p per head, William Glock later said: 'John Eliot Gardner appeared in all ten festivals with the Monteverdi Orchestra, mostly in Wells Cathedral. I have never heard such a wonderful performance.'

Mounting costs was the official reason for the festival abandoning the window display competition in 1975, but the truth was that no one could be found to undertake the leg work of walking round and bullying all the city's traders out of their apathy. That, together with an absence of flags and banners, left the city looking decidedly unfestive and brought calls for a revival of the carnival at festival time, including a 'Miss Bath' competition, an 'It's A Knockout' style tournament, and a young people's version of the 'Roman Rendezvous'. Youth council chairman John Hetterley, with the support of the mayor, Cllr Will Johns, backed the call. He said: 'It is about time that the youth of Bath joined with local organisations to help make the Bath Festival appeal to Mr and Mrs Average.'

It didn't take William Glock long to begin being adventurous with his beloved modern music. Speaking in 1998 he said: 'In 1976 I thought I would risk putting on Stockhausen's *Mantra*.' *Mantra* is an enormous, rarely heard, discordant work for two pianos and it was played in Bath by Bruno Canino and Antonio Ballista. The seating at the Assembly Rooms was arranged spaciously to accommodate a maximum of 190 and much to the organisers' delight, the event sold out. Glock said: 'Some enthusiastic people cheered. It was a battle won.' *The Bath Chronicle's* Morley Pooley found the 75-minute work all too much: 'After listening for 35 minutes I fled. And I am quite unrepentant. I would have shot anyone who made my piano make such unpianistic sounds.'

Sir William Glock had clearly stamped his impression on the festival's music programme, and it was a very different beat from either Menuhin's or Tippett's. While he continued with traditional chamber music concerts, such as the Amadeus Quartet, the harpsichordist George Malcolm, and the Beaux Arts Trio, Glock was nevertheless the master of the big, the brash and the new. An entire concert devoted to music by the American composer Elliot Carter, marking his country's bicentenary, found its way onto the programme, as did a concert of contemporary music at the Arnolfini in Bristol given by the John Alldis Choir entitled 'BBC Radio 3 at the Bath Festival'.

The 1976 festival's one big orchestral concert, given at the Colston Hall in Bristol, was a typically Glock programme and featured the BBC Symphony Orchestra conducted by Sergiu Comissiona playing Tippett's *Fantasia on a theme of Corelli*, Beethoven's *Piano Concerto No.4* with Alfred Brendel, and Stravinsky's *Rite of Spring*. Glock also had a flair for inviting big names to Bath. The flautist James Galway gave a recital accompanied by Anthony Goldstone. Sviatoslav Richter, one of the greatest pianists of the century, was engaged to close the celebrations. Sadly Richter pulled out. He had an engagement in Florence two days previously and had taken a dislike to flying.

Glock made his philosophy quite clear and stuck to it: 'The idea in drawing up a festival programme like this is not to put down anything that you yourself would not wish to go to.' He made his point by appearing as piano soloist himself in a concert at the Assembly Rooms with the Monteverdi Choir conducted by John Eliot Gardiner.

It was a heavyweight festival, made even more so by an Arts Council grant increased from £10,000 to £12,500, together with a further £6000 from them towards two performances of Monteverdi's *Orfeo* by Kent Opera conducted by Roger Norrington at the Theatre Royal. Industrial sponsorship reached £7000 and the new Avon County Council chipped in for the first time with a grant of £300. However, the city's contribution remained at a static £4500. Speaking at a festival lunch, the festival chairman Barbara Robertson said:

> Both the Arts Council and industry have recognised the facts of life and their support has kept pace with inflation. Unfortunately local authorities have not. Our local authority grant is one of the lowest. I think there are Bath City Councillors who wish they did not have such a musical cuckoo in their nest.

Bearing in mind that 21 years earlier, in 1955, the city had seen fit to award £5000 to Ian Hunter's come-back jamboree, she clearly had a point.

And to show her support for the festival that she chaired, Robertson opened up her home village of Combe Hay for an enormous 'at home'. More than 500 visitors trekked out to enjoy guided walks, lectures, games, sports and refreshments. The 1976 festival also included a festival book fair, claimed to be the biggest outside London; the Circus candles again heralding opening night with some 80 windows estimated to be aglow; and a 'Flappersupperpicnic' at Summerhill Park in Lansdown which attracted scores of festival devotees. After the previous year's success with Vera Lynn, the festival administrator, Luke Rittner, wanted to organise a 1912-style dance in the Guildhall Market with the theme of 'My Fair Lady'. His plan was to erect a marquee in the councillors' car park and serve supper at tables between the stalls, a little like the Covent Garden setting of *Pygmalion*. The city council accepted the idea subject to every trader being happy. Unfortunately for Rittner his plan was scuppered by just three of the 18 stall holders exercising their veto.

Fed up with the lack of public visibility of the festival, Naomi Buchanan reappeared and promptly resurrected the festival window display competition, attracting 150 entries from shops in and around the city. It took the theme from a Lionel Bart musical, 'Fings Ain't What They Used To Be'. She said it was a crying shame the competition had been dropped and told *The Bath Chronicle* in the spring of 1976:

> *One of the old complaints was that you could drive through Bath at festival time without knowing the festival was on. That was certainly true last year. The city looked dreary. It was a combination of factors. No window displays, bad weather and the fact that the city was late putting out its flowers. I told the festival I would organise the window competition if nobody else would. The next thing I knew I was landed with it.*

Barbara Robertson's five years as chairman ended in July 1976, and she handed over the mantle to a well-known musical organiser, but someone who was not at all local. Dione Digby, The Lady Digby, had been on the festival's board for a while and was undoubtedly well connected. Her series of concerts in country houses in Dorset had been copied across the country, and she had inspired some of the festival's concerts in local stately homes in recent years. She stated her philosophy from the outset:

> *I want the festival to be more fun. Music is not everybody's scene. We ought to be able to do something else. I should like to see late night entertainment, perhaps at the Theatre Royal. Don't let's be too highbrow – but let's have the best.*

The inflation which ravished the whole country in the 1970s also had a devastating effect on the festival. The costs of hiring musicians, booking venues and running the office had more than doubled since 1968, but the festival had been working to the same budget of around £40,000. With the 1977 festival in view, income had to grow significantly if it was to continue. Luke Rittner announced that an extra £10,000 in sponsorship would have to be found if the festival was to survive. He also wrote to *The Times* exposing the costs of putting on a major choral concert such as Beethoven's *Missa Solemnis* with the New Philharmonia Orchestra and Charles Mackerras, which was planned for 1977. The orchestra and chorus, he said, cost £4469; the conductor and four soloists' fees came to £1500, transport alone was £1200. And then there was hall hire and administration costs. With top ticket prices at £3, the maximum income the festival could expect was £2100. Fearing the worst, Rittner added: 'The sort of costs outlined above will, I suspect, ensure that in future London will be the only place where a major concert can be presented.' His missive brought a swift, if token, result. Charles Spencer, chairman of the New Philharmonia Orchestra, offered to waive the chorus's fee of £500.

With prices spiralling upwards and the festival's budget for 1997 set at £64,000, the Arts Council's grant shot up to £15,500. They also gave financial assistance towards a new opera by the composer John Taverner whose works were to be heavily featured in 1977. But before the 1977 festival, Luke

Rittner departed to establish the Association of Business Sponsorship of the Arts. It was to be the beginning of a meteoric rise for Rittner that eventually led to his appointment as Secretary General of the Arts Council and later as director of corporate affairs at Sotheby's. His successor was a local man, John Fisher, who had worked for the BBC and had a great love of singing.

Rallying to the call for greater private sector support, nine city centre shops came together under the umbrella of Bath Private Enterprise Sponsors to sponsor a concert. They were Duck, Son & Pinker, Fyson & Co, T R Hayes Ltd, W J Holloway & Sons, H & R Marsh, Membery Blackwell Ltd, Silcox, Son & Wicks, William Mitchell Ltd and Eric Snook (Bath) Ltd. The Festival Gallery also received financial help, this time in the form of a £1000 grant from Sotheby's, the auction house's first venture into cultural sponsorship.

The 1977 festival coincided with the Queen's Silver Jubilee, which was marked with a Jubilee Dance to the music of Humphrey Lyttleton and his band, and everything took on a slightly more informal air. Festival t-shirts made their début; the Festival Club, long a popular hang-out for artists and festival groupies, moved from the Hole in the Wall to Clarets in Kingsmead Square; and children's puppets made a welcome return. Even the traditional military brass band marching through the city centre at lunchtime on the opening day was replaced by a civilian one, the British Airways Brass Band. Unfortunately, when they played outside the Pump Room the band drowned out the festival lunch speeches being given by Peter Diamand (director of the Edinburgh Festival) and Sir Kenneth Robinson (chairman of the Arts Council).

The Bath Spa Band, directed by Russell Buckley, was invited to play on the bandstand in Victoria Park from 8.30pm on opening night, and from dusk windows in the Circus and Royal Crescent were lit with candles, to the accompaniment of madrigals. Many homes in Brock Street also joined in. The colonnade in Parade Gardens was transformed into a fascinating and atmospheric gallery exhibiting the work of local artists. Listeners found their senses wonderfully besieged as the roar of the River Avon assaulted their ears while their eyes tried to concentrate on the works before them. All was going swimmingly well. Neither *The Bath Chronicle* nor its readers could find anything to moan about: 'Now that the Bath Festival is no longer beset by debt or beleaguered by clashes of personality, there is nothing to talk about but the music,' said the leader column.

The programme in 1977 was a solid one, and made a particular feature of John Taverner. As well as his new opera *The Gentle Spirit* (performed alongside Stravinsky's *Soldier's Tale* by the Nash Ensemble, making their first visit to Bath), there was a performance in the Abbey of *Canticle for the Mother of God*, and at Bristol Cathedral of *Ultimos Ritos* and *Little Requiem for Father Malachy Lynch* by Southampton Youth Orchestra with Winchester Cathedral Choir conducted by Martin Neary. The 150th anniversary of Beethoven's death was commemorated by three exhilarating concerts given by the Bartók Quartet at the Assembly Rooms which impressed *The Bath Chronicle's* Morley Pooley:

This music floods the mind with its beauty and the Bartók [String Quartet] gave us an outstanding performance. They made it all look so easy – even those difficult entrances that have to be timed to the second if they are to come off. It was sheer precision all through from four players attuned to each other and to the music.

Richard Hickox and his singers and orchestra were taking over the regular slot enjoyed previously by the Academy of St Martin in the Fields, and before them the Bath Festival Chamber Orchestra. They gave the opening concert in Bath Abbey, in a programme that included Bach's *Magnificat*. Other artists included Trevor Pinnock performing Bach's *Goldberg Variations* on the harpsichord at the Guildhall, a concert by the London Sinfonietta at the Assembly Rooms contrasting works by Peter Maxwell Davies and Harrison Birtwhistle with fourteenth century music, and the Taverner Consort with Andrew Parrott in Parisian church music at St John's Church in South Parade. As a sop to those who were missing the long vanished jazz programmes, Glock included a concert at the Theatre Royal by the Jacques Loussier Trio.

The contrast with Menuhin's era could not have been greater. While Menuhin's name, rising fame and association with Bath brought the festival an international reputation, Glock's championing of contemporary composers (admittedly initiated by Tippett) and heavyweight programming, brought the Bath Festival a much needed element of respect among the international music *cognoscenti*. Challenging programmes and exciting names brought connoisseurs – including the long absent national and international broadsheet newspapers – back to Bath.

But it was all costing money, and inflation, as already mentioned, was rife. Although takings at the box office were rising, a deficit was accumulating once more and by the end of 1977 had reached £4500. The Festival Fringe Committee sprang into action and organised a series of winter events including concerts, lectures, produce sales and even a lottery, in a bid to pull the festival out of the red.

Bureaucracy and concerns over the safety of spa water saw the end of the 'Roman Rendezvous' after 1977. Although tickets had always sold well, it was a child of its time – the 1960s – and had evolved from the infamous 'Roman Orgy' of 1961. Nevertheless, a limited amount of bathing was permitted in the Cross Bath on three festival days in 1978. The swimming sessions were followed by a ploughman's lunch and beer. The blazing bank holiday Monday brought 56 bathers – the most the bath could hold. Other holiday weekend attractions included children's puppets at the Bath Technical College Theatre and a BBC Radio jazz festival in Parade Gardens.

The programme for 1978 was significantly larger than in previous years, and for the first time the number of fringe events – walks, talks, picnics – exceeded the number of musical activities. Together with the window-display competition – 140 entries along the theme of 'Going For A Song' – Bath acquired the feel of a festival city. The big social event was a 'Wife of Bath's Picnic' at Sheldon Manor requiring period dress. The lunchtime opening with brass band (the band of the Royal Corps of Signals) continued, as did the opening night magic and mystery of candles in the windows of the Circus, Brock Street and Royal Crescent. The police closed the roads, the council turned off the street lights, and an estimated 1,500 turned out to enjoy the spectacular. The lunchtime speaker, Gordon Richardson, Governor of the Bank of England, said: 'The economic return in the narrow sense – in terms of visitors and revenue taken – is obvious, but there is a further value in the investment in the artistic skills and talents for which this country is justly famous.'

There were worries about a rumoured closure of the Theatre Royal, which had fallen into new hands, but Glock ploughed on with his programming, and in 1978 avoided taking any concerts to Bristol. Speaking in 1998 he said: 'I decided not to go on with Colston Hall, preferring to concentrate on what Bath possessed. Music can be enhanced and invigorated by the right venue. Bristol is anti-Bath.'

The Theatre Royal turned out to be available and hosted a double bill of opera performed by Rye Opera – Pergolesi's *La Serva Padrona* and Mozart's *Der Schauspieldirektor*. The Academy of St Martin in the Fields under the directorship of Iona Brown also appeared there, as did the Canino and Ballista piano duo partnership who had shocked the festival with Stockhausen's *Mantra* a couple of years earlier. This time Stravinsky's arrangement of the *Rite of Spring* was the most risqué item on their programme.

The Theatre Royal was also the venue for an evening of show tunes called 'Just Friends', starring Marian Montgomery and Richard Rodney Bennett. Elsewhere, a 16-year-old pianist Stephen Hough, who had just won the BBC Young Musician of the Year competition and since then has become a household name, appeared at the Assembly Rooms playing Mozart's *Piano Concerto K449* with the Wells Cathedral School Orchestra. The pianist Cristina Ortiz joined the Medici Quartet and the double bassist Barry Guy for a concert that concluded with Schubert's *Trout Quintet*; the Arditti Quartet took the festival right to the cutting edge with classics by Schwertsik, Ligeti and Webern and the Lindsay Quartet gave the world première of Hugh Wood's *String Quartet No.3*.

Criticism that too many tickets were sold too far in advance to too many priority bookers were countered by holding some tickets back for sale on the door at each event, while in terms of media coverage, the success of 1977 was repeated. William Mann from *The Times*, who lived locally, produced several positive notices, while *The Daily Telegraph* summed up the festival in glowing terms, commending Bath for eschewing what we would today call the 'dumbing-down' of its programme:

At a time when certain of our music festivals show signs of drowning in a medley of mediocrity or have-a-go trendomania, Bath continues to impress, the city's 1978 summer festival already yielding something of a vintage crop. That much of this is due to Sir William Glock's judicious stewardship of the festival's artistic affairs can hardly be doubted.

The only sour note came when the festival became a victim of an ongoing dispute between the BBC and the Musicians' Union over fees for 'deferred relays', broadcasts that are transmitted a few minutes or up to half an hour after they are recorded rather than instantaneously. Consequently, the festival lost both valuable income and publicity.

Morley Pooley, who had outlasted anyone connected with the festival since his first mention on *The Bath Chronicle's* festival pages in 1949, continued to go to concerts featuring contemporary music, and never really began to enjoy them. This was illustrated by his review of the London Sinfonietta's concert in the Abbey, which included music by Robin Holloway and Olivier Messiaen:

> *I think everyone must have been delighted with the Sinfonietta's playing of Wagner's* Siegfried Idyll. *It was really delightful. Why are such determined efforts made to force modern musical peculiarities [Holloway and Messiaen] on to the British public? The vast majority hate them.*

However, David Cairns from *The Sunday Times* was enjoying his festival:

> *Since Sir William Glock's retirement from the BBC, the vision and rare common sense which transformed the Proms have been applied to the Bath Festival. It is difficult to put your finger on what makes it the unusually rich and enjoyable affair it is.*

William Glock's time should have been up after the 1978 festival but he had other plans. After five years he received much needed endorsement from the Arts Council of Great Britain which increased the Bath Festival's grant by 36 per cent. Glock was naturally delighted and extended the festival from ten to seventeen days. It was this vote of confidence, as much as anything else, which signalled that Bath had once more to be taken seriously. Speaking in 1998, Glock said:

> *They must have thought we were doing well. With that grant it changed. We started concentrating on composers especially, and artistically the festival became several times bigger.*

What actually happened was that at a festival lunch during 1978, Glock sat next to an Arts Council representative who suggested the two week/three weekend formula to him, and suggested the Council would buy the concept if it included a significant theatrical element. In the event, while the Theatre Royal was used for a number of musical events, the drama content in 1979 was somewhat low-key, and took the form of a week-long run of *She Would If She Could* by Sir George Etherege starring Paul Eddington and Ursula Johns. The emphasis in 1979 was still largely on producing a classical music festival, albeit a highly adventurous classical music festival. For some time any murmurings against this policy had been little more than that. But writing in the Day-by-Day column of *The Bath Chronicle* in February 1979, just after the programme for that year's festival had been announced, Horace Crocker resurrected an old gripe:

> *An international festival of music of this importance should do a lot more about jazz than just the Bank Holiday offering of the Midnite Follies Orchestra at the Pavilion. Haven't they heard in Bath of Stan Getz, Stan Tracey, John Surman and a host of other international jazz artists of repute?*

One of the other old gripes – visibility – also began to reappear on the letters page of *The Bath Chronicle*. Mr G Dodd from Corsham wrote:

> *On the eve of the judging of the Bath Festival shop window display competition I drove over ten miles to see the expected feast of especially designed displays. How can anyone be anything but disappointed by their insularity? Or are they [the shopkeepers] trying to strangle the organisers by apathy?*

In addition to these criticisms, the festival also had programming problems to contend with. The conductor Diego Masson pulled out of his concert after a gall-bladder operation, to be replaced by Lionel Friend. Peter Maxwell Davies pulled out of conducting a 13 concert tour, including Bath, of his own opera *The Martyrdom of St Magnus*. His place was taken by the American conductor Richard Dufallo.

With the increased largesse from the Arts Council and a total of £27,000 in industrial sponsorship, the budget for the 1979 festival soared through the £100,000 barrier to approximately £105,000. The candlelight opening night festivities were extended to include pedestrianised Margaret's Buildings with its quaint shops, while the trees in the Circus were floodlit to complement the candles in the windows. Later in the festival, members of the English Chamber Orchestra's Wind Ensemble ventured round to the Circus after their concert at the Assembly Rooms to give a free open-air performance.

The classical programme was vast, often extending to several events a day. Among the highlights were an all-Chopin piano recital by Vlado Perlemuter; a performance of *Die Winterreise* by Brian Burrows accompanied by William Glock; recitals by the pianist Peter Donohoe and the violinist Nigel Kennedy; a baroque performance of Bach's *St Matthew Passion* in the Abbey by the London Gabrieli Ensemble with Richard Hickox; and a performance of Handel's *Jephtha* in Wells Cathedral by the Monteverdi Choir and Orchestra and John Eliot Gardiner. Peter Pears, a regular visitor to the festival during the early years of the Menuhin era, had been due to appear in the oratorio *Jephtha*, but the 69-year-old tenor was advised to rest by his doctors and his place was taken instead by Brian Burrows. Disputes with the Musicians' Union behind them, the festival was able to invite the Royal Northern College of Music to the Theatre Royal for a one-off performance of Handel's *Orlando*.

The idea of a featured composer was beginning to catch on in festival circles, and Bath rose to the challenge by programming several works by Michael

Finnissy, most notably in a concert given by the Arditti Quartet. Finnissy's presence, however, was somewhat overshadowed by the heavily publicised world première of Sir Michael Tippett's *String Quartet No.4* given by the Lindsay Quartet. This alone brought much of the national press corps, as well as a couple of German newspapers, to the city, and reminded them of the festival's existence. Writing in *The Financial Times*, Max Loppert said: 'Even by its own standards, the Bath Festival has been this year a brilliant success, a mixture calculated to a nicety by William Glock to stir, stimulate, and delight on many fronts.'

The official fringe programme, if that is not an oxymoron, included vast numbers of walks, talks, cookery demonstrations and lectures. All were designed to dovetail with the main programme but, as in the past, they were complementing rather than providing any form of genuine alternative to the music programme. There were also children's concerts including one called 'Music for a Medieval Castle', which was a look at the music and instruments of the Middle Ages for over-fives. John Eliot Gardiner took time out of his schedule to conduct a visiting chamber group from Chethams School of Music, Manchester. The burgeoning collection of art exhibitions continued as venues across the city were pressed into service. On a more light-hearted note, Parade Gardens was the venue for a 'Naughty Nineties' picnic recreating the heady atmosphere of *fin de siècle* Paris, with frock coats and wing collars back in fashion. The tone was set by ladies from Bath Stage who performed the can-can as part of a Victorian cabaret.

And so, with this enormous expansion in 1979, the time-scale and basic structure of the festival as we know it 20 years later was established. By 1980 the amount of challenging and new music had risen considerably giving cause for some concern. Glock justified his policy saying that he had to include new works, otherwise the festival would 'veer dangerously towards being a museum piece.' He added, 'We are fairly unusual in choosing the programme before the artists. Other festivals tend to line up the artists and then find out what works they would be prepared to do.'

While the opening concert of 1980 in the Assembly Rooms was a sublime all-Schubert performance by the Melos Quartet of Stuttgart, the overall programme included works such as Stockhausen's *Stimmung*, featured composer John Casken's *Firewhirl*, and Iannis Xenakis's *Phlegra*. The Duchess of Kent visited the festival for the first time to see the Royal Northern College of Music perform *The Barber of Seville* – not the well-known Rossini version, but a now almost forgotten adaptation of the story by Giovanni Paisiello (1740-1816). The sets were designed to critical acclaim by John Pascoe, a name that would crop up a decade later as an opponent of the festival.

Extemporary Dance gave the première of a festival commission, *Pas De Deux*, choreographed by Vasco Wellenkamp, while the future artistic director, Nicholas Kraemer, was the harpsichord soloist in a concert given at the Theatre Royal by the Orchestra of St John's Smith Square and their founder John Lubbock. The theatre also found time to stage the Festival of Fringe with three 'alternative' theatre companies. Here was the first threat from within the city establishment to the festival's own official (and somewhat cerebral) fringe.

But in the 1980 festival itself, audience numbers were slipping. That could in part be attributable to the larger choice of events, the vicious recession of the time, and a strike at *The Bath Chronicle* preventing the proper dissemination of valuable publicity. But the esoteric nature of some of the programmes surely did not help. A 75th birthday concert for Sir Michael Tippett sold very slowly, in no small part because it was wall-to-wall Tippett with no other composer featured. Likewise, two piano recitals of contemporary music by Ursula Oppens also fared badly, with the sparse audiences mainly being made up of critics and metropolitan-minded new music devotees. With 48 musical events and 50 fringe events the festival was a major logistical exercise and required a budget of £135,000. The growth had been tremendous. But the city's contribution now stood at a meagre £6500 – little more than it had been 25 years earlier. In fairness to the city, the newly created Avon County Council was providing matching funding. However, with the Arts Council supplying £27,000 of the cost and industrial sponsorship now amounting to £35,000, the city clearly had not kept pace with an event that was an artistic success, provided entertainment for both local people and visitors, and promoted the name of Bath to the four corners of the earth. Union action at *The Bath Chronicle* wasn't the only industrial strife to affect the festival. Another dispute at the BBC meant there were no broadcasts, valuable publicity or management fees forthcoming. Explaining a sharp rise in ticket prices in the introduction to the festival programme book, the administrator John Fisher took a swipe at the unions:

> *In part, at least, the rising cost is due to understandable and doubtless well-intentioned union regulations, which may nevertheless in the long-term prove damaging to professional performers' interests.*

In 1981, the opening day's lunchtime brass band performance was followed with a formal opening speech given by the US ambassador, Kingman Brewster. The now traditional opening night candles, music and madrigals continued. They gained a new dimension with a parade through the streets of Bath starting at the Abbey and finishing in front of the Royal Crescent, based on the theme of Queen Elizabeth I. 'Elizabeth's Progress', as it was called, attracted large crowds onto the streets and into Royal Victoria Park. There was also an Elizabethan theme for the festival picnic, which took place at Longleat, marking the 400th anniversary of the stately home. But the biting effects of the recession and the nature of the programming were causing problems. The festival administrator John Fisher once again used the programme book to address the rising number of complaints about ticket prices:

> *We are very conscious of the need to keep ticket prices within the reach of the average person wishing to attend the festival. The cost of tickets for lunch-time and family concerts has been kept at the 1980 level and a whole new range of season tickets has been introduced for groups of concerts, which offer very worthwhile savings.*

Finance was indeed tough, and it was noted by several journalists that the 1981 programme was reduced in scope compared to previous years, although not enough to warrant the national press even considering abandoning Bath. One casualty was the souvenir programme, which for the first time only contained analytical notes for the new works. Another casualty was Wells Cathedral, which hosted only one concert, the Richard Hickox Singers performing Beethoven's *Mass in C*.

With a budget of £142,000 and only £32,000 of that coming from the Arts Council, industrial sponsorship was as important as ever. Now in her final year as chairman, Lady Digby noted that sponsorship had increased during her five-year tenure from £8000 to £32,000. Edward Blacksell of Sotheby's explained why his organisation continued to lend their support: 'Bath provides a much-needed centre of quality for the whole of the southwest. It is reliable and it is the best-run festival I know, including Edinburgh. It justifies sponsorship.' And while Sotheby's lent its name to the Festival Gallery at Linley House, arch-rival Christie's was supporting a new departure, the Contemporary Art Fair. Held at the Assembly Rooms, this remarkable innovation was the brainchild of the managing director of Pitman Press, Antony Rowe. It was matched in scope by only a handful of European and American cities and brought dealers and collectors from across the country, particularly London. Princess Margaret, who had attended the very first festival in 1948, opened the Contemporary Art Fair, only to be greeted by a long-haired female nude sculpture seated on a bench outside the Assembly Rooms. So contemporary was the art that the image chosen for the cover of the fair's brochure and its posters, by Rosemary Pass of Corsham, was printed upside down and nobody noticed until she pointed it out.

But there was a new threat to the festival – the beginnings of an Edinburgh-style fringe. Rob Hawdon of Bath Arts Association, which was formed in January 1981, explained the group's intentions:

> *At present the festival particularly appeals to the highbrow music buffs, and a lot of people felt there wasn't much for them. Hopefully we can now expand alongside the main festival until one day we could even have a jazz festival, or dance, or mime. Bath has the venues and is an ideal place for outdoor events as well.*

The reaction of the festival was to welcome the change as inevitable. But it meant that there would be two 'fringes': the complementary one organised by the festival, and the alternative one run by the BAA. It was an issue that would eventually have to be addressed.

Meanwhile, the 1981 festival proper got underway. The traditional military band playing in the city centre at lunchtime was dispensed with, and a cavalcade of clowns, together with children in fancy dress and face paints, paraded from Abbey Church Yard to Royal Victoria Park. Queen Square joined in the candles at dusk ceremony. The madrigals, sung as always in The Circus and the Royal Crescent, were extended to run from 9.30pm to 11.00pm.

The guitarist Julian Bream opened proceedings on Friday night and both that concert and a repeat performance the following evening were sold out. The first weekend had a strong contemporary element – to the extent of being a contemporary music weekend in all but name: Stephen Pruslin's piano recital at the Guildhall included the world première of Peter Maxwell Davies's new sonata; John Carewe conducted The Fires of London in the English première of Maxwell Davies's new opera, *The Lighthouse*; the cellist Rohan de Saram tackled music by Xenakis in an East-meets-West programme; and electronic music made its festival début in a concert for electronics and voices directed by the composer Denis Smalley.

The Times loved it: 'While most festivals are drawing in their contemporary horns, Bath continues to be a forum for new music.' *The Financial Times* also enjoyed the mixture: 'This remains, in blends of pleasure, adventure and instruction, and in siting itself in one of the world's most naturally festive cities, the leading English music festival.'

But the local media was voicing concern. *The Bath Chronicle's* Day-by-Day diarist pointed out that:

> *The 17-day festival is unashamedly highbrow, appealing to the discriminating music lover, usually from outside Bath – well outside Bath. Some 60 per cent of the audience is drawn from the rest of Britain and about 10 to 15 per cent abroad.*

The festival's new chairman, Robin Buchanan, was robust in his defence:

> *The important thing about the festival is that it works and it works well and we have to be very careful about injuring it in any way. Survival is more important than excitement.*

In the main programme, piano recitals from André Tchaikovsky and Cécile Ousett were among the notable events, while at the Theatre Royal a literary evening with P J Kavanagh and Laurie Lee attracted a fair amount of interest. Alas, a scheduled talk by Igor Stravinsky's son, Soulima Stravinsky, on his father's use of the piano was cancelled when the speaker fell ill. Amidst disliking the contemporary music and marvelling at the great classics, Morley Pooley found time to rally against artists who had started performing in casual dress. He said: 'I think that's wrong in a festival.' The subject features in festival council minutes when the board agreed they could not enforce evening dress by the artists, but an expression of preference was to be made known. Can an echo of the stagnation of the late sixties perhaps be heard in remarks such as these?

With a budget of £137,500 – of which £35,000 came from the Arts Council – the 1982 festival followed in a similar vein to the previous year. William Glock's programmes reflected the music of seven centuries and included a performance of Bach's *48 Preludes & Fugues* on the harpsichord over two concerts by Gillian Weir, the première of a new *Piano Trio* by Dominic Muldowney given by the Nash Ensemble, and a recital by the veteran pianist Vlado Perlemuter who was rewarded with a standing ovation from the delighted audience. The television newsreader Richard Baker joined Eleanor Bron for a performance of Walton's *Façade*, following which Baker signed copies of his new book on the life of Mozart. The book had been researched by a youthful Tim Joss, later to be the festival's artistic director.

The opening night celebrations were beginning to diversify a little further by 1982. A specific theme – weird and wonderful creatures, which encompassed astronauts, spacemen and visitors from outer space – caught the imagination of thousands of youngsters who processed in costume from Abbey Church Yard to Royal Victoria Park, where the Horizon Steel Band entertained them. The elements had different ideas when it came to madrigal time, but the downpour didn't stop the show from going on. However, with one theme for the opening night, another for the shop window competition – 'Comforts of Bath' (number of entries down to 75) – and none for the festival as a whole, the historian could be forgiven for sensing an element of fragmentation.

Magnanimous to the Bath Arts Association's 'fringe', and still promoting its own 'fringe', the festival carried publicity for BAA events in its own brochure for 1982. Rob Hawdon of the BAA reiterated his aims: 'We want to get a little more lowbrow for the ordinary man in the street who has no specific interest in classical music but who still wants to be part of the festival.' Well put, but did the festival in turn – now exclusively a classical music affair (albeit a world-class one) with a few extras tagged on – really want the ordinary man in the street to join the party? In hindsight, some might say that the theme of the festival's grand social event, a picnic in the grounds of Prior Park College, provided the answer – 'Rich and Famous'. However, it did bring fireworks back to the festival for the first time in many years.

The fringe issue was resolved in 1983 with the festival's own programme of walks, talks, lectures and other activities being relabelled 'festival events'. It was a sensible move; the term 'fringe' was increasingly associated with wild and wacky side-shows, as epitomised by the Edinburgh fringe. But the festival still maintained control of the opening night and in 1983 it grew enormously. For the first time there was no concert arranged for the opening Friday evening, allowing the park festivities to be a fully inclusive affair.

Some 10,000 people turned out in front of the Royal Crescent to enjoy the massed bands of the Light Infantry, the Avon Cadets in a military display, the Flying Bugles making a freefall parachute drop onto the lawn, and shire-horses from the brewer Bass. As dusk fell, candles were again lit in the windows of the Royal Crescent and surrounding streets. The massed bands sounded the retreat and, as flags were lowered over the Crescent, a bugler at each end of the historic driveway sounded the last post. Ten months after the nation's pyrrhic victory over Argentina to recapture the Falkland Islands, it was indeed a patriotic moment.

To its credit, the festival had taken note of criticisms about lack of visibility, and across Milsom Street were strewn row upon row of brightly coloured flags. Unmissable they may have been, but more than one person spotted the similarity to a Chinese laundry. As Florea Calo Coggan wrote in *The Bath Chronicle's* letters page: 'Thank you, festival team, you've shown us what money, good taste and *savoir faire* can do in the wrong hands.'

There was controversy at the third Contemporary Art Fair, where Yvonne Gilbert's painting of a female nude with vibrator in hand was hurriedly adapted on organisers' orders to show the subject holding a fan instead. It was probably just as well – the fair was opened by 13-year-old Henry Dimbleby, who stepped in at the last moment to replace his father, David, who was detained in London thanks to the mid-festival general election. Salman Rushdie, in his lesser-known pre-fatwa days, cancelled a festival talk due to pneumonia, and no fewer than three advertised lecturers died in the months between the publicity being prepared and the festival taking place.

Musically in 1983, the Amadeus Quartet returned celebrating their 35th year on the platform, Jeremy Menuhin became the first of that family to grace the festival stage since 1968, and Felicity Lott gave an enchanting recital at the Assembly Rooms. Both the music and the events programme were jam-packed with several activities each day. The fringe, with sponsorship from Sun Life, was similarly busy and included a jazz cruise, a kite festival and poetry.

Morley Pooley, whose first festival had been in 1949, and who had officially left *The Bath Chronicle* in 1969, finally decided that in 1983 he had seen enough, and retired once and for all. His last assignment was reviewing the Chilingirian Quartet at the Assembly Rooms.

With the Arts Council grant up to £36,500 and sponsorship sailing ahead to £46,000, all was going well until just two months before the start, when councillors at Avon slashed their contribution from £7300 to £3500. Based on the strength of advance ticket sales, the new administrator Richard Evans took the gamble – which paid off – of going ahead with the planned programme. But Robin Buchanan, the chairman, decided that it was time for Glock's reign to come to an end. His last year would be 1984. Buchanan has much admiration for the Glock years and speaking in 1998 he said:

> *Glock recognised that if we were going to have a concert that was difficult, we had it somewhere where you had 100 seats not somewhere with 400 seats and 100 people. He really understood the balance of cost versus income and the necessity of that.*

But Glock was reluctant to leave:

> *At the end of ten years, I did not want to leave. I could not see any reason for leaving. I was not ready to leave.*

Buchanan had no doubts:

> *He had been director for nearly ten years. I made it clear that ten years was enough for an artistic director. OK it was successful, but the most important thing was change. When I had influence, I said he had to go. He hated going.*

For the first time since 1955, when the suggestion of parading 20 deer through the city before spit-roasting them was quickly scotched, a question of ethics arose in 1984. The festival chairman Robin Buchanan was also the chairman of Bath District Health Authority, an organisation pursuing a campaign against smoking. But as chairman of the festival, Buchanan found himself with a concert sponsored by Imperial Tobacco. Both the festival and Buchanan came under pressure from the Government's Health Education Council to decline the sponsorship. The Health Education Council even offered to sponsor Imperial Tobacco's concert itself, a move Buchanan dismissed as a publicity stunt:

I would not insult the company which I consider one of the greatest sponsors in the country, not only of sport but of many more important things such as the arts.

The 1984 festival was a bumper occasion with 57 concerts (including 67 works written in the twentieth century), a total of 102 events, and a budget of £193,000 – of which Bath City Council's contribution rose from £8000 to £11,252. Ticket sales were £106,650. Alas, the Arts Council's largesse slipped slightly to £34,750, despite its chairman Sir William Rees-Mogg being asked to open the festival. A little embarrassed by the situation, he said:

The council's music panel has given festivals a lower priority than our main orchestral clients. There are considerable problems of orchestral pay which have put pressure on the musical allocation and our funds have been tightly squeezed.

As a way of boosting visibility and providing up-to-date information, the festival acquired half a dozen six-foot tall pyramids to be placed at strategic points around the city. They were used every year until 1997. Glock's 'maze and labyrinth' theme of 1984 proved popular, and the Beazer Maze near Pulteney Bridge stands to this day as a lasting monument to his idea. Great pianists adorned the programme. At the end of an all-Chopin recital, given on his 80th birthday, the audience regaled Vlado Perlmuter with a rendition of *Happy Birthday*. Barry Douglas appeared and so too did Alfred Brendel in an all-Schubert programme. András Schiff played Bach's *Goldberg Variations* at the Guildhall, and the featured composer György Kurtág gave a duet recital with his wife Marta. The Monteverdi Choir and Orchestra with John Eliot Gardiner ended Glock's reign as they had begun it, with a sublime performance of Monteverdi's *Vespers of 1610* at Wells Cathedral. Glock's own performing swansong was with the Endellion Quartet performing Mozart's *Piano Quartet K478*. The festival also included a production of Sir Michael Tippett's opera *The Knot Garden* given by Opera Factory at the Theatre Royal.

A festival cricket match pitted Ian Botham's Somerset XI against a Festival XI which included Tom Stoppard and Leslie Thomas, who scored an impressive 50 runs. Botham, however, was rushed to hospital after cutting his hand on a shattered champagne glass.

During his final year, Glock, a very senior and widely respected figure in the British music establishment, expanded on his thoughts about festivals:

> *People do ask what is the point of festivals. The answer is that a festival is an absorption of a great variety of music and a great variety of events which belong together. I am a great believer in that. Only in a festival can you find that unique quality.*

On the challenge of festival planning he wrote in the 1984 programme book that it is:

> *...a process that is partly intuitive, partly a matter of whatever knowledge and judgement one may possess... partly of never including anything that one wouldn't want to hear oneself, partly of being prepared from time to time to venture a few yards out to sea and of inviting the audiences to follow.*

Looking back on his ten years in office in 1998, Glock says proudly : 'There were three times as many concerts in 1984 than in 1975.' Thanks to this expansion, Glock's programming and, no doubt, his connections within the corporation, the BBC had been frequent patrons of his festivals and there remains a remarkable and largely unpublished archive of recordings. Glock was given a spectacular send off with players from the London Sinfonietta performing excerpts of contemporary music at the Pump Rooms. He was presented with a glass goblet in appreciation of his sterling work. Would he do things differently? 'If I was starting again, I would still do only music. Perhaps with an exhibition of paintings. Probably other things would come in.'

David Pratley sums up many people's opinion of that decade when he says: 'I have the view that during Glock's era it was very cerebral. A lot of great work was done and there were great events which I enjoyed.'

As in Menuhin's time, the Bath Festival was again a world player – but by now for reasons of content and style, rather than personalities. Where it would go from here remained to be seen.

CHAPTER EIGHT

After William Glock, the festival turned to *The Times's* distinguished music critic William Mann. His first festival was to be in 1985, but sadly it was an appointment that did not succeed.

Robin Buchanan, who was chairman at the time, was responsible for Mann's appointment. He says:

> *Bill Mann was living locally and he had sat at 25,000 concerts or 50,000 lots of music. Who better for the job? The council of management decided that he was the man and, as with all these things, you do not really know. He was entirely different from Menuhin, Tippett and Glock. But it just did not suit him at all. William Mann brought a lot to the festival and was a pleasure to work with. He certainly knew more about the festival than Glock.*

Speaking in 1998, Sir William Glock said: 'He was not very happy. It was a sad year with Bill Mann. But since then there have been some good years.'

Six months before his first festival actually took place it was announced that William Mann, casual dresser, self-proclaimed lover of the Beatles, and potential moderniser of the festival, had been ousted. Too upset to comment himself, Mann's wife Erika told the press: 'We have not been told the reason. As far as I understand it, the council thinks he has departed too far from the usual music programme.'

A clue to the putsch can perhaps be found in the minutes of the festival council meeting dated September 3, 1984, where there was great anxiety that barely half the programme for the 1985 festival was prepared. There was very little information with which to entice sponsors – and this in the classical music industry which has a two to three year lead time. The October minutes register that Mann presented his plans to the council. Thereafter – from November onwards – he is mentioned no more.

William Mann had listened to up to 21 concerts a week for 34 years, but was neither composer nor performer, nor had he previously programmed any form of festival or concert. When he eventually spoke about his ignominiously short tenure, he said he was standing down with relief: 'The plans I had for the Bath Festival weren't quite what they had in mind. It is all hard in-fighting. You have to struggle every inch of the way to get anything which isn't safe.'

The festival's administrator Richard Evans would only concur that there had been 'areas of disagreement' between Mann and the festival council.

Although he was by this stage no longer working for the festival, Luke Rittner watched the tragedy unfold:

It was a pretty disastrous appointment. I don't know why. I think he was probably not suited to the task of being an artistic director. And I think that the administration of it began to fall down a bit at that point.

Naomi Buchanan saw the disaster all too clearly:

He was one of the world's great idealists and he was possibly the most brilliant of music critics. The problem was all of a financial basis. He did not understand financial realism. I thought his programmes were good, but the festival simply could not afford to carry them out.

The festival put a brave face on the débâcle, and William Mann's programme for 1985 went ahead. With the tercentenaries of Bach, Handel and Scarlatti all being marked, it was the perfect vehicle for Mann to exercise his love of the baroque repertoire. Christopher Hogwood directed the Academy of Ancient Music in an all-Bach concert at St John's Church, Frome; Kent Opera produced Handel's *Agrippina* at the Theatre Royal, conducted by Ivan Fischer; and Malcolm Proud gave a harpsichord recital at Dyrham Park, featuring music by Bach, Purcell and Couperin. A decidedly Hungarian flavour hung over much of the programme, with works by composers such as Liszt and Bartók and performances by their compatriots such as György Pauk and Peter Frankl. Even the festival brochure had a dramatic red and black lithograph cover of Duke Bluebeard from Bartók's opera *Bluebeard's Castle*. Sadly there was neither the money nor the venue to stage that marvellous work.

In terms of scale, there was only one big event: Sir Michael Tippett returned to the festival to conduct the Leicestershire Schools' Symphony Orchestra in the draughty confines of Green Park Station, the first time the newly restored venue had been put to such a use.

And on the subject of size, the by now well-established opening night celebrations in front of the Royal Crescent included a cascade of fireworks to accompany Handel's *Music for the Royal Fireworks*. For subscribers to the 'there's nothing new under the sun' theory, it had of course happened many years earlier at the Recreation Ground. The opening night celebrations ended as before with candles, madrigals and the *Last Post* sounded by two buglers, one at either end of the Royal Crescent.

Musically, the 1985 festival was a packed programme full of big names – Radu Lupu, Olaf Bär and the Nash Ensemble. The repertoire covered everything from the aforementioned baroque to smatterings of contemporary music. And, for the first time in many years, Indian music was back in the form of a sitar recital by Nikhil Banerjee at the Theatre Royal. The national newspaper critics were attracted in droves, partly by Mann's featuring of several works by the promising young composer Simon Holt, and also, no doubt, to see how one of their own had fared, having, so to speak, gone native.

The budget for 1985 was £281,000 of which some £64,000 came through sponsorship. The Arts Council's grant remained static at £34,750 and the city's contribution rose by inflation to £14,047. The shop window competition inspired more than 100 entries, while the festival picnic which took place in the grounds of the Spa Nurses Home (now the Bath Spa Hotel) adopted a 'Pygmalion' theme. However the picnic was not without controversy. The resident nurses had to be issued with tickets to get in and out of their own accommodation, and were banned from having visitors on that day. Many who were due to work early the following morning were concerned that having their sleep disrupted by the party could jeopardise patients' lives.

Despite the overwhelming enthusiasm of the national press, *The Bath Chronicle*, while providing acres of supportive coverage, took the opportunity to prod at the classical music orientated nature of the festival. Diarist Simon Kinnersley telephoned festival organisers to ask what non-classical music was on offer and was sharply rebuked. He published the festival's response to his enquiry in full:

> *Well we've got George Melly for you – what more do you want? The Bath Festival is a classical festival. It's not about pop, jazz or folk. We're not trying to provide that sort of entertainment. You should realise that we're not that sort of festival. There's plenty of rock and pop festivals in the area already. If you're not satisfied with what we have to offer, and you want a pop festival, then you organise it.*

Despite Kinnersley's complaints, there were lighter elements to the programme. In addition to an appearance by George Melly, Joshua Rifkin performed a selection of Scott Joplin rags at the Theatre Royal. Six blocks of stone were lowered by crane into Parade Gardens for a sculpture competition which attracted widespread interest. Meanwhile, an 18-inch wide, one-and-a-half mile long pink ribbon was wound around the city's streets at a cost of £1500 to draw attention to the festival. Battered by high winds, it soon took on the look of a toilet paper advertisement. The plan had been to sell segments of the banner to members of the public as mementoes of the festival. Not surprisingly, there were takers for barely five metres. The controversial ribbon highlighted the presence of the Contemporary Art Fair, which by now was gaining almost as much national and international publicity as the music festival. For those who believed that the festival should be a festival of the arts in general rather than a festival of music with a few extras added on, the fair's success represented real progress.

Although William Mann was in evidence and appearances of civility were maintained, his successor had already been chosen by the festival council. On the day his departure was made public, the media were told that his replacement would be Amelia Freedman. She is the director of the Nash Ensemble, who during William Glock's era had become regular visitors to the festival. If the festival was looking for excellence in classical music, then Freedman was an inspired choice. But if they were looking for a multi-faceted arts festival of which classical music was just one part, she was not the right person. The problem was that, as Freedman was painfully to discover, neither the festival, the city, the press, nor even the public, really knew what they wanted.

CHAPTER NINE

Amelia Freedman is a strong-willed character with a remarkable list of contacts and enormously persuasive powers.

Her answer to questions on the disastrous William Mann era, of which she had to pick up the pieces, is succinct: 'I think William Mann was a very great critic and writer. It's very difficult for me to answer.'

Freedman had made some suggestions for Mann's 1985 festival, and so it was to her that the administrator Richard Evans, then effectively running the show in Bath, turned for help. Unfortunately for Evans, he had chosen a director with whom he could not get along. The ructions were furious and even today, many years later, Freedman finds it difficult to talk about the hurdles that she feels were placed in the way of her ambitious artistic programming.

But that was yet to come. How did Amelia Freedman feel about being asked to undertake such an important role?

> *There was a bit of a pause. I was very flattered and very excited about the prospect of being in a position of being able to work with an international festival of the calibre of the Bath Festival. It was one of the great festivals in England.*

Admittedly, she had done nothing on this scale before, but when Freedman went to meet the festival's chairman, Robin Buchanan, he had asked her what the Nash Ensemble's turnover was. She said: 'The Nash Ensemble's budget was larger in that year than the festival's, so they thought maybe I would have a good idea how to run it.'

Initially Freedman was asked to be artistic director for just three years. For guidance she turned to her predecessors:

> *I had the most wonderful moral support from both Sir William Glock and Sir Michael Tippett, who were quite marvellous to me. Before I accepted the post of artistic director I rang up William and he said 'yes, I think you would love it'. I love the Bath Festival and I think William had made it unique. It had its own special identity, and I respected that and developed it in my own way. You cannot be an imitator of something else. You have to have your own ideas. But that does not mean to say you cannot respect the good things that other people did. For instance, William was very interested in early music and the commissioning of new work, which I continued all through my festivals.*

But if she looked to Tippett and Glock, did Freedman also turn to Yehudi Menuhin?

No, he was no influence. My influences, or rather my spurs to develop the festival, were Sir Michael Tippett and Sir William Glock, because I think they made it an international festival. With Yehudi it was very much Yehudi and friends. It was a lovely, vivacious festival but it was based very much around the baroque repertoire.

Amelia Freedman started with a blaze of artistic glory, as she remembers:

One of my great moments was when we put on the Turangulîla Symphony *in Wells Cathedral in 1986, and both Michael Tippett and Olivier Messiaen were there. It was my first festival and I didn't know what the audience were going to do. Simon Rattle was conducting the City of Birmingham Symphony Orchestra, and at the end of the symphony there was silence, and then there was clapping, and then Simon turned round and Messiaen walked slowly to the front and people, to a man, stood up and cheered. They cheered for 10 minutes non-stop. It brought a tear to my eye. I was so thrilled that we had this great man and we had enjoyed a magnificent performance.*

It was indeed a high point in a festival full of high points. The festival had a predominantly French theme – Freedman's links to French culture were well known. Two years previously she had been appointed a *Chevalier d'Honneur* for her services to French music. The cross-Channel *entente cordiale* came as a result of a financial contribution totalling some £40,000 from the *Association Française D'Action Artistique*, enabling more than 100 French musicians to visit Bath. The festival team were not slow to point out that this meant that overseas funding was exceeding our own Arts Council's offering of £36,000. With commercial sponsorship topping £135,000, a scheme of matching funding from the British Government (an incentive to first-time sponsors to get involved with the arts) brought in an additional and very welcome £25,000.

Freedman made other great waves in her first festival. She re-introduced jazz to the programme, and it wasn't just a token gesture. There were no fewer than eleven performances by artists as diverse as the Stan Tracey Big Band, Keith Tippett, Loose Tubes and the Jacques Loussier Trio. The jazz programme was organised by Nod Knowles, a local jazz concert promoter and agent who, belying his laid-back approach, would over the coming turbulent years act as a major source of continuity and stability within the festival.

Even though venues in Bath were bursting at the seams, Freedman was determined to expand further. The festival returned to Bristol, and this time for more than just a couple of big orchestral concerts. Freedman ran a whole series of Bath Festival chamber music concerts at St George's, Brandon Hill, in the centre of Bristol. Looking back, Freedman admits that her forays into Bristol were probably too much. Persisting with concerts in Bristol was a controversial policy. As every Bathonian knows, Bristol and Bath may look close on a map, but culturally they are miles apart. Being a Londoner, Freedman thought that the two cities could be brought together in an artistic collaboration. She soon found out it would not be so easy. Although Bath Festival audiences felt comfortable journeying to Wells, Bradford-on-Avon and Frome, when it came to Bristol they took a different view. For the big orchestral concerts which Freedman was determined to include in the programme, there was nowhere suitable in Bath. Wells did not always suit the repertoire, so she used the Colston Hall in Bristol.

One such concert in Bristol in 1986 was given by the Ensemble Inter-Contemporain and their director Pierre Boulez at Clifton Cathedral. Other great names appearing outside Bath but in the Bath Festival included the cellist Paul Tortelier, the pianists Shura Cherkassky and Anne Queffélec, and the violinist Augustin Dumay.

The festival 'events', formerly the fringe, were sharpened up and designed to bring more relevance to the festival's overall theme, with talks by such musical luminaries as the broadcaster John Drummond and the writer Felix Aprahamian. Likewise, the Contemporary Art Fair, held over four days at the Assembly Rooms, was staggering in its magnitude, drawing dealers and collectors from all over Europe. The media coverage in 1986 was enormous. BBC2 broadcast a series of late night shows from the festival, Radio 3 practically lived in the city, and newspapers as far afield as the South China Morning Post in Hong Kong ran features.

The opening night of the festival continued its meteoric growth, and began to focus more on local celebrations. For example, in 1986 the displays in front of the Royal Crescent celebrated the 150th anniversary of the Bath police force and included demonstrations by past and serving members including the mounted police, dog handlers and police bands.

A survey of audiences during Freedman's first festival produced some surprising results, debunking the myth that the festival provided stodgy classical music for middle-aged people. Nearly a quarter of the 4800 people who completed the survey were under 35, 57 per cent were women, and a great many considered themselves 'trend-setters' who read *The Guardian* newspaper and subscribed to everything from *Dirt Bike* to *Oggi* and *The Beano*. The festival survey also showed that concert-goers spent more than £400,000 on accommodation, meals, shopping and tickets.

In terms of programming, 1986 was a truly enormous affair including events as diverse as Britten's *Curlew River* in Wells Cathedral, a recital by the soprano Elly Ameling, and a concert performance of Jean-Marie Leclair's opera *Scylla et Glaucus* at the Theatre Royal. One of the big ideas of 1986 was to complement the well-established opening night with a similarly popular closing night party, keeping alive the social side of the festival which had existed since the days of the 'Roman Orgy'. Bath racecourse was the chosen venue and the theme was 'Asterix the Gaul'. Sadly, only a couple of hundred people ventured up to the dizzy heights of Lansdown to brave the cold and cheer a few bedraggled pantomime horses across the line. This was the last time there would be a major end-of-festival event until 1999.

Overall, Amelia Freedman's first festival went down well, and glowing reviews from the national press proved a welcome boost. Away from the musical programme, there was a substantial exhibition of sculpture – not all of it uncontroversial. Although most was classical in style, the appearance of several hundred car tyres in the shape of a Polaris submarine outside the Assembly Rooms, created by the artist David Mach, made a very definite political point. The exhibit was equipped with 24-hour security – which was more than could be said for other exhibits in the city. A spate of vandalism, particularly to the exhibits in the Circus, caused festival organisers some headaches. A legacy from that festival is a work entitled 'Hanging Nails' by the artist Peter Logan. It is a 24-feet high collection of aluminium tubes floating in the wind that stands today by the entrance to the Homebase store, behind Green Park Station. It was based on a similar model by the artist called 'Hanging Pencils' that was originally displayed outside the Holburne Museum during the festival.

The net result of Freedman's first festival was ticket sales of £45,000 and a turnover of £500,000. For their troubles, the festival, which had raised £135,000 from sponsorship, was rewarded in December 1986 with recognition from the Association for Business Sponsorship of the Arts (ABSA) as the most effective arts organisation in Britain at raising business sponsorship. Although the path is never smooth for the arts, the Bath Festival, in many respects, had never had it so good.

After Amelia Freedman's first festival, a new chairman was appointed to succeed Robin Buchanan whose five years were up. Tony Garrett, a former chairman of Imperial Tobacco, a vice-chairman of HTV and a founder member of the Association of Business Sponsorship of the Arts, lived in Thornbury and was well known for his artistic interests. He said he wished to change little of Robin Buchanan's direction but added: 'One of the things I am positive about is increasing business sponsorship of the arts.'

The 38th festival in 1987 capitalised on the growing trend among festivals throughout the country for celebrating particular nationalities. After the success of Freedman's first year, she turned to the twin peaks of Russia and Italy for 1987. Politically it was an astute move: 'perestroika' and 'glasnost' had entered the vocabulary but the Berlin wall still stood. Demonstrating solidarity with Freedman's programming, the Italian government poured some £22,000 into the event. Our country's own Arts Council, however, felt unable to stretch beyond £36,500.

Freedman's doomed quest to unite the West Country in celebrating the arts led to her taking twenty-two events to Bristol. While Bath could not match Bristol in terms of a setting for orchestral events – the Bournemouth Symphony Orchestra and the Royal Philharmonic were scheduled to appear – the use of Bristol for chamber music events felt ever more uncomfortable. When Bath had such glorious settings as the Assembly Rooms and the Guildhall, why use St George's, Brandon Hill? Freedman's determination to make the Bath Festival into a regional event, meant that one-third of the festival's entire artistic budget was spent on events taking place in Bristol. Although this caused displeasure among a few long-term festival-goers, Freedman's contacts brought some great names to the West Country, including the Russian bass Paata Burchuladze, the conductor Gennadi Rozhdestvensky, and the violinist Anne-Sophie Mutter.

But first came the 1987 opening night celebrations in front of the Royal Crescent. Thousands of people ignored the rain to see the author Jilly Cooper, a last minute stand in for the actress Jane Seymour, declare the festival open. And beneath a shower of fireworks a military band played while along the surrounding streets local residents placed hundreds of candles in their windows. The jazz programme was beginning to flex its muscles with the Orchestre Nationale de Jazz appearing with Courtney Pine, just one of the dozen or so participants. At Bath Abbey, the blind organist David Liddle won a loud round of applause from the 600-strong audience for his recital. This led to an unholy row as the rector, Prebendary Geoffrey Lester, furiously insisted his ban on clapping had to be observed. He said: 'Some people like applause and some don't – we don't. I don't have to explain the decisions of the Parochial Church Council to the general public. The church is not a public place.' Reacting to the rector's demand that people should show their appreciation by simply standing in silence, David Liddle said: 'I was glad they all applauded. I think God gave performers their talents, and in applauding them you are applauding God.'

But there were more serious headaches than hand-clapping for festival organisers to contend with in 1987. Three days before their scheduled concert at the Theatre Royal, the Moscow Virtuosi demanded – and were offered – an extra £1000 on top of their fee. Then came a further demand from Gosconcert, the Soviet artists' agency, for yet another £5500 towards transportation costs. It was too much for the festival organisers, who refused to bow to the Russians' demands. At the last minute the festival managed to secure instead the services of the Polish Chamber Orchestra who were already touring the UK. A second scheduled concert by the Moscow Virtuosi was replaced with an appearance by the London Mozart Players conducted by Jane Glover.

Another Soviet hiccup came when a string quartet commissioned from the composer Sofia Gubaidulina by the BBC, and due to be heard in the festival, was dropped because the composer hadn't finished writing it. There were also cancellations on the Soviet front by the Borodin Quartet, the cellist Natalia Gutman and the pianist Victoria Postnikova, creating countless problems for the festival administration team. But there was a Soviet success in the 1987 festival: the commissioning and first performance of Edison Denisov's piano quintet. It contrasted, according to *The Guardian's* Gerald Larner, with another new work written for the Guildhall String Ensemble by Nigel Osborne called *Esquisses*. Larner described the Denisov work as '...complicated to play and, because it is so short and apparently so inconsequential, not very rewarding to hear.'

While 1987 brought a catalogue of irritations, the overall event was a remarkable artistic success. But when the figures were worked out, the net result was an enormous loss for the year of £58,000. Although great moments still lay ahead, with hindsight a deficit of such magnitude can be seen as the beginning of what was almost the end. Tony Garrett's chairmanship did not work out, and Robin Buchanan was brought back in for a year. Speaking in 1998, Amelia Freedman said: 'The thing about Tony Garrett was that he just didn't understand the politics of the game. He was a decent man but it didn't work.'

Freedman's plans for 1988 were blighted by the great storm of October 1987 which closed the Assembly Rooms. Losing this important venue – one of the three most important concert halls in the city along with the Abbey and the Guildhall – was a major blow. Freedman turned instead to Christ Church on Julian Road, which sufficed because it had a very good acoustic, but she felt distinctly disadvantaged by its location near a busy road junction. She said:

I will never forget the Beaux Arts Piano Trio trying to put on a performance of Schubert while the firemen were going past with their sirens. It was a great blow, because we had to move all our major chamber music and solo artists into Christ Church. We didn't have the Forum at that point either.

Other alternatives didn't come to mind very easily:

Bath Abbey is a wonderful venue, but of course you have to be discreet as to what you put on there. Some things work and some things don't. It was quite a struggle, not because it stopped us from putting on major artists, but because it was quite difficult to persuade audiences to go that bit further up to Christ Church.

The Contemporary Art Fair was also left homeless by the closure of the Assembly Rooms, but relocated to Green Park Station where it blossomed.

Thanks to Freedman's decision to make the USA her theme for 1988, the festival attracted an unprecedented £250,000 in sponsorship – most of it from across the Atlantic. Although welcomed by the festival organisers, the overseas fund-raising success exposed miserliness at home. In March, just two months before the festival was due to begin, Bath City Council reneged on an agreement to give a grant of £36,000 to the festival. After much discussion, a Liberal-Labour pact led to civic support for the festival totalling just £28,000. Despite this blow, the festival scraped home with a surplus of £2900. But it hadn't begun seriously to tackle the previous year's deficit.

The New York Times headlined the migration of arts from the New World to the Old as 'Yankee Doodle Goes to Europe', and this time actress Jane Seymour, who owned a house near Bath, managed to make it from America to declare the festival open during festivities in front of the Royal Crescent. In total, some 450 American musicians and artists pitched up in the city, including the composers Elliott Carter and George Crumb, the entire Atlanta Symphony Orchestra and Chorus, the dance company Lar Lubovitch, and the jazz greats Sweet Honey In the Rock. Other visitors included the Orpheus Chamber Orchestra, the veteran broadcaster Alistair Cooke and, delighting a new generation of jazz lovers, the seasoned festival artist John Dankworth with his wife Cleo Laine.

Freedman's growing international outlook led the festival chairman Robin Buchanan to rename it the 'Bath International Festival'. Closer to home, a new venue, the Michael Tippett Centre at Newton Park near Bath, was opened by the composer as part of the 1988 festival. Eleven years later, the re-opening of the expanded and enlarged centre is to be a highlight of the first weekend of the 1999 festival. But the festival being the festival, it could not allow its 1988 fortnight of glory to pass without some controversy. A life-size wire sculpture of two copulating horses by the artist Sophie Rider, who had previously worked on a stud farm, stood proudly outside Green Park Station, attracting complaints. Graham Loader, who worked in a nearby office, said: 'Some people might find it amusing but I think it's distasteful. I live in the country and see it all the time. There are going to be people who are far more outraged than me.' Like the art or not, it proved the launch pad for a revival of the elitism debate. Cllr David Gregory led the tirade in a letter to *The Bath Chronicle* calling it 'pretentious, elitist and irrelevant.' He went on to lambast the Conservative-led city council: 'They have not got the money to pay for council house repairs but they have it to sponsor an up-market peoples' festival.'

The American success was to be a contributing factor in the near downfall of the festival. The enlightened view of American patrons and sponsors led festival chiefs to believe they could continue to capitalise on that market place in the future, even when Amelia Freedman's artistic theme had nothing to do with the United States. The festival believed it could raise regular income from across the Atlantic, and opened up an American base. It was to prove a dangerous and expensive expedition. The future chairman Ken Broadhead explained, during an interview in 1998: 'They tried to get a Friends organisation going in the United States but all they did was spend money.'

The emphasis of the festival returned to Europe in 1989 when, celebrating the 40th anniversary of the post-war state, West Germany was in the spotlight. It led to the West German government, through the office of its ambassador in London, Baron Hermann von Richtofen, donating £30,000 to the celebrations. It was at this point that Ken Broadhead, a former bank manager and classical music enthusiast, picked up the reins as chairman. What he found behind the veneer of artistic success was a crumbling and over-staffed structure, as well as a dreadful deficit hanging around the festival's neck. Speaking in 1998 he said: 'When I took over we had not given returns to Companies House, and we were struck off and not able to trade. That was in my first three months.'

Despite the absence of results from its American venture, at the beginning of 1989 the ambitious festival established a completely separate fund-raising organisation in Britain, the Bath Festival Foundation. Complete with office, equipment and staff, it was chaired by Bristol solicitor Richard Smerdon and headed by Richard Evans. This paved the way for Christopher Head to move in as administrator of the festival. The Foundation's sole aim was to raise and invest £2m over a three-year period, which would generate up to £200,000 in annual income. The objective of the exercise was to avoid the annual, time-consuming and humiliating begging-bowl routine to city council, county council and Arts Council. Ultimately, the Foundation achieved practically nothing and, in the final analysis, cost more to run that it ever made. By October 1989, Richard Evans, who at the outset of the Foundation went on a six-week fact-finding mission to the United States, had landed himself a post in New York at the National Arts Stabilisation Fund.

While the fund-raising continued on an ad-hoc basis and London-based Amelia Freedman planned the programmes, Ken Broadhead tried to keep the whole show together. Although Broadhead, being a music-lover, was undoubtedly her favourite chairman, Freedman is cordial about her relationships with past-chairmen. She said:

> *I worked with Robin Buchanan and had a very friendly relationship with him. He left the festival after 1986. Then Tony Garrett came in, and he didn't quite work. Robin came back for a year in 1988, then Ken Broadhead, who I loved. I have a great deal of respect and admiration for him.*

But as the expansionary years of the late 1980s evolved into the recessionary years of the early 1990s, money was increasingly to become a major issue. The festival was not helped by great inflationary pressures in the classical music industry. Artists' fees had begun to soar as large American management companies moved into the British market place. Speaking in 1998, Freedman said:

> *There's no point in having ideas if you haven't got any money to put them on. The thing about Ken Broadhead is that he is a musician himself. He sings in the Festival Chorus and Bath Bach Choir, so I was talking to a kindred spirit. Robin Buchanan always wanted a fine festival. But his forte was the business side, as opposed to the artistic side.*

Broadhead's appointment as chairman gave the festival a direct – and crucial – link to its bankers, NatWest, whose generosity in extending the festival's overdraft now kept the festival alive. The lending was secured on the festival's headquarters, Linley House, a building which was itself showing signs of dilapidation. And while lovers of the arts in Bath had reason to be grateful for the bank's benevolence, such generosity merely served to postpone the day of reckoning.

For the fortieth festival in 1989, the year in which she was awarded the MBE for her services to music, Amelia Freedman arranged a star-studded line-up including Ute Lemper and Georgie Fame. Together with the growing Contemporary Art Fair, there could be no mistaking that the festival was evolving into a celebration of the arts generally rather than classical music in particular. Visual art was well established, performance art cropped up with increasing regularity, and Nod Knowles's jazz programme was even beginning to rival the classical programming in terms of popularity. The 1989 programme saw performances by such greats as Nina Simone, Dizzy Gillespie and the David Murray Trio. But, as with the classical programme, a lot of the jazz was taking place in Bristol. While superficially it seemed to make sense, it actually caused a degree of underlying resentment. There was more discontent among audiences when the festival dispensed with the souvenir programme, and instead produced flimsy programmes for every event – each priced separately.

On a happier note, the film star Jenny Agutter was brought in to declare the 1989 festival open in front of the Royal Crescent. Although the opening night programme was beginning to loosen up, it still had the feel of a military tattoo with salutes being taken, retreats being beaten and a march past by the Royal Marines. It was supposed to be a 'dry' opening night. The city's new on-street drinking laws prohibited revellers from consuming alcohol outside bars and pubs, leaving a popular opening night watering-hole, the Vendange in Margaret's Buildings, with no choice other than to shut for the evening in case drinkers stepped outside the doors and risked the establishment's licence. Despite the new rules, there was no shortage of alfresco drinking both in Margaret's Buildings and in Royal Victoria Park, leading to claims that wine drinkers were receiving preferential treatment over beer drinkers.

Opera, the *bête noire* of many a Bath Festival, poked its head into the programme again with a visit by Kent Opera performing Monteverdi's *The Return of Ulysses* and Britten's *Peter Grimes*. Meanwhile, the conductor Simon Rattle brought his City of Birmingham Symphony Orchestra to the party, and Vladimir Ashkenazy appeared with the Royal Philharmonic Orchestra. Other stars of 1989 included the violinist Nigel Kennedy, the singer Margaret Price, and the veteran pianist Jorge Bolet. Lending his support to the fortieth festival celebrations was the Prince of Wales, who turned up to hear a concert by the Melos String Quartet from Stuttgart, Germany, at Christ Church, Julian Road. His Royal Highness also agreed to become the festival's new patron.

Entrants to the shop window competition had to arrange their displays on the theme of 'echoes of romanticism', while the Festival Friends organisation launched a new recruitment drive to build up support for the festival. They were led in their efforts by Brenda Beeton, the wife of a former chief executive of Bath City Council. Meanwhile the fringe, presented by Bath Arts Association, continued to work in tandem with the international festival, presenting events such as poetry readings, theatre, bands and films.

The 'lack of visibility' criticism reared its ugly head again in 1989. David Nice, owner of Edouards wine bar in Lansdown, claimed that the festival had not brought him any extra trade. As a sign, perhaps, that things were turning, *The Bath Chronicle* did not leap immediately to the festival's defence. It wrote:

> *At least last year there were those copulating wire horses to focus attention on the festival. This time round, everything has been in remarkably restrained good taste... the Bath International Festival might as well be held on the moon.*

Financially, however, 1989 was another disaster. How much of a disaster did not become apparent until almost the end of the year when a loss approaching £100,000 was revealed. The hunt for sponsors was renewed with vigour.

There was some solace when, on the eve of the 1990 festival, there came a four year sponsorship deal with BMW (GB) Ltd, which brought in £12,000 a year to shore up the festival's finances. It was the first of a number of long-term sponsorship deals. While these were crucial to the festival's ability to pay its bills and manage its cash flow, they alone were not enough to guarantee survival. The biggest disasters in 1989 had been the concerts in Bristol. Already budgeted to lose money, the Colston Hall was less than half full, creating a loss approaching £10,000 on one event alone. Speaking at the end of the 1990 festival, administrator Chris Head put a brave face on the financial situation. He said: 'The long term aim is to make a surplus. Next year should see the first step on the road.' Those words had been heard before. For how long would the people and politicians of Bath continue to stomach a classical music extravaganza which, although one of the greatest of its kind in the world, was financially a lame duck?

The festival returned to Bath Abbey in 1990 with a concert by the City of London Sinfonia, featuring soloists Jill Gomez and Stephen Varcoe. The rector Geoffrey Lester had retired, and his successor Richard Askew was not prepared to reconsider the ban on applause until the church council met – after the festival had finished. Nevertheless, applaud they did. The music of Spain formed the backbone of this festival and the Abbey concert included the suite from Bizet's opera *Carmen*. Highlighting the continuing divide between those who wanted their festival to be a musical one and those who wanted their festival to be one long party, this opening concert clashed with the festivities in the park where the poet Pam Ayres formally declared the festival open.

The rest of the festival included performances by several Iberian artists, including the flamenco star Paco Pena, the Spanish clarinettist Joan Lluna and his compatriot the cellist Lluis Claret. Jazz star Courtney Pine, the pianist Alfred Brendel, and the acclaimed baritone Thomas Allen all gave performances. So too did the American organist Carlo Curley, who arrived in the country to discover that restoration work on Bristol Cathedral's ancient pipe organ was not complete – he had to use a computerised instrument instead.

Far away from the high art of classical music, the 'Festival Fun Run' for vintage and classic cars proved to be a popular crowd puller. The 55 vehicles, with drivers and passengers dressed in period costume, left Green Park Station for a tour around the Cotswolds, returning to a Glenn Miller-style welcome from the Wells Cathedral Brass Band in Royal Victoria Park.

After the poor showing in previous years, large-scale orchestral concerts in Bristol were temporarily abandoned. But while there were cuts in that area, the tenth Contemporary Art Fair, at Green Park Station, was moving from strength to strength, and featured a staggering 800 artists with works ranging in price from £50 to £50,000.

Nevertheless, the fact remained that the festival was still primarily a classical music showcase attracting a stereotypical audience. And while surveys showed that the majority of that audience was indeed from the local area, an underlying resentment was building up in the city at large. Why were non-musical events tagged on to the festival rather than an intrinsic part of the whole thing?

As the curtain fell on the 1990 festival, Amelia Freedman attempted the same type of public relations exercise tried by Sir Thomas Beecham when the 1955 results became apparent. Speaking to *The Bath Chronicle* of her desire to make the Bath Festival feel less exclusive, she said:

> *I am only elitist in that I want the very best for the city. We already have a huge variety of things happening for the festival, but I want people to*

feel more involved with it. It is not just a series of concerts that is plonked down for people coming into the city from far away who then go away again. I want people to feel there is something special for them in the Bath Festival.

The genie was out of the bottle. Amelia Freedman had spoken the 'e' word. The charge of elitism – which Sir Michael Tippett, Sir William Glock and William Mann had all managed to some degree to suppress – was set to haunt Freedman and her festival for the remainder of her time in Bath.

The 1991 festival was saved by a stroke of good financial luck when, thanks to chairman Ken Broadhead's contacts, Beazer plc injected £100,000 to become title sponsor. Beazer became accredited as the 'principal sponsor' of the Bath International Festival. It was intended to be the first part of a five year deal but Beazer was taken over, its enthusiastic executives disappeared, and the Bath Festival was left abandoned by its sponsor after just one year. On an overall budget of £683,000, the 1991 festival scraped home with a £4000 profit. It was not helped by the result of a concert given by the Philharmonia Orchestra with conductor Leonard Slatkin and pianist Barry Douglas at the Colston Hall in Bristol, which sold less than 900 of the 2000 available seats and consequently lost around £10,000. The city's contribution was £42,000 while the Arts Council's offering was £43,000. However, with an accumulated deficit of £216,000, it was highly unlikely the festival was going to trade its way out of trouble. There was more expense with the inclusion of another Achilles heel of the festival – opera. A group called Opera 80 gave performances of Mozart's *Magic Flute* and Donizetti's *Don Pasquale*.

Opened in Royal Victoria Park by the actor Anthony Andrews, the 1991 festival with its theme of 'Beyond Vienna' brought some 900 artists to the city, including many who had never previously been allowed to travel from the former Soviet bloc when it was under Communist rule.

The opening night celebrations again clashed with a major concert. The Royal Liverpool Philharmonic Orchestra, conducted by their Czech maestro Libor Pešek, performed Brahms's *Violin Concerto* with Kyung-Wha Chung in Wells Cathedral. Later that evening Nigel Perrin's Bath Camerata gave a candlelit concert at St John's Church in South Parade.

The pianist Mikhail Pletnev, the violinist Josef Suk, the Vogler String Quartet, and the Franz Liszt Chamber Orchestra were typical of the Eastern bloc artists who were suddenly able to travel with greater ease. All the same, there were cultural misunderstandings to be overcome. The Franz Liszt Chamber Orchestra performed Mahler's arrangement of Schubert's *Death and the Maiden*. With Mahler's music still in copyright, and royalties still being paid to his estate, the British publisher could not understand how the orchestra had acquired their music without his knowledge. He attended the group's rehearsal at the Theatre Royal and followed the score note by note satisfying himself that the handwritten and photocopied parts on their music stands were indeed the same as Mahler's work. Confronted on the issue, members of the orchestra tried to insist that it was their arrangement of Mahler's ideas, but eventually they capitulated and agreed to pay the publisher for the music.

Nod Knowles's jazz programme was by now a solid and well-established part of the festival, interwoven with the classical ambitions of Amelia Freedman. In 1991, he arranged for John Dankworth and Cleo Laine to make a return visit to the festival. Also on the programme were the National Youth Jazz Orchestra, the Northumbrian pipe player Kathryn Tickell, and a programme of modern jazz led by Keith Tippett. Falling both inside and outside of the classical and jazz programmes was the Kronos Quartet, an American group that had made a name for itself by breaching such boundaries and conventions. Their concert at the Forum, featuring only music by living composers, included spectacular lighting and sound effects.

The festival's position as a purveyor of high – dare one say elite? – arts, was exaggerated by the absence of a true fringe in 1991. While to those in the know the festival and the fringe are two very different beasts, to the public at large they are often seen as one and the same. Consequently, the lack of fringe activities made the festival appear to some as nothing more than a highbrow event. With the rise in fame of the Edinburgh Fringe, which in terms of publicity has sometimes eclipsed the main Edinburgh International Music Festival, there were calls for Bath to have something along similar lines.

The seeds of discontent were growing. Severely hit by the recession of the early 1990s, the festival countered the accusations of elitism by making demands for public funding to be increased from £42,000 in 1991 to £110,000 in 1992. The administrator Christopher Head raised the stakes by publicly announcing that it was a case of all or nothing. If the council wouldn't put up the entire £110,000, there would be no festival. At the same time, councillors were busy studying a report written by musicians in the city claiming that the festival had cultivated an aura of exclusivity, and didn't seem to care if the public bothered to go to concerts or not.

The waters were muddied because some of these local musicians were seen as using the festival's weaknesses to further their own ambitions. The short-lived Bath City Orchestra and its conductor Simon Ible, the opera designer John Pascoe (who had previously designed sets for the festival opera) and the local impresario Tom Clarke, were all among those seeking council funding for their promotions. And all three spoke out vociferously against the festival.

The festival was defended by the local conductor and former King's Singer, Nigel Perrin, who argued that the festival's prestige both in this country and overseas made it a worthwhile event. He said: 'I don't believe that these people who are criticising the festival have actually been to the concerts.' Perrin was rewarded for his support by the revival, under his direction, of the Bath Festival Chorus for 1992. As he pointed out, it was a tangible way of involving more local people in the festival. *The Bath Chronicle* (August 30, 1991) similarly stuck by the festival: 'Whether or not you agree with criticism that the festival is elitist and that its long term future needs to be considered, the fact remains that the city would be poorer, in every sense of the word, without it.'

Eventually the festival struck a deal with Bath City Council in October 1991, which provided a bailout of £110,000 to save the 1992 festival. In return, the festival had to succumb to scrutiny from a working party, which would include some of its sternest critics as well as representatives from other arts organisations.

The Liberal Democrat leader on the city council, Cllr Sue Sutherland, said: 'The festival is viewed as being elitist by an awful lot of people in the city who are now going to be asked to pay for it.' Festival chairman Ken Broadhead argued that the council was reaping the cost of not investing properly in the festival in the past. He said: 'I am very well aware of what happens in Cheltenham and Leeds, and that those councils are far more generous.'

As a prelude to the working party, four students were drafted in from the University of Bath's School of Management to undertake a survey of arts groups in the city, and to ascertain the views of the public in Bath. Their findings revealed that 93 per cent of respondents were in favour of the festival continuing – in one form or another. Doing its part to either fan the flames or stimulate debate, depending on your point of view, *The Bath Chronicle* organised a festival forum at the Guildhall in February 1992. Some 300 people turned up, and one after another called for more fun, more fringe events and less elitism. Days later, despite the Natural Theatre Company being brought in to provide light-hearted entertainment at the official launch, Nod Knowles and Amelia Freedman announced a programme for 1992 largely full of classical music. There would also be Knowles's jazz programme, a Georgian treasure hunt, and a project presented by the Society for the Promotion of New Music looking at the fusion of modern music and architecture. However, for the festival's image the timing could not have been worse.

At the height of the controversy, the festival administrator Chris Head left for unconnected reasons to join a Bristol charity. Fortuitously, his place was taken on an interim basis in March 1992 by Nod Knowles, whose position as jazz director meant he was allied with the more accessible image being advocated by the festival's critics. His long relationship with the festival also paid dividends in the months of turbulence that lay ahead.

By May 1992, the city's director of leisure and tourist services, Denis Easterby, had considered the festival and its future. In his report to councillors he attributed the problems to 'inadequate management control and conceptual extravagance in the late 1980s.' He added that to give the festival a broader appeal it would need further substantial cash injections. On his advice, councillors voted in June 1992 to extend a second £110,000 lifeline to the beleaguered festival. However, by early 1993 a clear and decisive business plan would have to be in place. The Arts Council demonstrated its support for the 1993 festival by increasing its grant to £50,000. While grass roots opinion was sharply divided, arts professionals clearly felt the Bath Festival was, in principle, a good thing.

Despite the ongoing debate, a festival did actually take place in 1992. It exploded into life with a massive evening of entertainment, including fireworks, in front of the Royal Crescent, and was opened by the actress Fiona Fullerton. A coup for the festival came when Bath was the only venue outside London to use an original piano that once belonged to Beethoven. It was played by Melvyn Tan in a concert with the London Classical Players conducted by Roger Norrington, and attended by the festival's patron, the Prince of Wales. Another memorable highlight of 1992 was a performance of the former festival director Michael Tippett's oratorio *A Child of Our Time* in Wells Cathedral.

For her theme in 1992, Freedman turned her attention to home. England and the effect our own culture has had on music in the rest of Europe was the basis of the festival. It included performances by the percussionist Evelyn Glennie, the pianists Joanna MacGregor and Alfred Brendel, the guitarist Julian Bream and the Bournemouth Symphony Orchestra.

In 1992, the Contemporary Art Fair returned to the now-repaired Assembly Rooms, while the long-empty Empire Hotel was pressed back into service as a joint club and information point for both festival and fringe. The fringe, newly constituted, began addressing the demand in the city for alternative and light-hearted forms of entertainment. At the same time, festival organisers made a concerted effort to get the message across that there was a festival happening in the city, with gimmicks such as having a string quartet play inside the Marks and Spencer store.

By the end of the festival Amelia Freedman was claiming that the controversies had merely served to strengthen the festival, and that the sold out notices proved that people in the city wanted the core of the festival – first rate classical music – to remain unchanged. She said: 'The silent majority voted for the international class programme to continue. What we needed was the fringe to be re-established and for the whole festival to have a much higher profile.'

By the end of the year the tensions were clearly visible once again. The country was deep in recession and Freedman, like Menuhin 25 years earlier, had ever rising and ever more expensive ambitions. Unfortunately, popular support was not on her side. Despite the council's intervention and bailouts, the festival would have to live hopelessly beyond its means if it was to keep pace with her demands. Financially it was still in as much of a mess as ever. Ken Broadhead persuaded his former employers to extend the festival's overdraft way beyond any reasonable limits. He said: 'We enjoyed it [the festival] until we got all the bills. Often we were holding back and only paying at the last minute. We held back until the writs were coming in.'

With limited political support and muted public support, there was no real future for the Bath Festival in its existing form. There was just enough will-power to stage a festival in 1993, but few people expected anything more. Artistically, Amelia Freedman put on a brave face. She turned to Norway, a country celebrating the 150th anniversary of the birth of its most famous composer, Edvard Grieg. His music was contrasted with several works by the English composer Robin Holloway, who was celebrating his fiftieth birthday. Among Holloway's pieces was the world première of *Partita* for solo horn given by Freedman's own group, the Nash Ensemble, at the Guildhall.

Yet again, Freedman programmed a concert in Wells Cathedral that clashed with the opening night celebrations. With vast crowds now turning up in front of the Royal Crescent to enjoy the party, there was something undeniably elitist about the festival's top brass distancing themselves from the great Bath public. While the St Petersburg Philharmonic raised the roof in Wells with Rachmaninov's *Symphony No.2*, fireworks were raising the skies in the centre of Bath. The message about being inclusive clearly had not penetrated to the heart of the festival. And even the prestigious opening night festivities were having problems recruiting sufficient sponsorship. In January 1993, the organiser Pamela Wordley told *The Bath Chronicle*: 'If we don't get a bit more money together, I am getting to the stage where we cannot put a show on.' Fortunately it was saved, but even the opening night format was looking a little jaded. A parachute drop by the Royal Marines and a military drill display were not really the type of entertainment the city wanted to party to. Reserved seating for the great and the good, leaving the rest of the city to mill around the park, widened the chasm between those who were part of the festival and those who were not.

Elsewhere in Freedman's final festival, there was a good cross-section of different music, including a concert by The English Concert with Trevor Pinnock in Bath Abbey, an all-Schubert piano recital by András Schiff, and an appearance by the Borodin Quartet. There was also sitar music from Budhaditya Mukherjee, two generations of Dankworths – John and Alec – appeared at the Pavilion, and the classical pianist Joanna MacGregor teamed up with the jazz pianist Django Bates for another of those events that didn't really fall into any category.

Even today people have widely differing views on Amelia Freedman's directorship. Although many found her programmes to be stimulating and imaginative, her style of being an absentee director was one more befitting the Menuhin era. In many respects, Bath still did not really know what it wanted from its festival: visiting international artists, the participation of local people, a blend of the two, or some higher and more imaginative approach.

But Freedman had had enough, and she was lured away by a post at the Philharmonia Orchestra in London. Although she had continued to find new ideas by adopting countries or nationalities for her themes, which admittedly made extracting money from national governments, embassies and cultural institutions relatively easy, the concept was wearing thin and many of the same artists were coming back year after year. It had all become a little routine. 'In the end, it all ran away with itself,' says Ken Broadhead.

Just like the city council in the 1950s, Yehudi Menuhin in the 1960s and to a lesser extent William Glock in the 1980s, Amelia Freedman had tried to repeat a once-successful formula. And that in itself was not enough to carry the Bath Festival any further forward after her initial achievements. With her difficulties compounded by the many outside forces detailed above, in February 1993 Freedman announced her departure after that year's festival.

CHAPTER TEN

Amelia Freedman had seen the writing on the wall. Although upset to be taking the blame for the city's inability to determine what it wanted from a festival, she was ultimately relieved to step down after the 1993 festival. Speaking in 1998 she said:

> *It became apparent because of the recession that the festival couldn't really survive unless it was taken over by the city council. Quite a lot of the earlier sponsorship had dried up because companies had either left Bath or been swallowed up by very big conglomerates. Therefore, the independence of the festival became quite difficult. The council had to make a decision. Did they want a festival? And if they did, they needed to put some real money into it. It seemed at that point that it was the end of an era. I was partly identified with the past, but I was also identified with the independent organisation. I feel the festival is one of the great festivals of England, and I was very proud to have taken it over from Sir William Glock and Sir Michael Tippett. I am very glad to be part of that band of very creative and visionary people.*

The financial problems were compounded by an anti-elitism storm being raged at the same time by the festival's detractors. While aimed more at the festival generally than at Freedman directly, she nevertheless took it as a personal attack on her work. Freedman's non-residency in Bath was another major disadvantage and, like Menuhin before her, gave her critics further ammunition.

But ultimately her experience in the city, her intimate acquaintance with the local venues, and her pre-eminence on the world's musical stage, left her ideally placed to take over at the autumnal Bath Mozartfest in 1995, where she has been an outstandingly successful artistic director.

The festival's financial position was deteriorating all the time, and the reasons were only too clear to the chairman, Ken Broadhead. He said: 'It comes back to the fact that we were over-manned. We were paying five people to raise money. We were better off without them.'

During 1992, while the financial and elitism arguments had been raging, David Pratley was appointed as the city's arts and tourism officer, succeeding Denis Easterby. An arts professional with a law degree from Bristol University, and long aware of the Bath Festival from his student days when he had helped out as an assistant stage manager, Pratley was convinced of the artistic viability of the festival. On his first day in the job, June 29, 1992, Pratley was confronted by the Arts Council wanting to undertake a funding appraisal of the festival, a daunting proposition as he recalled during an interview in 1998:

It had an accumulated deficit and Amelia Freedman had one more year as artistic director. The festival was feeling tired and the city council was extremely ambivalent. The Arts Council was saying to me: 'You are an arts professional. If you cannot sort it out, then it is time to pull the plug'. The Arts Council was also about to devolve the funding to South West Arts, which would not accept Bath Festival with such a deficit.

Pratley was given three months by the city council's chief executive, Clive Abbott, to come up with an appropriate strategy. Up until this point, the city had been acting in much the same way as it had since 1955 – enjoying seats on the board of a limited company that every year went to the council, begging bowl in hand, for cash. It was no way to run a modern business with planning times of two or three years.

David Pratley's approach was to establish a partnership between funder and recipient rather than the traditional council officer's role of handing out money to arts organisations. He said: 'The city council were doing nothing other than giving out grants – £10,000-£20,000 for the festival.'

The situation had reached crisis point. The city was not big enough to provide year round arts facilities, but it could certainly be a stimulating centre of culture. Speaking in 1998, Pratley said:

Bath is a very small city. It is a city that culturally thinks it is world-class. But on a population of 80,000 or so it could not possibly support a year-round programme; it could not support an orchestra; it could not support a repertory company. But it seemed to me that Bath was uniquely placed to support short bursts of artistry, and therefore support the notion of a year round festival city. The dilemma was how to do it.

Pratley believes that local authorities are very good with strategy and money, but not very good at day-to-day organisation. If he could sell a strategy to the city council and come up with the cash, it should not be too difficult to find the right person or people to do the job, and save Bath's much admired, but jaded, festival. In addition to dealing with an apathetic public, a weary council and a sometimes hostile press, Pratley had the problem of Bath Festival Society Ltd, a separate entity in its own right. He needed its members' support, while encouraging the Society to sign its own death warrant. And, if for nothing else, it is for this particular accomplishment that he deserves credit. He said:

One of the barriers to change was the city council's perception that the Festival Society was elite and represented only one sector of society. In addition, the festival was perceived as being run by people from outside Bath. It was remote. The people who ran the festival were not part of the city. There was a need to alter things.

Pratley's vision was two-fold. Firstly, he believed it was essential to keep the continuity of the Bath International Music Festival. Whatever internal changes there might be, the flagship festival had to go on. Secondly, he wanted to create an organisation that would be set up on a long-term basis, have assured funding for a decent period of time, and that would be soundly managed while providing the year-round artistic bursts – including the music festival – which he sought. Bath Festival Society Ltd was clearly beyond redemption. A totally new organisation, with a new identity and a new mission, would be needed. It would have a contract with the city council that would require the delivery of certain key tasks, an international music festival being the prime one. In return, the city would guarantee payment of an agreed fee for several years ahead. Financially it would need money, real money, not just the handouts of a few thousand pounds each year.

In the early 1990s, before the advent of the Bath and North East Somerset unitary authority, Bath City Council was a relatively wealthy authority. While the county council (Avon) levied a domestic charge to cover education, social services, road maintenance and the like, the city council was setting a zero domestic council tax. Vast property investments kept the city solvent. By deft internal re-organisation of his department, Pratley could find the money he needed to make Bath Festivals Trust a reality without having to call upon the city's council tax payers. He said:

> *I was undertaking a major restructuring of the department and seeking to make economies wherever I could. By the end of three months, I had identified £500,000 that could be freed up and used for new developments.*

The money wasn't simply a one-off saving. It was revenue funding removed from other projects. Pratley allocated £200,000 to the establishment of a tourism bureau in the city. The balance would be the seedling money for the new Bath Festivals Trust. However, Pratley still had the job of selling his plans to the politicians, many of whom remained, at best, unhelpful. Fortunately, there were some people on the council's Spas Committee, to whom Pratley answered, who were sympathetic to the festival. The Conservative representative was Elgar Jenkins. Pratley said: 'If you proved that you were someone with ideas, initiative and energy, and that there was kudos to be taken, then Elgar was supportive.'

Jeff Manning (Liberal Democrat), the opposition spokesman, was also relatively easy to win over. Pratley said: 'Jeff was probably the more sympathetic, and therefore I had bi-partisan support.'

Labour, although with very few seats on the council, also proved helpful. 'The refreshing thing about that committee was that it was ideas led,' recalls Pratley appreciatively. All this happened at a remarkable pace. Looking back, Pratley says: 'In the first six months I just got on with it.'

And Pratley was not without useful friends in high places. The chief executive of Bath City Council, Clive Abbott, was particularly helpful in getting Pratley's plans approved: 'He became a little difficult about the human aspect of the changes, but was broadly supportive.'

On the one hand Pratley did not wish to repeat the mistakes of municipal provision which had led to the degeneration of the festival during the first half of the 1950s; on the other hand, complete independence of the festival – Ian Hunter's dream which had led to many inspired events – was clearly no longer sustainable in the dire economic climate. But there were to be casualties along the way, the most high profile of whom was, as already mentioned, Amelia Freedman.

The new Bath Festivals Trust didn't just need an artistic director at its head; it needed a strong chief executive. Pratley said: 'It had to be headed by a chief executive who was part of Bath.' It is hard not to feel sympathy for Freedman. At the very moment when the city had finally seen the light and found a way to provide the substantial funding for the festival she had long demanded, Freedman was not to be part of it. Pratley, who has great respect for Freedman's artistic credentials and programming abilities, said: 'Her departure was very difficult. I am not sure Amelia has forgiven me, but it was clear a new appointment was needed.'

With all her other commitments, including head of music at the South Bank Centre, Freedman is today relaxed about her departure from Bath:

> There was a lot of conflict in the city as to whether they wanted a Salzburg Festival or a community-based festival. At the end of my time it had become destructive, and so I felt happy to move on. I couldn't have gone on, simply because it had to be a new regime, a new start. I think most of all you have to have someone living in Bath.

The other members of the Festival Society were, according to Pratley, only too happy to be relieved of the mounting pressures of an ever-rising overdraft, public and political apathy (and sometimes opposition) and the burden of the festival's 45-year heritage. The Festival Society, with its insoluble £200,000 overdraft, had to be cut adrift. Reluctantly, Ken Broadhead, the society's chairman, agreed. He said: 'It was necessary to set up a completely new entity.'

But the society still owned Linley House, the one-time home of the composer Thomas Linley and the festival's base for many years. This presented David Pratley with a diplomatic tightrope. He needed offices for his new Bath Festivals Trust, and he also needed the Society's friends, supporters and goodwill which, despite the continuing vociferous opposition in some quarters of the city, were still plentiful. He said:

> We agreed with NatWest that they would freeze the overdraft and, as part of the contract between the city council and Bath Festival Trust, the city council would rent Linley House. The sum paid in rent would, magically, be the same as the interest due. In other words the city acted as guarantor of the Festival Society's debt.

Continuity, both visibly and in the boardroom, was important to Pratley's scheme. After Ken Broadhead's departure as chairman of the Bath Festival Society, the new Bath Festivals Trust appointed a member of the society, property developer Paul Perry, as its new chairman.

To Pratley's surprise and delight the city council either swallowed his scheme or didn't fully comprehend what they were agreeing to. For a while, the new Bath Festivals Trust lived in Linley House. However, over the years the structure of the building had been allowed to deteriorate into a dilapidated condition. Sad though it would be to leave a building with such important musical connections, a modern festival management team needed to be in modern offices. Once he could see the wood for the trees, Pratley pressed ahead with part two of his plan for Linley House. As long as the Festival Society was letting out the building and the rent covered the interest, NatWest would not foreclose on the debt. But the situation could not go on indefinitely. As Pratley explained, the building was eventually sold, although not for enough to cover the Society's outstanding liabilities. He said: 'At the end of the day, there was a debt of around £70,000 and NatWest wrote it off. Somewhere there are some good guys in NatWest.'

Bath Festival Society Ltd, free of assets and liabilities, and no longer trading, was quietly wound up.

David Pratley, like many before him, could identify one of the festival's main problems: long term stability. But he was the first person to be in a position to be able to do anything about it. Bath Festivals Trust, with a remit to expand the festival in many different directions, break down the cultural barriers, and transform Bath into a year round festivals city, including a major new literature festival, came into being.

Ken Broadhead agrees that Pratley did the right thing:

> *He put it on a proper footing. It was a positive move. He did quite a good job. He persuaded the council that we needed the money, and since then it has improved.*

Pratley is in no doubt as to what the consequences of failure in any aspect of this complex deal would have been:

> *If it had not worked, the festival would have died. The Arts Council would not have helped. I am not being melodramatic. The festival in 1992 had only just happened and I suspect that 1993 would have been the last.*

Meanwhile, there were only a few months to go before the city and the arts world, both largely ignorant of all the wheeling and dealing that had been going on to save the world famous Bath International Music Festival, would expect a 1994 event. Someone had to take charge and present an image of normality. David Pratley seized the reigns: 'With no chief executive [for the festival] we had to decide what to do.'

Pratley chose to employ an artistic triumvirate, an idea that had been used, with limited success, in 1955 and again in 1969. There was Nod Knowles who had undertaken a great deal of festival administration over the years. He held the 1994 festival together. Known for his contribution to the jazz programme, Knowles was spared the criticism of elitism and remoteness that haunted other members of the Festival Society. Pratley was grateful for Knowles's long association with Bath: 'He moved heaven and earth to make it happen,' said Pratley.

Another local musician, Jolyon Laycock, renowned for the imaginative nature of his avant-garde 'Rainbow over Bath' series of concerts staged at the University and Bath College of Higher Education, was asked to programme the contemporary elements of the festival. But someone was needed to programme the flagship classical music programme. As the festival was at this stage in the hands of the city council, Pratley, in line with local government red tape, was obliged to advertise for a director. Helped in his choice of candidate by Richard Pulford, a director of the South Bank Centre in London, Pratley selected his old friend the conductor Nicholas Kraemer – but he made it quite clear to Kraemer this was to be a one year appointment only. He said:

> *Nicholas was nominally the senior of the three. He knew how things worked. Nicholas more than anyone else made the 1994 programme. It may have been transitional, but it was very good. There was a very different buzz and it seemed to me to play to Bath's strengths, the eighteenth and twentieth centuries. We did eschew the nineteenth century which really does not work in Bath.*

With the stopgap solution sorted, it was time to find a chief executive to take the longer view. Enter Tim Joss, manager of the Bournemouth Sinfonietta. He described his appointment and the approach he subsequently took during an interview in 1998:

> *One of the great things about working for the Bournemouth Orchestras was being able to programme a chamber orchestra, actually shaping the programmes and matching artists and conductors with repertoire that I knew they would play well. But I was only working with the chamber orchestra repertoire, and was just longing for an opportunity to work over a wider musical canvas. I was also interested in developing an involvement in other art forms.*

Ironically, the only other art form Joss was familiar with was dance – one that he wouldn't immediately be required to display an extensive knowledge of in Bath. He had at one time been music and dance officer at North West Arts. By his own admission, Joss was reasonably ignorant of the Bath International Music Festival and its history: 'I might have been no more than half a dozen times.'

What particularly excited Joss was the prospect of developing Pratley's vision of Bath as a European festival city. But first he had to be Pratley's knave in guiding the Festival Society towards its final demise.

Tim Joss joined the embryonic Bath Festivals Trust on October 4, 1993, and was immediately under pressure to deliver on many fronts very quickly:

On the one hand I was fired up with enormous enthusiasm. I thought this was a great opportunity and a fabulous chance to start something afresh. But on the other hand I think the expectations of the organisation were, for the amount of money that was available, too high.

The first nine months of Bath Festivals Trust, July 1993 to March 1994, had no scheduled events. Joss used the time and the funding to put his staffing structure in place and to ensure that the groundwork for the 1994 festival was complete. Even then he was operating with one hand tied behind his back. The city council expected him to deliver, but their funding for a full scale operation was limited, as Joss described:

It was suggested we would have one person doing both marketing and fund-raising, but I told them that if they wanted a properly set up fund-raising operation and a properly set up marketing operation, they would need to have two separate posts.

Joss was partially successful. He negotiated for increased funding and at the same time lowered some of the wilder and more unrealistic expectations among his new political masters. But even at that stage he didn't employ someone to work on the Trust's education and community programme, a major element of the new festival organisation's brief. He justifies his stance:

I thought it was very important for me to lead on that. Education and community work should not be a bolt on. I wanted to avoid a situation where I had a fabulous international festival and an unrelated, and perhaps not even very high quality, education and community programme. I wanted the education and community work to emerge out of the festival programme or vice versa.

Before the 1994 Bath International Music Festival could go ahead, Tim Joss had to remember that it was a festivals city that he was now promoting, with an emphasis on year round festivities. There was to be a public consultation on what a literature festival should or should not be about. It took place in December 1993. Joss said:

The meeting came up with conclusions such as: wouldn't it be wonderful to have a gloriously diverse festival with cookery writing, science fiction, poetry, serious literary novels, fantasy, fiction, travel writing, screen writing for television and film, all of that. The other thing was, wouldn't it be wonderful to develop a strong focus on young people?

If Bath was to hold a literature festival, the timing of it would be crucial. Consideration had to be given to other festivals in Bath and other literature festivals around the country. If young people were really to be integrated into it, school calendars would have to be consulted. And the new Bath Festivals Trust team would need to pace their own work. As Joss said: 'We didn't want the literature festival in June, straight after the music festival, thank you very much.'

February/March was the agreed time of year for a literature festival, which went down well with the tourism bureau because it would be before Easter when the city's tourist season starts properly.

With the first literature festival set for February 1995, Tim Joss and his new team had to manoeuvre themselves safely and carefully through the 1994 music festival – not least bringing in some sponsorship to cover the actual cost of the artists. Jonathan Miller's spectacular and much talked about production of Bach's *St Matthew Passion* at Green Park Station was at the centre of the festival; but the team were committed to the event before they had the means to pay for it. This taught Tim Joss a lesson about budgeting for future festivals:

It put it in my mind that you must never make special projects contingent on risky funding. Ever since, I've had the opposite policy – that what you must do is get the core programme that you really believe in and then look at how much it's worth from a fund-raising point of view. Patronage and Friends income does not vary much. As long as you are producing a quality festival, patrons will be supportive. It's the sponsors who want to associate their name and their effort with a particular event who are harder to predict. It's actually a great art being able to forecast sponsorship income for the festival.

This close shave also underlined to Joss how important it is for the person who is spending the festival's money to be aware of how it is raised. It was a concept that had never previously been fully understood in the history of the Bath Festival. Joss said:

My view is that in the late nineties, with the pressures that we have on public arts funding, the idea of just having an artistic director who can have ideas and then someone else goes and raises the money for it, just doesn't stack up very well. I, as chief executive, don't do much of the fund-raising directly myself. But I am responsible for the fund-raising operation.

As chief executive of the new Bath Festivals Trust, Tim Joss was handed the programme for the 1994 festival on a plate by Nod Knowles, Jolyon Laycock and Nicholas Kraemer, and it was a programme he had to live with. He says diplomatically:

Programming festivals is a very personal thing and that festival was not a Tim Joss festival. I think the Matthew Passion *was wonderful; I think having Nicholas Kraemer was interesting because he had such a strong early music background. If you look at festivals in the eighties and early nineties, early music was not one of the highlights. Then along came Nicholas, and he brought in a lot of early music, which I thought was good. He also took part.*

One sign of the difficulties that the festival had got into was in the lack of contemporary music. Tim Joss analysed the amount that was being played, and claims that it had reached a point where, in 1993, there were only two contemporary concerts. He said:

There had previously been very little. Jolyon Laycock's role meant that there was a lot more contemporary music. There was a jump to about seven contemporary concerts as a result of him becoming involved.

There was also some one-off funding from Bath City Council to promote a feeling of continuity and inheritance in the festival. To retain a sense of identity with audiences, friends and sponsors, and also to demonstrate that the line of tradition was not being broken, the festival mounted an exhibition of its history in the Assembly Rooms. Tim Joss said:

David Pratley was concerned to help in all sorts of ways with the management of change. The idea was to say: 'Let's celebrate and remind ourselves of where this festival has come from'.

A significant setback for Tim Joss came just before the 1994 festival. John Drummond, then director of the BBC Proms, wrote a scathing article in *The Daily Telegraph* in which he was critical of the festival, the state it had got itself into, and the programme for 1994, without (apparently) being aware that a new team was being established. Joss, who has clearly never forgiven Drummond for his outburst, admits that in the context it was justified, but regards the episode as decidedly unhelpful to his attempt to create a new style and image for the festival. He said:

It sent a buzz round the music business that we were going down-market. At a time when our public relations were very fragile, there had been all those local criticisms of elitism, and only one national critic was coming to the festival, I didn't find the article at all helpful.

Although Joss was not able to influence the artistic programme in 1994, he did arrive in time to make significant changes to the traditional opening night celebrations in front of the Royal Crescent. Until this point it had been run by volunteers and was intrinsically military in style, with hovering helicopters, the taking of the salute, ratings running up rigging and similar activities. Although it was fun in its day, it was not the image Joss wanted for the mid-1990s. He said: 'My simple view was that this is a music festival, and we should be having lots of music.'

It was not just marrying up artists and music that attracted Joss to the potential of the opening night, it was also marrying them up to the location, a key part of any programming. He said:

It's actually responding to these lovely spaces and, for someone who doesn't know Bath very well, having a proper look at the Royal Crescent and Royal Victoria Park. I thought 'Isn't this a wonderful space.' We responded to the space. It went down very well and it was the start of what has turned into a very special event in Bath's calendar.

Joss's main opening night initiative was to use what happens on the main stage as a window for what was going to happen in the festival as a whole. He said:

Obviously you are sensitive to context. You cannot put a string quartet up there. But you can put certain jazz artists, you can put certain world music artists, and you can put contemporary artists up there.

The opening night has also become an opportunity to draw in many of the educational strands of the festival. Joss said:

One of the great things about festivals is that they provide a platform for the results of education work and, given the high profile of every-thing that is going on, it is a fabulous way of celebrating and giving them a really great sense of occasion.

The opening night now includes an extraordinary procession of colour from the Circus, along Brock Street and around the Royal Crescent. In 1994 the opening night attracted sponsorship from *The Bath Chronicle*, support which has grown each year. Early in 1999 a major three year sponsorship deal was agreed between *The Bath Chronicle* and the festival covering the opening night until 2001.

Tim Joss also decided that he would make the opening night celebrations a fully inclusive event. No longer would an orchestral concert in Bristol or Wells clash with the city's big party, separating music lovers from the rest of the city.

As for the programme of the 1994 festival, the triumvirate took the theme 'Ancient Echoes'. It featured two of the best known names of contemporary music at that time: Henryck Górecki, whose third symphony had recently become a bestseller, and Michael Nyman, renowned for his music for the film *The Piano*. Opera, for so many years the *femme fatale* of the Bath Festival, returned, but in a very limited form. Kent Opera were invited to give three performances of Benjamin Britten's *The Prodigal Son* at St John's Church in South Parade.

At a concert in the Abbey on the first Saturday of the festival, the Tallis Scholars and their director Peter Phillips marked the 400th anniversary of the deaths of composers Giovanni Palestrina and Orlando de Lassus. The Shobana Jeyasingh Dance Company from Southern India were at University Hall, Bath Camerata sang Allegri's *Miserere* by candlelight at St John's Church, the pianist Joanna MacGregor gave two recitals covering repertoire from Bach to John Woolrich, and in Wells Cathedral the Bath Festival Chorus sang Górecki's *Beatus Vir* and Walton's *Belshazzar's Feast*.

The complementary events, now known as the 'Walks and Talks' pro-gramme, were boosted to include street entertainment, dancing in the park and Sheboom, a 21-piece all-female drum orchestra from Scotland who performed around the city over two days. Was the festival answering its critics and becoming more visible? Or was it muscling in on the type of events expected of the fringe?

With a chief executive in place but no permanent artistic director, Bath Festivals Trust had to move quickly if ideas for 1995 were to be formulated in the 12-18 months it takes to put a festival together. In December 1993, Tim Joss, a shrewd political operator, was ready to consolidate his powerbase. Still in a 'honeymoon' period and without even his first festival under his belt, he moved quickly to secure the prime position: artistic director of the Bath International Music Festival. Joss had done his homework. He had lobbied board members and bounced his idea off David Pratley, the Arts Council and other influential operators. When he came to present his plan – which undoubtedly made a great deal of sense – he had no trouble in being appointed as 'artistic director and chief executive'. Tim Joss would still employ artistic directors for specialist areas such as jazz, contemporary art and literature on a freelance basis, but he would now take artistic responsibility for the main festival.

In his original plan, David Pratley had envisaged an artistic director separate from, but working closely with, the chief executive. However, Pratley was content with the new arrangement. He said:

> *Tim Joss is a musician and a programmer, and it seemed sensible that he should take on the role, but it was not absolutely necessary. There could be a different structure in the future. There were those who felt that Tim should not be artistic director.*

On the one hand this is the way that modern festivals should be, with he (or she) who spends the money held responsible for earning it. A less charitable view would be that, in occupying both positions, Joss would never find himself in a situation where he risked a public falling out with a high profile artistic director over the lack of money needed to carry out the artistic director's ambitious plans.

With the Trust's first music festival out of the way, it was time to turn attention to the first ever Bath Literature Festival in February 1995. The children's author Laurence Staig was brought in on a three-year contract – later extended to five years – and put together a programme of readings, talks and discussions on the theme of 'story lines'. The concept of a literature festival in Bath was so new that attracting financial support was almost impossible. Consequently the publicity for that first festival was printed in black and white. The opening speaker at the first festival was the Poet Laureate, Ted Hughes, whose death was sadly announced shortly before this book went to press.

* * *

Amid the long list of piano recitals and string quartet concerts in the 1994 music festival, there had been an appearance by the cellist Steven Isserlis accompanied by the fortepianist Melvyn Tan, hero of the Beethoven Broadwood piano tour in 1992. Their recital gave Tim Joss an idea for the future. He said: 'I spoke to a lot of people in Bath and outside in the music business, and other people in the know. One of the things that local people who had been coming to the festival for a long time loved was the Menuhins in residence.' Joss set about familiarising himself with the city's venues and contemplating the kind of music that would suit them. He decided to try and update the feeling of Menuhin and his friends spending a significant amount of time in the city. Although Menuhin had brought his Bath Festival Orchestra to the city, Joss felt that as professional orchestras had now achieved such high quality, putting a festival orchestra together would be inappropriate. However, he felt that a group of international artists in residence, present in the city for several days, would recapture some of that spirit. He said: 'It would be so different from the flying in, give your concert, run back to London, and won't see you again for another year at least.'

The first 'International Artists in Residence' series in 1995 brought an eclectic group of musicians led by Steven Isserlis, who spent a great deal of time with Joss planning the programmes for their ten concerts. They included the violist Tabea Zimmerman, who gave a wonderful unaccompanied recital in the Octagon, the violinists Joshua Bell and Pamela Frank, the guitarist Eliot Fisk and the pianists Pascal Devoyon and Jon Kimura Parker. Their concerts formed the backbone of the classical programme in the second week of the festival, and among the many highlights were a pair of late night virtuosic concerts entitled 'Paganini in the Pump Room'.

For his first festival in 1995, Joss adopted the theme 'Utopias'. While the concept of an abstract theme puzzled some people, it was most eloquently expressed in one of the most memorable artistic events of his tenure, the appearance of the Val Reef Choristers from South Africa, a country newly liberated from the tyranny of apartheid. Their visit was both colourful and spectacular. Although they didn't do education work as such, the choir appeared at the opening night festivities and were engaged in street work the following day. They sang in the festival service at the Abbey on Sunday and later at the Festival Club. Finally, they gave a full concert at the Forum on Monday.

The opening night brought large crowds onto the streets to enjoy a fine evening's weather and entertainment. With the perfect backdrop of the Royal Crescent, it seemed like the whole city had turned out to party. It was a colourful and exciting evening and established, come rain or shine, the format for the opening night in future years. Families flocked to the park in droves to enjoy the first picnic of summer and await the 10pm fireworks spectacular. While there was music on both the main stage, erected in front of the Royal Crescent, and on the permanent bandstand at the bottom of the park, there was – for the first time in Tim Joss's era – a controversy that attracted real, if short-lived, public emotion. The Bristol-based artist Robert Bradford had built a 25-foot high fire sculpture. It was a kneeling angel designed to be burnt as an act of art. Hours before the opening night was due to begin, a group of fundamental Christians objected to what they saw as a blasphemous act, and threatened to mount a protest. In the end, their demonstration failed to materialise and the display went ahead, although there was a minor scare as the burning head fell from the torso and rolled towards the crowd. Fortunately, it stopped short of the thousands of people behind the safety barrier.

The 'utopias' theme was also pertinent in that 1995 was the year the nation marked the fiftieth anniversary of the ending of the Second World War. The festival itself had been a casualty of the conflict when Charles B Cochran's plans for a 1939 celebration of the arts in Bath were scrapped. The half a century of relative peace in Europe was marked by two concerts in Wells Cathedral. In the first, the Royal Liverpool Philharmonic Orchestra performed Beethoven's powerful *Symphony No.5* and Richard Strauss's meditation on the rubble of Germany, *Metamorphosen*, while in the second the Bournemouth Symphony Orchestra looked to the future with Beethoven's *Symphony No.9* and its 'Ode to Joy'.

As these two concerts showed, although Tim Joss was determined to take the festival out into the community, he refused to let the festival's artistic heritage disappear. The opening concert on Saturday morning at the Guildhall was given by the Borodin String Quartet, including the group's founding cellist from 1945, Valentin Berlinsky. In the un-soundproofed Banqueting Room the musicians found themselves battling against building work from the nearby Empire Hotel and a peal of bells from the Abbey. Nevertheless, their mesmerising programme of music by Borodin, Shostakovich and Beethoven was rewarded with a rare (in Bath concert halls) standing ovation.

Determined to continue building up a strong contemporary music strand to the festival, Tim Joss invited Jonathan Harvey, a musician who enjoys including electronic sounds in his works, to be the festival's featured composer. Nine of Harvey's works were featured including a world première (*Fanfare for Utopia*) and two British premières. Meanwhile, Nod Knowles, who had been able to give up his administrative duties and return to what he felt most comfortable with, programming jazz, arranged a programme for 1995 that included the Sophia Domancich Trio, the Chainsaw Sisters, Howard Riley and Sonny Rollins. For a crossover treat, an audience at the Forum was presented with a thrilling first-time collaboration between percussionists Evelyn Glennie and Nana Vasconcelos.

While the 1995 festival was Tim Joss's first as artistic director, it was the second in his well-planned strategy. With the fiftieth anniversary (1998) and the fiftieth festival (1999) looming on the distant horizon, he knew in which direction he wanted to head, and was already establishing the foundations for a very different type of festival to that which had previously been seen in Bath.

* * *

The departure of David Pratley from local government in 1996 left not just Tim Joss, but the Trust as a whole, feeling somewhat lonely. At about the same time, Bath City Council, Wansdyke District Council and Avon County Council were abolished. A new unitary authority, Bath and North East Somerset (B&NES) was established instead. Bath Festivals Trust could have become isolated, but Tim Joss had seen the changes coming. He said:

> *When I arrived in 1993, I could see that this was going to happen, and*
> *so we laid down a very firm guideline, which was that all our education*
> *and community work should be divided 50/50 between Bath and*
> *Wansdyke. That's a divide that actually reflects the population split.*
> *There had been a tradition of putting on concerts in places like*
> *Malmesbury and Bradford-on-Avon, neither of which are in B&NES.*
> *We immediately started developing music festival concerts in Chew*
> *Magna, Keynsham and Midsomer Norton. We also created a community*
> *venue circuit and made sure those concerts were divided equally*
> *between Bath and Wansdyke.*

But it wasn't just worrying about where to present performances that presented Joss with a diplomatic and political tightrope. The more politically correct members of the new authority were far from keen to see the name Bath used in isolation in the festival's name. Joss said:

> *When B&NES council came into being all sorts of ideas were around,*
> *such as it had to be B&NES Festivals Trust. It has been a big challenge*
> *for us to do our best in terms of developing things across the whole*
> *authority. Given the important emphasis that we lay on education and*
> *community work and the way it is integrated into the whole of what we*
> *do, I'm not pessimistic about the future.*

But if Bath City Council, a reasonably wealthy authority, hadn't moved the financial goal posts, B&NES certainly did. Tim Joss found this extremely frustrating, but says he understands the council's reasoning:

> *If you're going to have to make cuts then, as you build up your budget,*
> *you're going to naturally have to start with the thing that you are*
> *required by law to provide and, to my regret, the arts are not a statutory*
> *function of local government.*

B&NES Council found itself unable to balance the books and looked to Bath Festivals Trust for a saving of some 25 per cent. It was a cruel blow to an organisation that believed it had a firm contractual agreement with the council until the year 2000. Band concerts, children's events and – most painful of all for Joss – contemporary art, were all cut in 1996. Apart from the heavy heart that goes with making anyone redundant, Joss was aware of two other factors. Firstly, there was the dark shadow of history repeating itself. Secondly, when he had first arrived, Joss had successfully argued against a plan by David Pratley to establish a separate contemporary art trust. Joss claimed that the medium would be better served by a larger arts organisation. He said: 'If there had been a separate contemporary art trust, would it have been cut? I don't know.'

But before those cuts took effect, Joss was able to present the most visible contemporary art programme the festival had seen for some years. Five large scale bronze statues by the Polish sculptor Igor Mitoraj were brought overland from his studio in Italy and erected in Queen Square, Beauford Square and Abbey Church Yard for the duration of the festival.

Jazz had been an element of the festival with varying degrees of importance for almost four decades. But it had often been little more than either a token gesture or a bolt on. There had never been a true sense of the medium being equal in stature to the classical music programme. Tim Joss set out to change that with the help of Nod Knowles, a long-standing member of the festival team whom Joss had beaten for the post of chief executive. Joss said:

I had got to know Nod and had enormous regard for his particularly imaginative approach to jazz programming. I then looked at what had happened in the jazz programme prior to my arrival, and there had been around ten to twelve concerts.

Joss credits Nod Knowles with the idea of transforming the middle weekend of the festival into a focus weekend of European contemporary jazz:

The programme grew to about eighteen concerts. Some of those were double and triple bills, so the number of ensembles or acts appearing in the jazz and folk programme doubled to about twenty-five. Although we decided that the weekend would be a focus for European contemporary work, it wouldn't stop us having other folk and jazz throughout the seventeen days.

The insurance giant Clerical Medical, who had supported the festival in the past, spotted the opportunity to raise their profile in the city, and the now prestigious jazz element became the Clerical Medical Jazz Weekend, a tribute to an enlightened sponsor and an exciting programme.

The overall theme of the 1996 festival was 'migrations', and what more appropriately named group could there be than the Trio Wanderer to open it? Their programme included Haydn's *Gypsy Trio*, another link to the festival theme.

The migrations theme was reflected in the opening night procession when local children dressed as fish, birds, mammals or fantasy creatures. They made their way from the Circus, along Brock Street, around Royal Crescent, down Marlborough Lane and into Royal Victoria Park. But there was a more serious, thought-provoking side to the theme. Many migrations are forced ones, such as that caused by the Holocaust. Even voluntary migrations cause a yearning for home, as was reflected by the inclusion of Dvořák's *New World Symphony* and Gershwin's *American In Paris* in the festival programme.

Continuing his policy of bringing new music to the festival, Tim Joss invited his former orchestra, Bournemouth Sinfonietta, to give the première of a work he had commissioned when he was manager there. Heinz Karl Gruber's eccentric work *Zeitstimmung* was performed at the Forum with the composer taking the part of *chansonnier*, or narrator, in texts by H C Artmann.

After the success of the International Artists in Residence series in 1995, Tim Joss offered the British accompanist Roger Vignoles the opportunity to put together a similar series in 1996. Vignoles brought with him a group that included the pianist Barry Douglas, the violinists Dmitri Sitkovetsky and Yuri Zhislin, the cellist Ralph Kirshbaum, and the singers Louise Winter and Tiffany Jackson. For Jackson, the American soprano, it was her British début and she was greeted with wild acclaim. Olaf Bär's recital with Vignoles of Schubert's song cycle *Die Winterreise* was similarly widely appreciated. And recreating the type of specialist programme performed by Yehudi Menuhin in his early days, such as when he played a solo recital in the Abbey, Tim Joss invited the Dutch cellist Anner Bylsma to play all six of Bach's solo cello suites during two afternoon concerts at the Holburne Museum. The cycle drew cello connoisseurs from all over the country to appreciate the artist's effortless interpretation.

Following the success of the jazz weekend, Joss decided to develop the idea of using all three weekends of the festival for particular themes. Speaking in 1998, he said:

> *I thought we could make a special feature of each of the weekends, because that's the time when people might be willing to travel from further afield, and we ourselves can offer something which is unique. We now have the contemporary weekend, which is unique in the way that it has a couple of focuses each year, and we are well on the way to having a world music weekend.*

In fact the world music strand effectively began in 1995 with the visit of the Val Reef Choristers from South Africa. However, despite his best efforts, by 1998 Tim Joss had still been unable to develop this as a fully-fledged element.

Where the 1996 festival perhaps went wrong was in one of the ways it reached into the community. It has long been a problem that collectively the city has never known whether it wants visiting international artists in its festival, or the very best of local talent. While the grumbles are forthcoming about too much of the former, that is undeniably where the biggest ticket sales lie. The 1996 festival included a few too many performances by local groups, and not always of the quality to be expected in an international music festival. Among the local artists who appeared – and not always before large crowds – were Bath Baroque, the Apollo Ensemble and Avon Schools' Orchestra.

But the audience in 1996 did take one musician to their hearts. The teenage cellist Dmitri Tsypkin appeared as a member of the Chamber Orchestra of the Belarussian Music Lyceum in a concert at Midsomer Norton. Midway through the performance, the group's director Vladimir Perlin got carried away and crashed into the cello section, breaking Tsypkin's bow. With the orchestra already busking between concerts to pay their travel costs, it looked like a major disaster, until the audience held a spontaneous whip-round and raised £267 on the spot to pay for repairs.

With the 1996 festival out of the way, it was time for the festival to leave Linley House, its home since 1962. For the following year or so, the administrative offices were in a comfortable modern building at Midland Bridge belonging to the solicitors' firm, Thrings and Long. Meanwhile Bath

Festivals Box Office, fast becoming a commercial enterprise in its own right by selling tickets for numerous other arts organisations all year round, found a perfectly positioned home just south of the Abbey.

Dead insects and raw meat found a place in the 1997 festival with an exhibition by the Flemish artist Jan Fabre in seven different locations. Fabre devised a trail through Bath, beginning in the grounds of the Holburne Museum and taking in a room under the colonnade in Parade Gardens, a former mortuary chapel in Walcot, and a flooded cellar belonging to the City of Bath College. At each location visitors could see constructions built with Fabre's unusual materials.

The Clerical Medical Jazz Weekend was now considered to be Europe's largest jazz festival. It took over the Guildhall and the Pavilion, providing music from late morning until the early hours. Carla Bley, Abdullah Ibrahim, Keith Tippett and Nikki Yeoh were among an enormous list of artists who drew thousands from across the country to enjoy their music.

By now Tim Joss's Bath Festivals Trust was beginning to penetrate beyond formal concerts in formal venues. If audiences couldn't come to the music, the music was sent to the audiences. Performers went to old people's homes, community centres and libraries across the B&NES region; every school in the region was given the opportunity to take part, either in the opening night or by having a visit from an artist. The Festival Club – which had been spluttering along barely noticed in the Pump Room – was established in the 1805 Rooms above the Theatre Royal. But perhaps because it was a joint venture with the fringe, it didn't particularly appeal to festival-goers.

Given the growth in the festival, the number of venues available for the fringe was diminishing. It was also realised that audiences were no longer 'festival' people or 'fringe' people, but often one and the same. Consequently fringe organisers decided in 1997 that they would start one week later than the festival and run on for an extra week, which fitted very nicely with the laid-back image of a fringe. The fringe culminated in an enormous party in Walcot Street, dubbed Walcot Nation Day, with the theme 'Walcot waives the rules'. It attracted thousands and was a fitting climax to three weeks of festival and fringe festivities.

The festival had, at long last, found itself in a situation where it could welcome the light-hearted and the frivolous without feeling threatened. The two elements – a concentrated pursuit of high artistic ideals and an all-out party – could live side by side and, indeed, feed off each other. A rapport was developing between festival and fringe.

In February 1997 the Literature Festival leapt to a new level. Major new sponsorship from the regional power supplier SWEB meant the director Laurence Staig could present a far stronger programme – and publicise it in a full colour brochure. High on the list of priorities was an extensive series of events for children and young people designed to interest them in the written word. For their parents, Helen Fielding spoke about her best selling book *The Diary of Bridget Jones*, the former Beirut hostage Terry Waite gave a harrowing insight into his time in captivity, and Beryl Bainbridge discussed 'chance and humour' with her fellow novelists Jonathan Coe and Nicholas Royle.

The theme of the 1997 Bath International Music Festival was 'Resurrections'. It brought works such as Penderecki's agonising *Threnody to the Victims of Hiroshima* followed by Messiaen's jubilant *Et Expecto Resurrectionem Mortuorum* performed by Sir Simon Rattle and the City of Birmingham Symphony Orchestra at Wells Cathedral. Sir Simon wasn't the only household name in town. Both the flautist James Galway and the jazz legend Dave Brubeck drew capacity audiences to their concerts at the Forum.

Tim Joss felt that 1997 was the year to push the festival forward into a new dimension. Having launched the jazz weekend as a pivotal part of the festival, he wanted to give similar treatment to his beloved contemporary music. Although the classical programme continued – largely with the International Artists in Residence series led by Imogen Cooper – the closing weekend was devoted to the music of the Greek composer Iannis Xenakis, who visited Bath from his home in Paris for the occasion. Joss's predecessors, particularly Glock and Freedman, had tended to follow established practice and sandwich 'difficult' contemporary music between well-known works that would shore up the box office. While Joss had indeed followed that formula on occasions, the contemporary music weekend, like the jazz, would be unashamedly full on. New music specialists such as the Twentieth Century Ensemble, the New London Chamber Choir, and the Graham Fitkin Group, were brought in to ensure that the standard of performance was the highest possible. It proved to be an overwhelming success. Clearly, cutting-edge contemporary music has a limited appeal to the world as a whole, but in the context of a festival that was doing a great deal on so many other fronts, criticism was muted. And, as with the jazz, the audiences contained a broad mixture of both local people and aficionados who had travelled great distances.

Had Tim Joss finally stumbled on a formula that had eluded Sir Ian Hunter, Bath City Council, Sir Thomas Beecham, Yehudi Menuhin, Sir William Glock and Amelia Freedman? In terms of popular support – essential when asking the taxpayer to pay for a large part of the bills – Joss's success could be compared to that of Sir Michael Tippett in the early 1970s – the only previous artistic director to live locally.

* * *

Fifty years after the first Bath Assembly, held in a city far different from the one we know today, the Bath International Music Festival used 1998 as the springboard for its golden jubilee celebrations. Having missed 1956 and 1957, this was still only the 49th festival. But there was a lot to celebrate including new offices in Broad Street, right in the heart of the city.

The appointment of the well-known broadcaster, author and local resident Jonathan Dimbleby as chairman in succession to Paul Perry, brought renewed vigour and enthusiasm at the top. Dimbleby, in turn, was able to secure a visit – the first for several years – from the festival's patron, the Prince of Wales. His Royal Highness spoke to the audience in Bath Abbey, reminding them of the importance of the Bath Festival. He also used the opportunity to launch the 'Fifty Festivals Development Fund', a bold endeavour to establish an endowment of up to £5m to provide a secure income for future festivals. Tied in with the Fifty Festivals celebrations was a sponsored Scarlatti marathon in which pianists, each playing three of the composer's 555 sonatas, performed for visitors taking tea at the Pump Room. They didn't perform them all, but Tim Joss played the first three, the international pianist Anne Queffélec gamely volunteered to take part, and *The Financial Times's* music critic Stephen Pettitt secured sponsorship from his fellow writers on the national press for his rendition.

But before all that was the opening night, now so established that it would be impossible to imagine Bath without the famous party in the park. On a balmy evening, an estimated 30,000 people stood shoulder to shoulder filling almost every available square foot of grass in front of the Royal Crescent. As far as the eye could see, there was an ocean of humanity enjoying the bands on stage and, later, the biggest and most spectacular firework display the city had ever seen. Once the party was over, 100 flags were erected in front of the Royal Crescent by the artist Angus Watts. During the course of the festival, they were gradually changed to show a constant movement of colour.

With the jazz weekend and the contemporary music weekend well-established, Joss began to put in place, in all but name, his idea for a third themed weekend. Evolving out of the opening night celebrations, which by their nature were inclined towards music from other cultures, would be the world music weekend. A series of Flamenco performances and workshops, and a pair of Indian concerts during the first few days of the 1998 festival, set a pattern which Joss hoped would develop into a themed weekend with as much prominence as the other two weekends.

The 1998 festival was overshadowed by the death of Sir Michael Tippett in January that year who, long after leaving office in 1974, had proved a stalwart supporter. He was remembered with a performance of his *String Quartet No.5* in the opening Saturday morning concert by the Lindsay Quartet, whom he had introduced to Bath when they were completely unknown in the 1970s.

It is tempting when dealing with recent history to gloss over the things that didn't quite work. We shouldn't – although they must be seen in the context of a festival that was undeniably a success. A joint concert at the Forum by the percussionist Evelyn Glennie and the King's Singers drew large crowds in anticipation of something familiar. They were rewarded with a performance of uninteresting and difficult contemporary music – a marriage made in the boardroom. HTVs three festival programmes broadcast live from the Assembly Rooms on the three Friday evenings of the festival, brought embarrassment and complaints. The presenter Henry Kelly was clearly not properly briefed on his subject. And Kent Opera's staging of Monteverdi's *Orfeo* at the Theatre Royal was disappointing and stagnant.

But look beyond such annoyances and there was the marvellous discovery of the hitherto little-known Ukrainian pianist Anna Kravchenko, who gave a late-night Chopin recital at the Pump Room, the bass Willard White's selection of spirituals at the Forum, and the International Artists in Residence series led by the world's greatest viola player Yuri Bashmet. Did anyone tell Bashmet that he was treading the same boards as the previous world's greatest viola player, Lionel Tertis, half a century earlier? Bashmet's recital with Mikhail

Muntian was a performance of startling intensity culminating in a remarkable performance of Shostakovich's *Viola Sonata*, completed on the composer's deathbed in 1975.

For jazz supremo Nod Knowles it was time to take his final curtain call – although not quite. After 13 years with the festival, Knowles was appointed music director of the Scottish Arts Council. Throughout some of the festival's most turbulent years, Knowles had been a steady constant in a changing world. Sad to be leaving, it soon transpired that he would be continuing to programme the jazz weekend, which in 1998 included Jools Holland, Lemn Sissay's Firepeople and L'Orchestre Nationale de Jazz from Paris.

The 1998 fringe squeezed into the headlines with the legalisation of cannabis being advocated by local councillor Keith Lunt in a debate on the subject. With a re-run of the Walcot Nation Day, it seemed that after two years the great fringe street party was here to stay.

* * *

Approaching the 1999 festival, Tim Joss is by all previous reckoning at least halfway into his term as artistic director. Measured in ticket sales, diversity of programming, goodwill around the city, media coverage or any other tangible scale, there is no doubt that overall his tenure has so far been a success. David Pratley, the man who in 1993 sold a grand plan to the city that saved the festival, said:

> *I think Tim has succeeded extraordinarily in fulfilling the brief he got. He has made the Trust part of the landscape, and that is no small achievement. He has given the music festival a very high profile in terms of its activity.*

Pratley also believes the Trust's diligence in involving young people in education work, children's concerts and outreach work with musicians has been a great success, but he admits that there are areas where the Trust has deviated from his vision:

> *The Literature Festival has not grown as I had hoped and, as before, visual art has more or less died. The Trust has got to do it. By now I would have liked to see two weeks of literature with more identity and a year round programme at major visual arts venues.*

Pratley agrees that financially things have been tough and that the council has reneged on elements of its agreement:

> *Too many of their resources are going into the music festival. I am sure the finance has conspired against them, but I would hate the Trust to get sucked into the same rut as the Festival Society was. I believe that city and political support would disappear. It would be disappointing for that barrier to be re-erected.*

Tim Joss agrees it has not been plain sailing. He said:

> *It goes back to this thing about high expectations from the council. We were trying to deliver on more than just rebuilding the music festival and establishing the new Literature Festival. In the end it all had to work not by having extra council money, but simply by having project budgets that would work free of council money.*

One of the earliest casualties was a monthly winter chamber music series that Joss had attempted to establish. It ran for two seasons from 1994-96 with concerts at the Assembly Rooms featuring world-class artists. As things worked out, the strengthening of the privately funded Mozartfest with Amelia Freedman, Joss's predecessor, at the helm, has provided a welcome autumnal diversion for classical music lovers. Tim Joss said:

> *I thought it would be lovely to have a winter series to keep in touch with our classical audience. As things have turned out, I don't regret the passing of the chamber music series because the Mozartfest [in November] has made some good advances.*

A more embarrassing failure for the Festivals Trust was the 'Larks in the Parks' in 1995, an attempt to cash in on the popularity of the opening night by providing summer activities in the park for children. Joss said: 'The opening night celebrations had been so successful, we thought it would it be fun to have an event a bit like it, but that we could charge for. It would be another strand to making a festival city.' But opening night audiences don't like paying for their entertainment, as Joss discovered. He said: 'It was a miscalculation. People are prepared to turn out for a big free event and one that is well lodged in the calendar, but they were not prepared to come to something that actually cost them money.'

There is no doubt that 'Larks in the Parks' was an attempt to appease those politicians who still felt the Festivals Trust was little more than the old Festival Society in new clothes. Joss said: 'We were being encouraged to have a go at something like this. We duly did, but failure for us hurt. We look back on that as something that was an experiment. It didn't work. We failed.'

As a political creation, Bath Festivals Trust is very dependent on the view held of it by the elected representatives of the people of Bath and North East Somerset. Tim Joss is aware that, despite his efforts, some councillors continue to harbour doubts while others are simply prejudiced. He fears that despite all that his team have done in terms of programming, ticket pricing, education and community work, and general communication, there are still councillors who think the festival is elitist and not for local people. However, there is also a solid core of councillors who actively support the festival's work. Meanwhile, others are happy with the festival's work but at a time when there is so much pressure on the overall local authority budget they find it difficult to justify giving the festival £300,000 a year. Joss said:

They're not for us, they're not against us. But they have a wider agenda to cope with and we haven't got them to a point where they truly understand the value that we play, certainly artistically and culturally, but also economically. We are the only council service which is delivering economic benefits, education benefits, and community benefits. If you look at the vision and values that the council has, and how that has been elaborated, we are right in there.

Roughly speaking, the council's annual grant only covers the running costs of the festival office, about one third of the festival's budget. Ticket sales provide a further third, and the remainder of the income comes from sponsorship, patronage and donations. In charge of ensuring this side of the festival budget is up to scratch for the past five years has been Tim Hobbs. David Pratley said: 'Tim Hobbs is nothing but a genius. He is very successful.'

Sir William Glock, who remains president of the festival, is supportive of its evolution. He said: 'It is an interesting festival, not at all the same as mine. There are special weekends I never thought of having, such as jazz.' Refusing to be drawn on whether the current festival is a dilution of the former music festival, William Glock said: 'I don't want to criticise it.'

Former chairman Ken Broadhead: 'Tim Joss is here. People see him around. He has done a good job and he is on the spot.' But Broadhead argues that Joss lacks his predecessor's pulling power: 'It is good, but what we have not got is the quality of artists that Amelia could get. You see that in the Mozartfest.'

Naomi Buchanan, who has been associated with the festival for almost as long as anyone living in Bath says: 'They are only re-inventing the wheel. There is nothing new. We had a film festival, we had jazz.'

Amelia Freedman, while supportive of her successor's work, says much the same: 'There's nothing I haven't imagined; nothing Tim Joss has imagined that I haven't already imagined and tried to do.' But Freedman does hit on a very important point. A festival's success is not just how you do it, but how you satisfy the politicians who pay for it. She said: 'Tim has done a very successful job in persuasion, and making people understand how important it is to have a festival that continues to have its own identity. It wobbled for a few years. One didn't quite know what was going to happen.'

* * *

As this book goes to press, the fifth Bath Literature Festival, Laurence Staig's last as programme director, has just finished. With the backing from SWEB remaining, it has brought a wide selection of writers in many mediums to the city, including soap opera scriptwriters, poets and comedians. Famous names included the feminist author Germaine Greer, the poet Andrew Motion, and the broadcaster Rabbi Lionel Blue. In 2000 the Literature Festival will take on a new look altogether with a wider interpretation of the meaning of literature and greater input from the Festivals Trust's chairman Jonathan Dimbleby and his wife Bel Mooney.

The 1999 Bath International Festival of Music, the fiftieth of the modern era, has been long in the planning and is set to be 25 per cent bigger than its predecessor. It will cover an enormous array of musical disciplines and artistic cultures including the three strongly branded weekends – world music, jazz music, and contemporary music. The 1999 International Artists in Residence series will be led not by a soloist but by an entire orchestra, the Orchestra of the Age of Enlightenment. The rest of the classical music programme features a diverse and renowned selection of artists with equally wide ranging repertoire. Great things are promised for the opening night, while the programme of community events and the 'Walks and Talks' series are as rich and varied as ever. For the first time in many years, a closing event has been planned involving the writing of a new piece of music to be played from windows and balconies of The Circus by up to 200 musicians. Another of the highlights of 1999 will surely be a visit – the second in as many years, and thirty years after his first visit – by the festival's patron, the Prince of Wales.

At the time of writing, Bath Festivals Trust's service contract with B&NES Council beyond the 2000 festival is still being discussed. With demands on public money for things like housing, health and social security as great as ever, who can tell what the future will hold, but the festival has clearly become an important – some might say essential – part of the fabric of Bath. With the first fifty festivals now complete, the planning – and the budgeting – for the next fifty years of the Bath International Music Festival is already well underway.

CONCLUSION

Since the opening notes of the National Youth Orchestra's concert on April 21, 1948, the festival has travelled further, higher and faster than its founding fathers could ever have imagined.

But so too has the world we live in. And in order to retain its freshness and vitality, the festival has regularly found it must change, develop and evolve – often very quickly.

Late in 1998, Bath Festivals Trust produced a *Visions* document, which sets out a series of inspired moves that it hopes to follow. Key among these is the development of a Festivals' Centre, a multi-purpose space in the centre of the city that will house the box office, a performance space, a bar/cafe and the festival's own offices. Such a move will be a natural progression, establishing the festival at the heart of the community in which it belongs.

The reopening of the spas as part of the city's millennium celebrations will provide a further platform for the festival to evolve, primarily in contemporary art, an aspect of its remit which has been somewhat moribund of late.

The *Visions* document also speaks of reviving the Contemporary Art Fair, developing the Literature Festival, and improving the education and community programme. All these are important aspects of the festival's work, which must be given due prominence in the months and years that lie ahead.

When reviewing more than fifty years of festivals, one becomes aware of common factors that surface time and time again. On a matter of detail, the inclusion of opera in a festival programme has often been more trouble than it is worth. Looking at the broader canvas, change is an absolute must – both in the shape and content of the festival as well as in the leadership. Six or seven years is long enough for an artistic director to forge an identity, create an impression and head towards stagnation – and with the exception of Sir Michael Tippett every director of the Bath Festival has, unintentionally of course, managed to outstay his or her welcome.

The problem of funding has long been a millstone around the neck of festival organisers, and we must hope that the somewhat unrealistic dream of creating a £5m endowment to pay for future festivals can be achieved by the current festival administration. Although a handful of dissenters remain, both the local council and the community have generally accepted the value of the festival to the city of Bath and the surrounding districts. The reputation of the festival, which is talked about in all corners of the world, may be unquantifiable, but the enormous impact it has on spending, employment and tourism cannot be underestimated. Would an advertising programme costing the same as the council's current expenditure on the festival (about £300,000 per annum) bring the same return? I suspect not.

But what attracts people to the Bath Festival from all over the world isn't so much the cleverness of the programme, the imagination of the theme, the quantity of events, the number of premières, or the breadth of the educational work. Instead it is the opportunity to hear and see some of the world's greatest musicians in the setting of one the world's most beautiful cities. It is easy to get distracted from this simple fact, and most festival directors, particularly towards the end of their tenure, have been guilty of pursuing an overtly personal agenda.

The great difficulty for all directors is the balancing act between drawing in crowds of visitors, and satisfying local feeling. It is possible for the two to run in harmony, but it requires supreme effort, particularly when dealing with the community here in Bath. Taking the trouble – as Luke Rittner and Anthony Tootal did in the early 1970s – to meet resident's associations and other local groups and listen to their hopes, wishes and fears is something all festival directors have been particularly bad at. Another great failing is the boundary created by their own imagination. It should not be perceived as an act of weakness to either accept criticism or to implement the ideas of people who genuinely wish to support the festival. Indeed the festival is *their* festival. A director is but a temporary guardian, entrusted with the opportunity and the responsibility to pass it on to his or her successor in better shape than when they inherited it.

Today we live in an era where the festival must be more things to more people than it has ever been before. This is reflected in the diversity of content which in 1999 will include three themed weekends for the first time – world and folk music, jazz music, and contemporary music. The Literature Festival has been held five times and from 2000 will have a new – and as yet unknown – format and programme director. The city also boasts festivals celebrating food, cricket, Shakespeare, Mozart, guitar music and film, not to mention the fringe. They may be run independently from the International Music Festival, but their presence and success needs to be wholeheartedly embraced by Bath Festivals Trust, which was established to unite these diverse expressions of creativity under the umbrella of a festivals city.

On the eve of the fiftieth festival, the Bath International Music Festival is as strong as it has ever been. It has come through some dark days and horrendous crises, and yet change remains important.

Does the present board, dynamically led by the Bath-based author and broadcaster Jonathan Dimbleby, represent a wide enough range of society to properly reflect the needs and aspirations of the community they serve?

The council has recently been more supportive than at other times in its history. Nevertheless, its financial input is still a fraction of that given to other international festivals of far less significance. Does the local authority fully understand what a bargain it receives?

Sooner or later a successor to Tim Joss will need to be found. Is it not about time that he or she came from the local area? There are many people in this region who are well-placed to face the daunting challenge of the directorship of this festival. And while writing documents, theses and papers on the future shape of the Bath Festival is all well and good, they must be translated into action otherwise they are worthless.

Over the years, change has been the only constant in the Bath Festival and there is little to suggest that the future will be any different. But despite the doubters and the philistines, the Bath International Music Festival has been one of the city's – and the country's – great post-war artistic successes. Long may it continue to entertain and challenge both visitors and residents alike.

APPENDIX – Dates

1948
Bath Assembly: April 21-May 1
chairman: Cllr Alleyne Berry
artistic director: Ian Hunter MBE

1949
Bath Assembly: May 15-28
chairman: Cllr Alleyne Berry
honorary artistic director: John Boddington

1950
Bath Assembly: May 7-20
chairman: Cllr Alleyne Berry
honorary artistic director: John Boddington

1951
Bath Assembly: May 20-June 2
chairman: Cllr Alleyne Berry
honorary artistic director: John Boddington

1952
Bath Assembly: May 22-31
chairman: Cllr Alleyne Berry
honorary artistic director: John Boddington
theme: Roman Bath

1953
Bath Assembly: May 11-23
chairman: Cllr Alleyne Berry
honorary artistic director: John Boddington
theme: Royal Occasions

1954
Bath Assembly: May 15-29
chairman: Cllr Alleyne Berry
honorary artistic director: John Boddington
theme: John Wood and his times

1955
Bath May Festival: May 11-21
chairman: The Mayor of Bath, Cllr William H Gallop
artistic directors: Sir Thomas Beecham *Bart*, Oliver Messel, Hugh Beaumont
theme: devoted in character to the arts of the eighteenth century

1956
No festival

1957
No festival

1958
Bath Festival: May 29-June 7
chairman: The Mayor Bath, Cllr Hugh Roberts
festival direction: Harold Holt Ltd (managing director Ian Hunter)

1959
Bath Festival: June 3-13
a festival arranged with Yehudi Menuhin
chairman: The Mayor Bath, Cllr Hugh Roberts
festival direction: Harold Holt Ltd (managing director Ian Hunter)

1960
Bath Festival: May 18-28
a festival arranged with Yehudi Menuhin
chairman: Cllr Hugh Roberts
festival direction: Harold Holt Ltd (managing director Ian Hunter)

1961
Bath Festival: June 1-11
a festival arranged with Yehudi Menuhin
chairman: Edwin Leather MP
festival direction: Harold Holt Ltd (managing director Ian Hunter)

1962
Bath Festival: June 14-24
a festival arranged with Yehudi Menuhin
chairman Sir Edwin Leather MP
festival direction: Harold Holt Ltd (managing director Ian Hunter)

1963
The Bath Festival: June 6-16
a festival arranged with Yehudi Menuhin
chairman Sir Edwin Leather MP
festival direction: Harold Holt Ltd (managing director Ian Hunter)

1964
The Bath Festival: June 3-14
a festival arranged with Yehudi Menuhin
chairman Sir Edwin Leather MP
festival direction: Harold Holt Ltd (managing director Ian Hunter)

1965
The Bath Festival: June 8-20
a festival arranged with Yehudi Menuhin
chairman Sir Edwin Leather MP
festival direction: Harold Holt Ltd (managing director Ian Hunter)

1966
The Bath Festival: June 15-26
artistic director: Yehudi Menuhin
chairman: Lord Strathcona and Mount Royal

1967
The Bath Festival: June 7-18
artistic director: Yehudi Menuhin
chairman: Lord Strathcona and Mount Royal

1968
The Bath Festival: June 19-30
artistic director: Yehudi Menuhin
chairman: Lord Strathcona and Mount Royal

1969
Bath Festival: June 13-29
artistic directors: Sir Michael Tippett, Colin Davis, Jack Phipps
chairman: Lord Strathcona and Mount Royal

1970
Bath Festival: June 5-14
artistic director: Sir Michael Tippett
chairman: Lord Strathcona and Mount Royal

1971
Bath Festival: May 28-June 6
artistic director: Sir Michael Tippett
chairman: Barbara Robertson
motif: butterflies

1972
Bath Festival: May 26-June 4
artistic director: Sir Michael Tippett
chairman: Barbara Robertson
motif: parasols

1973
Bath Festival: May 25-June 3
artistic director: Sir Michael Tippett
chairman: Barbara Robertson
motif: crowns

1974
Bath Festival: June 21-30
artistic director: Sir Michael Tippett
chairman: Barbara Robertson
motif: hot-air balloons

1975
Bath Festival: May 23-June 1
artistic director: Sir William Glock
chairman: Barbara Robertson

1976
Bath Festival: May 28-June 6
artistic director: Sir William Glock
chairman: Barbara Robertson

1977
Bath Festival: June 3-12
artistic director: Sir William Glock
chairman: The Lady Digby

1978
Bath Festival: May 26-June 4
artistic director: Sir William Glock
chairman: The Lady Digby

1979
Bath Festival: May 18-June 3
artistic director: Sir William Glock
chairman: The Lady Digby

1980
Bath Festival: May 23-June 8
artistic director: Sir William Glock
chairman: The Lady Digby

1981
Bath Festival: May 22-June 8
artistic director: Sir William Glock
chairman: The Lady Digby

1982
Bath Festival: May 21-June 6
artistic director: Sir William Glock
chairman: Robin Buchanan

1983
Bath Festival: May 27-June 12
artistic director: Sir William Glock
chairman: Robin Buchanan

1984
Bath Festival: May 25-June 10
artistic director: Sir William Glock
chairman: Robin Buchanan
theme: the maze and labyrinth

1985
Bath Festival: May 24-June 9
artistic director: William Mann
chairman: Robin Buchanan

1986
Bath Festival: May 23-June 8
artistic director: Amelia Freedman
jazz director: Nod Knowles
chairman: Robin Buchanan
theme: France

1987
Bath Festival: May 22-June 7
artistic director: Amelia Freedman
jazz director: Nod Knowles
chairman: Tony Garrett
theme: Italy and Russia

1988
Bath International Festival: May 27-June 12
artistic director: Amelia Freedman
jazz director: Nod Knowles
chairman: Robin Buchanan
theme: America

1989
Bath International Festival: May 26-June 11
artistic director: Amelia Freedman
jazz director: Nod Knowles
chairman: Ken Broadhead
theme: Germany

1990
Bath International Festival: May 25-June 10
artistic director: Amelia Freedman MBE
jazz director: Nod Knowles
chairman: Ken Broadhead
theme: Spain

1991
Bath International Festival: May 24-June 9
principal sponsor: Beazer
artistic director: Amelia Freedman MBE
jazz director: Nod Knowles
chairman: Ken Broadhead
theme: beyond Vienna

1992
Bath International Festival: May 22-June 7
artistic director: Amelia Freedman MBE
jazz director: Nod Knowles
chairman: Ken Broadhead
theme: England

1993
Bath International Festival: May 21-June 6
artistic director: Amelia Freedman MBE
jazz director: Nod Knowles
chairman: Ken Broadhead
theme: Norway

1994
Bath International Music Festival: May 27-June 12
artistic directors: Nod Knowles, Nicholas Kraemer and Jolyon Laycock
chief executive: Tim Joss
chairman: Paul Perry
theme: ancient echoes

1995
Bath International Music Festival: May 19-June 4
artistic director and chief executive: Tim Joss
jazz director: Nod Knowles
contemporary art programme director: Jane Connarty
chairman: Paul Perry
theme: utopias

Bath Literature Festival: February 25-March 5
programme director: Laurence Staig
theme: story lines

1996
Bath International Music Festival: May 17-June 2
artistic director and chief executive: Tim Joss
jazz director: Nod Knowles
contemporary art programme director: Jane Connarty
chairman: Paul Perry
theme: migrations

Bath Literature Festival: February 24-March 3
programme director: Laurence Staig
theme: journeys and places

1997
Bath International Music Festival: May 16-June 1
artistic director and chief executive: Tim Joss
jazz director: Nod Knowles
contemporary art programme director: Jane Connarty
chairman: Paul Perry
theme: resurrections

Bath Literature Festival: February 22-March 2
programme director: Laurence Staig
theme: chance

1998
Bath International Music Festival: May 15-31
artistic director and chief executive: Tim Joss
jazz director: Nod Knowles
contemporary art programme director: Jane Connarty
chairman: Jonathan Dimbleby
theme: fifty festivals

Bath Literature Festival: February 20-28
programme director: Laurence Staig
theme: boundaries and frontiers

1999
Bath International Music Festival: May 21-June 6
director: Tim Joss
jazz director: Nod Knowles
contemporary art programme director: Jane Connarty
chairman: Jonathan Dimbleby
theme: fifty festivals

Bath Literature Festival: February 26-March 6
programme director: Laurence Staig
theme: tales of sound and vision

INDEX